DECLARATIONS OF INTERDEPENDENCE

This important work goes beyond conventional accounts of the recognition of indigenous rights. Building on critical pluralist theories, Anker challenges us to re-imagine ways of thinking law(s), and in so doing takes us to the heart of the problem of legal encounters which has proven such an intractable issue in Australia, Canada and elsewhere.

Shaunnagh Dorsett, University of Technology, Sydney, Australia

In this book, Anker provides a comprehensively researched, beautifully written and passionately argued case for adopting her innovative critical discursive legal pluralist approach to the question of the legal relationship between indigenous peoples and the modern state.

Anthony J. Connolly, Australian National University, Australia

Cultural Diversity and Law

Series Editor:
Prakash Shah, School of Law, Queen Mary, University of London, UK

Around the world, most states are faced with difficult issues arising out of cultural diversity in their territories. Within the legal field, such issues span across matters of private law through to public and constitutional law. At international level too there is now considerable jurisprudence regarding ethnic, religious and cultural diversity. In addition, there are several layers of legal control – from communal and religious regulation to state and international regulation. This multiplicity of norm setting has been variously termed legal pluralism, inter-legality or inter-normativity and provides a fascinating lens for academic analysis that links up to cultural diversity in new and interesting ways. The umbrella of cultural diversity encompasses various population groups throughout the world ranging from national, ethnic, religious or indigenous groupings. This series particularly welcomes work that is of comparative interest, concerning various state jurisdictions as well as different population groups.

Also in the series

Legal Reform and Business Contracts in Developing Economies
Trust, Culture, and Law in Dakar
Julie Paquin
ISBN 978-1-4094-4488-6

Minorities and Nationalism in Turkish Law
Derya Bayir
ISBN 978-1-4094-2007-1

Socio-Legal Integration
Polish Post-2004 EU Enlargement Migrants in the United Kingdom
Agnieszka Kubal
ISBN 978-1-4094-3699-7

Judging in the Islamic, Jewish and Zoroastrian Legal Traditions
A Comparison of Theory and Practice
Janos Jany
ISBN 978-1-4094-3716-1

Declarations of Interdependence

A Legal Pluralist Approach to Indigenous Rights

KIRSTEN ANKER
McGill University, Montreal, Canada

Routledge
Taylor & Francis Group
LONDON AND NEW YORK

First published 2014 by Ashgate Publishing

Published 2016 by Routledge
2 Park Square, Milton Park, Abingdon, Oxfordshire OX14 4RN
711 Third Avenue, New York, NY 10017, USA

First issued in paperback 2016

Routledge is an imprint of the Taylor & Francis Group, an informa business

British Library Cataloguing in Publication Data
A catalogue record for this book is available from the British Library

The Library of Congress has cataloged the printed edition as follows:
Anker, Kirsten, author.
Declarations of interdependence : a legal pluralist approach to indigenous rights / By Kirsten Anker.
p. cm. – (Cultural diversity and law)
Includes bibliographical references and index.
ISBN 978-1-4094-4737-5 (hardback) – ISBN 978-1-4094-4738-2 (ebook) – ISBN 978-1-4724-0626-2 (epub) 1. Indigenous peoples – Civil rights. 2. Legal polycentricity. 3. Sovereignty. 4. Self-determination, National. I. Title.
K3247.A55 2014
342.08'72–dc23

2014005598

ISBN 13: 978-1-138-63764-1 (pbk)
ISBN 13: 978-1-4094-4737-5 (hbk)

Contents

Acknowledgements

The Australia I grew up in was, in my tutored imagination, an empty place before the arrival of the British: nameless before the explorers filled in their maps, unproductive before the crops were planted, and unowned before the advent of fences and title deeds. To a large extent, this book stemmed from a desire to address my own ignorance and to learn to see the land as full: named, known, law-producing and loved. I would like to start, then, with an acknowledgement of the Haudenosaunee and Algonquin peoples who have shared the land on which I now live, and, in echo of the Haudenosaunee thanksgiving address *Ohenten Kariwatehkwen* – the words that come before all else – an acknowledgement of my ultimate gratitude to the earth, water, air, animals and plants in all the places that sustain me.

The book itself has indebted me to scores of people, and in the most wonderful ways. The seeds of enquiry were planted when I taught an introductory law course at the University of Sydney in 1996 that included a case study on native title. I thank the course designer Jenni Millbank for her prescience in insisting on the importance of native title for Australian law. Early inspiration came from the work of (I will acknowledge only those I have met!) John Borrows, Peter Fitzpatrick, Nicole Graham, Ghassan Hage, Richie Howitt, Rod Macdonald, Val Napoleon, Paul Patton, James Tully and Jeremy Webber. I would like to thank John Borrows for graciously allowing me to borrow my title from his chapter 'Landed Citizenship: An Indigenous Declaration of Interdependence'. Chapter 5 was published in a slightly different form as (2005). The truth in painting: cultural artefacts as proof of native title. *Law Text Culture*, 9(1), 91–130, and I appreciate the permission to reprint parts of that article here.

From its initial stages as a doctoral dissertation, through three continents, two children and several years as a professor at McGill, the work in writing this book has been enriched by innumerable conversations with peers and colleagues, and the whole process made that much more enjoyable by their friendship and community. Particular thanks go to those who have read and commented on drafts: Mark Antaki, Terry Carney, Annelise Godber, Alyson Grant, Aidan Johnson, Ian Kalman, Rod Macdonald, Victor Muñiz Fraticelli, David Newstone, Bradley Por, Alex Reilly and Kristen Rundle. I am very grateful, also, for the conscientious and detailed comments of my three thesis examiners, Margaret Davies, Peter Fitzpatrick and Richard Mohr. Having people engage critically with one's work to that extent is, I am realizing, a rare gift. During the dissertation research, my interviewees were generous and welcoming, including Richie Howitt, the late Rick Farley, Justice Tony North, and Mary Edmunds. Thanks, too, to barrister Patricia

Lane and to Paul Hayes, formerly of NSW Native Title Services, for taking me into the daily life of native title processes.Finally, I have enjoyed working with the editorial team at Ashgate, who have been professional and patient.

Above all, my sincerest thanks go to Desmond Manderson, exemplary supervisor, inspiring colleague and valued friend. His love of ideas and commitment to an intellectual community has been infectious, and it has been a privilege to have benefited from his generous and enthusiastic engagement with my research over the years. His ideas and input are inextricable from the text that follows, and his supervision was a performance of the idea of dialogue at the heart of this book. I am particularly grateful that he pushed me to make the thesis into the most expansive educational experience possible, and for him leading me to McGill, and beyond.

To my family for daily reminders of interdependence, and particularly to Alice and Lucien: this book is for you.

Kirsten Anker, Montreal

Chapter 1
Introduction

> In a dream where there is no fear of retribution Nungas face the Australian state and ask, 'By what lawful process have you come into being?' 'An Act of State', says the High Court, and it is as though doctrines of state supremacy conjure a magic that absolves centuries of unlawfulness and violence against Indigenous peoples. The question is – now that *terra nullius* is 'known' to be dead – what constitutes the state? This question is met with the silence of an unrecognized violence – a power of the state to annihilate all that is different (Watson 2002: 265).

> This is the radical question of justice, too: not 'How much do I get?' but 'Who are we to each other? What place is there for me in your universe, or for you in mine? Upon what understandings, giving rise to what expectation, do we talk? What world, what relations do we make together?' These are the questions we ask our law to answer (White 1990: 233).

The Project

When the Australian High Court's decision in *Mabo and Others v Queensland [No 2]*[1] (1992) (*Mabo*) came out and the debate over 'native title' hit the media, I was studying undergraduate property law. Naïvely, I remember feeling relief at the decision – well finally! Indigenous rights have been recognized, so everything should be okay now. The false 'doctrine of *terra nullius*' which had treated Australia as a land without owners had been rejected,[2] and something about that magic word 'recognition' promised resolution, authenticity and justice. Whenever the recognition of Indigenous rights[3] has taken place, from the constitutional recognition of Aboriginal rights and the federal government's land claims policy in Canada, the state acceptance of the Sami parliaments in Norway and Sweden, and the host of constitutional reforms in South America, to the signing of the United Nations Declaration of the Rights of Indigenous Peoples (2007), it carries the sense that governments and courts are progressively doing the right thing.

And yet, as the Australian native title debates ensued, everything was not okay. Miners and farmers were not happy. Maps of Australia appeared with menacing

1 The first common law recognition of native title in Australia.

2 Although there is considerable debate about the role of *terra nullius* in the *Mabo* case (see Ritter 1996), I refer here to the popular conception that this was the effect of the High Court's decision.

3 I use the term generically to cover self-determination, land title and cultural or other practices.

black patches of potential 'lost' land; backyards were threatened on national television.[4] My relatives, farming what I later learned was Yorta Yorta country,[5] complained that everyone had gotten along fine until native title stirred up trouble. Others felt that native title gave special rights and divided the community. Native title undermined the Commonwealth of Australia by recognizing Indigenous law as if it were the law of a foreign country in our midst. Native title promoted a 'black armband' view of history[6] and destroyed national pride.

Even the beneficiaries of native title, Indigenous Australians, did not think everything was okay. Not only did they have to weather the backlash of anti-native title vitriol, but the promises of recognition did not materialize. Native title was just available over the remnant land that the Whites[7] didn't want. Made weak and inferior by easy extinguishment, native title represented racist inequality under the law. More profoundly problematic for the possibility of justice through legal recognition, though, was the claim that recognition is a twisted colonial trick. While purportedly based on an existing and authentic 'true' Indigeneity, culture and law, the criteria of authenticity are always and forever set by the agents of colonial power through academic expertise, parliament and the courts. The structure of this claim lent itself to criticisms of *mis*recognition and *mis*representation, where the forms of native title as it made its way through the system were compared to a more genuine version, an Indigenous perspective on land which found the official version of native title wanting.

My sense that there was something crucial in the complexities of these debates, and that they might teach us something important about law in postcolonial polities, drew me to undertake the research culminating in this book. Why was recognition so appealing (or so threatening)? Why did it fail? If the key concern was equality, well then, equality of what? Equal treatment of our (different) property, simply begged the question of what property was and how far those differences would extend. What did it mean to say that the common law and Indigenous laws co-exist? Could authentic Indigenous perspectives ever be represented in the legal system?

---

4 There was a misunderstanding purveyed in the media that ordinary suburban blocks would be the subject of native title claims, when it was clear in the *Mabo* decision that any grants of freehold had extinguished native title. The fear-mongering continues, with the recent successful Nunga claim over Crown land that included areas in metropolitan Perth greeted as a 'land grab' over cities (Peatling 2006).

5 I have adopted this Aboriginal English expression for land or territory which, as I will explain in later chapters, has resonances that challenge Western conceptions of land and our relation to it: see Rose (1996a), who notes that in Aboriginal English, 'country' is a proper noun as well as a common noun, it is a living entity that has consciousness, it is lived in and with (7).

6 A phrase coined by historian Geoffrey Blainey (1993) to indicate a perspective in which Australian history is principally characterized by imperialism, dispossession of Indigenous peoples, exploitation and genocide – the stuff of mourning.

7 Used colloquially to refer to non-Indigenous Australians of European origin. See p. 13 below for a discussion on naming.

And what exactly were the reasons for resistance to the idea of Indigenous law? The recognition debate seemed to go to the heart of James Boyd White's radical justice question: Who are we to each other, and what space is there for Indigenous peoples in the universe of national law? Seeing the recognition of native title – a form of land title with its source in Indigenous legal traditions – as effecting a perceptible constitutional shift in the nation, as Justice Gummow of the Australian High Court famously said (*The Wik Peoples v Queensland; The Thayorre Peoples v Queensland* 1996 (*Wik*): 230),[8] implies this sense of the relations we make together, and the spaces made for the co-existence of different universes. But what struck me, on closer inspection of the native title debates in Australia, was the asymmetrical nature of the shift: national law admits only change over which it has firm control. It maintains the prerogative of the final decision. It recognizes rights derived from Indigenous law but determines the meaning of that law and the parameters for recognition. It never submits itself to the potentially disruptive process of asking, 'What place is there for *me* in *your* universe?'

The purpose of this book is to imagine a law capable of taking this risk. Such a law cannot claim to be the only law, nor rest on the unquestionable sovereignty of the state. It cannot rely on aspects of its universe – whether notions of history, fact, language or space – as if they are universal. It cannot mistake its power for the truth. In focusing on prominent aspects of legal discourse and process, this book seeks to set state law in front of its own reflection in the mirror of Indigenous rights. Dimly, in the reverse image in the glass, there is the possibility of another law: that of Koori, Murri, Nunga, Gitxsan, Mi'kmaq and Inuit peoples.[9]

But despite this haunting image, the monism of the one law persists, solid and pervasive. It can be found in the doctrine of sovereign monopoly, the rule of law, and the one humanity equal before the law. It is there in the idea of law as a systematic and ordered package of rules and principles with stable and determined meanings, unified by a single and central organizing principle. It is a key characteristic of the positivist and empiricist rationality with which modern law 'thinks' in finding the world composed of stable facts and objects, a separate thing to which it can then be applied. In modern Western legal theory, legal monism (law as a singular system or kind of object with a monopoly in a given territory), legal positivism (the possibility of identifying law according to pre-existing criteria, a property that is taken to give it impermeable intellectual boundaries) and legal centralism (the formal criteria for law are located in state action) make up a consensus about the nature of law (Macdonald 1998; Davies 2005). The corollaries of monism, then, are unity, coherence, autonomy, stability, objectivity and reification.

8 See also French 1997: 1.

9 Local language names for Indigenous peoples from, respectively, Southeast NSW and Victoria, Southeast Queensland, Southwest Australia, around the Skeena River in British Columbia, the maritime provinces in Eastern Canada and the Arctic region of Canada.

People who experience an 'other' law, like Nunga legal academic Irene Watson (cited in the epigraph), have no difficulty in pointing out the 'Just So'[10] quality of the State's answers to existential questions. Not only do these answers attempt to brush over the violence with which the State's supremacy was established, but they deny the ongoing colonization of Kooris, Murris, Nungas and others by insisting that there is ultimately one law, one knowledge and one truth. In this context, any claim for 'recognition' then happens in the epistemic language of settler law that will try to name and fix Nunganess as a *fact*. To do otherwise would be to risk acknowledging partial legitimacy, an incomplete domination, the shifting foundations of knowledge, and the possibility of obligation to another *law*. So conversely, to start to see another law and to call for thinking in terms of legal multiplicity is to welcome indeterminacy, fluidity, relation, subjectivity and contestation.

It is this call that *Declarations of Interdependence* answers. In the chapters that follow I diagnose some of the implicit assumptions about law that have directed the development of the law and practice of Indigenous rights in certain ways, and suggest an alternative way of thinking about law that may well offer less stability and coherence (the 'certainty' clamoured for in native title debates) but more honest answers to better questions about justice. The analyses in this book are deeply grounded in a series of Australian – and to a lesser extent, Canadian – case studies, and their strength and richness lies in their specificity. However, the terms with which they engage – recognition, pluralism, translation, proof and negotiation, as well as sovereignty, difference, authenticity, continuity and change, objectivity and subjectivity, dialogue – resonate in other places in which justice for, by and with Indigenous peoples is at stake, and beyond that, where the development of a general critique of Western law and jurisprudence is of interest.

It will be my argument that an approach to law known as 'legal pluralism' provides a more apt language for treating 'the justice question' of the place of Indigenous law than orthodox legal theory because, in the way I conceive it, a legal pluralist recognition is an engagement about the nature of law and not about a formal relationship between two fixed entities. A first premise of legal pluralism is that state law is not the only legal order in any given social space. In scholarship this premise has been largely supported by social science techniques and analysis. The argument against the monopoly of state law is thus supported by evidence of multiple forms of social control by 'unofficial' legal orders. A second premise has been developed by critical legal scholars and others – attacking the monism of modern law from the inside – who argue that state law does not have a monopoly on legal meaning because language is indeterminate; that its stable, coherent

10 The *Just So Stories for Little Children*, published by Rudyard Kipling in 1902, gives fantastic accounts of how various natural phenomena came about. The phrase is now used to describe a theory of human or animal traits or behaviour that is unverifiable and unfalsifiable. It has been used in relation to stories of sovereignty in Australia by Dorsett and McVeigh 2002.

foundation is a myth; and that the reification of law is a denial of the human element, of relation, interpretation, symbolism and embodied practice.

My argument will develop these two legal pluralisms, the first seemingly 'looking out' to other laws and the second 'looking in' towards the nature of state law. In that my approach is sceptical of the objective reality in which law is assumed to operate, it is a critical legal pluralism. I perceive law as constructing, and being constructed by, notions of time, space and subjectivity. In that I am interested in semantic, symbolic and relational dimensions of law, and hope to develop my idea of law through a conversation with many interlocutors, both Indigenous and non-Indigenous, it is a discursive legal pluralism. Together these two dimensions of legal pluralism express the interdependent qualities of law.

This book draws on a broad base of scholarship in addition to legal theory, from philosophy, literary studies, anthropology and social theory, to Indigenous studies, literature and art, all of which can help us to think against the grain in law and to seek the 'unofficial' law of native title, the law that is not dictated by the official organs of the state. It is an approach that takes pluralism – the minimum condition for the 'recognition of difference' – to be not just the co-existence of multiple legal *systems*, but a plurality in the very nature of law. In contrast to the unity of monism and the objectification of positivism, law can also be seen as inherently partial, fragmented and shifting, its meaning never given but rather derived from an inherently dialogic process. Instead of a solid edifice of rules, I show that law's structures of fact and law, property and sovereignty, traditional and modern, Indigenous and Australian or Canadian, are made not of concrete but of the dynamic play of human discourse: symbolic and embodied exchanges on which we act, and acts which make our world meaningful.

This is not so much a book about 'Indigenous law' as it is about the processes of interaction which produce an entity that becomes known as 'Indigenous law'. In critiquing those processes the book also puts into question the constitution of what I know as my own law. Uncovering the blind spots, the 'Just So' stories, and the paradoxes is the first step in challenging them. This introduction first provides a brief history of the advent of 'native title' in Australia in order to describe the problem I am addressing in legal pluralist terms. It then goes on to lay out the conceptual, methodological and ethical concerns of my project. The final part introduces some critical resources that will serve the rest of the book, and shows how they relate to a theory of legal pluralism.

Native Title and Legal Pluralism

Unlike in North America and New Zealand, there was no history of treaty-making in Australia. The first case claiming traditional rights to territory, *Milirrpum v Nabalco* (1971), failed on a number of bases, one of them being that the common law of Australia did not recognize traditional title in the absence of acts of recognition by the Executive. Although a number of state and territory-based land rights statutes were enacted following this decision, it was not until the *Mabo* decision in 1992 that *Milirrpum* was overruled, and native title was recognized as the inherent rights and interests in land, held by communities of Aboriginal peoples and Torres Strait Islanders and deriving from traditional laws and customs, that survived the Crown's acquisition of sovereignty. The core of the definition of native title was reproduced in the Native Title Act ('NTA' or 'the Act') the following year, and a National Native Title Tribunal ('NNTT') established to manage the claims process and act as mediator in disputes.

The majority of commentary on native title addresses itself to the fairness of the Native Title Act and the interpretive choices made by the courts – whether the categories of existing land titles that extinguish native title are too broad, for instance, or whether the requirements of continuity with a pre-existing traditional law are too strict. The focus is often on the workability of the system and the benefits it delivers, in real terms, to Indigenous communities or to the 'national interests' of certainty and resource development. Even for those more likely to see the situation in terms of postcolonial justice, the focus is on the practical impact of statute law and judicial decisions. The arguments employ the powerful, accessible language of equality before the law, but tend to take the structures of the state legal system and the concept of law more or less as givens.

But without questioning the conceptual architecture of law, critics miss the intricate ways in which Western law is tied up in a colonial project that either excludes or assimilates others to its terms (Fitzpatrick and Darian-Smith 1999: 1–3). For instance, the claim of misrecognition implies that one ought to aim towards better representation, in the law, of an Indigenous reality. However, it thereby re-imprints a European epistemology about the knowable, ascertainable nature of the world that accompanies positive law: the one commanding people through the edicts of state officials, the other ordering the world of phenomena through scientific discipline. The law is applied to the facts, but the facts are always and already compromised, mediated through colonial institutions, Western science, common law technologies of proof and the English language.

If attempts at recognition by the law appear as an endless trajectory, leading down a hall of mirrors reflecting one European perspective after another (Howitt and Suchet-Pearson 2003: 557), and if the inevitability of this ethnocentricity is an inherent limitation in the law, then for many the solution must be political. Justice in Indigenous land claims can only be resolved through negotiated settlement, and the legal aspect of the project abandoned. I agree with the focus on negotiation, but contend that law will not go away by making the matter a pragmatic or political one. We have only shifted the problem. In any case, the idea that law is separate from politics is itself one of those European mirrors.

Indigenous critiques of the Eurocentric nature of state law are plentiful, including those who compare the changeable, arbitrary 'book law' of the Europeans to the strength of a moral law that is literally grounded in the land. In academic circles, it is frequently anthropologists, historians or political theorists who have some occasion to question the orthodoxy of positive law in Indigenous rights jurisprudence, for instance, because these writers are qualified to challenge the assumptions that judges and others make that touch on their domains in native title matters: the nature of 'fact', the value of texts as a window on historical truth, or the separation of the legal from the political. Very often, however, they are just as happy to leave the definition of non-Indigenous law to the lawyers, and to assume that, in its own domain at least, the common law is as positivist and monist as it claims to be.

One brief example will suffice. Christos Mantziaris and David Martin, in their book *Native Title Corporations: A Legal and Anthropological Analysis* (2000), conceptualize native title as the overlap of 'the Australian legal system' and 'the system of relations ordered by traditional law and custom'. This is visually represented as two intersecting circles, and builds on Yalanji lawyer Noel Pearson's well-known characterization of native title as a 'recognition space' (9). This is seen to be a progressive characterization in that it posits a non-hierarchical relationship between the two systems, and an existence for Indigenous law beyond or in spite of official recognition. However, in situating recognition of native title in the 'history of relations between Indigenous and non-Indigenous societies in Australia [which] has produced a complex zone of political, social and economic interaction' (3), Mantziaris and Martin notably omit 'legal interaction' from this list. This point is made more emphatically later, when the diverse meanings attributed to native title by Indigenous groups are said not to 'assist in defining the *legal* content of the title. This is primarily a task for conventional legal analysis (12)'[11]

Again, in the extensive discussion on the problems of defining law, of assuming that traditional laws and customs constitute a 'legal system', and of translating them into other terms, Mantziaris and Martin note that translation 'may result in the *transformation* of practices and values generated through the direct interaction of people, to practices and values generated from the exegesis and interpretation of written texts' (42–3).[12] We are approaching a stronger sense of interaction here, but it is still one-sided: the common law is not similarly re-interpreted and transformed. The imbalanced use of pluralist themes like this is common in much social science commentary on Indigenous rights, which, similarly, tends not to allow that the interactions might be considered *legal*, and also tends to be blind to reciprocal processes and effects on the state legal system.[13] It is my conviction that answering the radical justice question in Indigenous rights – who we are to each other – requires taking on some of these blind spots in order to ask how Indigenous and non-Indigenous law might be seen to co-exist. It requires thinking around the doctrine of the monopoly of sovereignty, the unified structure of law as a system of rules with an objective existence, and the account of legal change via the exercise of sovereign will. That is, it requires a critical and discursive legal pluralism.

11 Emphasis in original.

12 Emphasis in original.

13 One exception is Weiner 2006.

As a label used by social scientists, legal pluralism emerged in the 1960s, but traces its roots back to the work in the early twentieth century of Boas, Malinowski and Mauss. Although the assumption that law and the state are coterminous had been dominant in the West since the early nineteenth century, these ethnographers found it difficult to accept that tribal and village peoples in the acephelous (stateless) societies they observed were not behaving as if they had law. The new emphasis on fieldwork in anthropology at this time brought the gaze of theory to the concrete world of everyday life and away from abstract principles and codes, and thus to focus on law in terms of its function – dispute resolution, social order – rather than the forms and institutions that were particular to European law. Law was, in functional terms, argued to be a universal phenomenon in human societies, not limited to particular 'stages of development' or types of political organization.

Further, even where there was a politically centralized authority – such as in the colonial nations in which most early ethnography took place – it was readily observed that 'paper' laws promulgated in the distant capital penetrated only partially the lives of Indigenous peoples whose own rules and processes carried on. In Indonesia, for instance, where the terminology of pluralism was first used in the colonial context, the arrival of European law was merely another element added to the earlier legal complexity brought about through centuries of invasion and migration (Vollenhoven 1918; Furnival 1939; Geertz 1983: 226). Legal pluralism thus began to be identified in situations in which the same person could be subject to more than one legal order (Benda-Beckman 2002: 60).

Studies in the legal sociology of European societies had also separated the idea of law from the state. Max Weber (1954), for example, argued that private organizations generate their own legal orders, with internal customs and rules, and a means of coercing or inducing compliance (56). Eugen Ehrlich (1975) identified a 'living law' practised by the many different social groups whose actual norms of conduct, he thought, often conflicted with the written law or the norms used for decisions by judges. Later sociologists of law developed the idea of legal diversity to challenge the 'state centralist' model of law, among them Georges Gurvitch (1932) and Leopold Pospisil (1971), who identified various levels or types of law co-existing in the same society. A 'new legal pluralism' began to develop which no longer referred to the traditional issues of relations between colonial law and colonized groups, but to the overlap of interacting and competing normative orders belonging to the range of collectives in contemporary democracies: religious and ethnic minorities, trade unions and industry groups, localized communities and other social networks and institutions.[14] Thus, as John Griffiths argues, while the ideology of 'legal centralism' had been effective in supporting the aspirations of the modern state to be the exclusive source of law and to ultimate political hegemony through a unified set of institutions, researchers should not be blind to the reality of law as 'an unsystematic collage of inconsistent and overlapping parts' (1986: 3–4).

14 Merry (1988) cites the work of Sally Falk Moore, Laura Nader, Carol Greenhouse, Harry Arthurs and Murray Woodman, among others, as examples of 'new legal pluralism' (872).

But the idea that diverse forms of law could be identified based on criteria, functional or otherwise, undermined a pluralist ethic because, in an essentialist fashion, it suggested there could be a universal understanding of law. This had imperial overtones for Indigenous or non-Western peoples whose languages often have no ready equivalent for 'law' or to whom the categories implied by the criteria (rules, disputing, order) were not sensible in their ways of thinking. As Boas and others realized, a cross-cultural enquiry into Indigenous law would have to confront the fact that law takes place in a world where knowledge, people, place and things are configured in specific ways and that perceptions of unifying characteristics of law across cultures depends on the perspective of the observer. In ethnographic accounts, any exposition of 'Indigenous law' unavoidably implicates what the researcher already thinks law is, but also what the Indigenous informants understand the researcher to mean by law. Each attempt to fit data into a conceptual frame of reference provokes questions; behind each question is a further frame of suppositions that may not fit: not just 'what is law?' but 'what is a human being?' and 'what are time and space?'

This conundrum in comparative research was addressed by the 'interpretive turn' in the social sciences in the latter half of the twentieth century that led to an understanding of law as a linguistic and symbolic practice which had to be interpreted in order to be meaningful. Anthropologist Clifford Geertz, in particular, emphasized the hermeneutic process by which an outsider must seek to grasp the 'distinctive manner of imagining the real' of which law is a part, by beginning with the key local vernacular linguistic and symbolic terms in which legality might be approached by insiders (1983: 173).

With law as a discourse or system of signs, legal pluralism can then be seen not as a conflict between sets of social norms, but, in Günther Teubner's (1992) terms, as a 'multiplicity of diverse communicative processes' with which individuals observe social action in terms of law and non-law (1443). Legal pluralism is thus a lens for looking at the world which helps constitute a plural state of affairs to observe. Legal sociologist Boaventura de Sousa Santos's case studies (1977; 1987) show people living in 'interlegality', and drawing on various normative and symbolic resources that frame reality in particular ways, where each frame informs others. Legal orders are, as encapsulated in Sally Falk Moore's *Law as Process* (1978), neither static nor distinct but involved in a constant process of creating norms and developing discourses that borrow from, and react to, other norms and discourses. Legal pluralism in this sense sees not co-existing and distinct orders, but rather a pervasive mixedness in legal phenomena.

Legal theory also felt the impact of the interpretive turn in the social sciences, and in the work of Lon Fuller, Robert Cover and Ronald Dworkin to name but a few, the possibility for multiple and equally cogent interpretations of texts lays the grounds for a critique of the idea that law and legal rules can exist objectively prior to interpretation (Fuller 1958: 661–9, Dworkin 1986: 238), or outside of cultural narratives which locate them and give them meaning (Cover 1983: 4). But while Dworkin privileges judges as the interpreters of law, Cover's argument is that we each contribute to the creation of legal meaning through our invocation of and commitment to cultural narratives. Conversely, the power of discourse to construct reality has led critical legal and critical race scholars, feminists and those influenced by poststructuralist philosophy to attack law's claim of separateness from social life, to critique the role it plays in perpetuating and creating inequality and oppression and to argue for the better inclusion of diverse perspectives in the law. Part and parcel of this approach is a critique of the self-sufficiency of legal language and the determinacy of legal reasoning, which are seen instead as rhetorical ploys that cloak the position and interests of the powerful in the clothes of neutrality and fairness. While these internal critiques of law tend not to identify as 'legal pluralist', Margaret Davies (2005) has argued that, along with the empirical or socio-legal approaches, they form a broad *ethos* of pluralism in legal thinking that has ethical, ideological and aesthetic dimensions.

The term 'critical legal pluralism' was coined by Martha-Marie Kleinhans and Roderick Macdonald (1997) who incorporate some of these critical insights into a theory of legal pluralism. Rejecting the reification of law and communities in social science approaches to legal pluralism, as well as the criteria-based approach to law and the prescriptivist idea of law as something applied *to* its subjects, they focus on individuals – those who follow, use, invoke and interpret law – as productive sites for its symbolism, sense and normativity. This approach, they argue, 'endows legal subjects with a responsibility to participate in the multiple normative communities by which they recognise and create their own legal subjectivity' (38).

Other theorists are concerned that versions of legal pluralism inspired by poststructuralism lead us either to the idea that 'law' is meaningless, or to an incapacitating relativism. Brian Tamanaha (2000) promotes a conventional linguistic definition: the meaning of law is to be discovered from whatever people identify as law in their speech and other referential practices (306). Emmanuel Melissaris (2009) makes a case for contextualism as the only defensible form of pluralism: not that there can be no true statements about law, that all statements about law are equally true or that any choice made between them rests on arbitrary preferences, but that a commitment by any person to an understanding of law as true in a particular context and given their experience will be open to the falsification of that understanding (47–50). In order to have any kind of conversation about law, there needs to be a 'thin' sense in which we hold to an overarching or a-contextual common-point of reference, but it should be understood as provisional, partial and incomplete.

This rather impressionistic and brief account of legal pluralism has not done justice to the subtleties of all these theories nor given much attention to the disagreements among them, so I return to some of them in Chapter 3. The purpose of this survey was to briefly set the scene for my argument, which is that critical, discursive legal pluralism allows law to remain relevant to Indigenous rights because it contemplates diverse authorship in law that renders the 'Just So' stories relative and subjective, and therefore makes a multitude of other perspectives legally cogent. Because an understanding of different perspectives and accounts of law comes about through dialogue and encounter, those accounts are responsive and provisional, and so discursive legal pluralism anticipates the possibility of change. And because legal pluralism acknowledges the creative propensities of these encounters and conversations, it encourages a different sense of responsibility for decision-making that does not just respond to the world but creates it. By choosing to highlight the dynamic and discursive nature of law, legal pluralism is better placed than other approaches to law to open up the question of intercultural justice and stimulate a dialogue between legal traditions.

The Ethics of Research Method

The dialogue between legal traditions I am advocating has implications for research methods, particularly in a project that might be seen as trying to identify 'Indigenous' and 'non-Indigenous law' as elements in native title. Research concerned with the ways in which Indigenous peoples were different from Europeans was and remains behind some of the most repressive colonial policies, but later also assisted the emancipation of Indigenous peoples by showing an intricate and rational culture deserving of respect and recognition. In either case, since the time of the great 'voyages of discovery', scientific scrutiny of Indigenous peoples and their lives has largely operated under a research paradigm in which the civilized European self is the 'knower', and the savage non-European other is, like objects of nature, part of the 'known'. Indeed, a larger point can be made that the history of European sciences has been a process of creating a European subject at the expense of colonized ones (Spivak 1988: 280).

The Western research paradigm mostly continues to elide Indigenous peoples as *subjects* of research, as thinkers, theorists and philosophers. And although they are the most researched minority group in Australia, Indigenous peoples have the highest indicators of poverty, illness and social disadvantages. The principal benefit of research seems to some to be the increase in scholarly status and expertise. On the other hand, even where a research project is intended to benefit the members of a community, the 'benefits' may, from the community's perspective, be ill conceived or tempered by other scales of value.

Ethics standards in research and higher education institutions in places like Australia and Canada have begun to reflect these concerns. Guidelines issued by the Canadian Research Councils, for instance, highlight the need for consultation, negotiation and informed consent, the involvement of Indigenous researchers, individuals and communities as research collaborators, and respect for Indigenous knowledge systems and processes, for cultural and intellectual property rights, and for the diversity among Indigenous individuals and groups.[15] National ethics guidelines in Australia have also adopted the core values of reciprocity, respect and responsibility (among others) in research concerning Indigenous peoples (NHMRC 2007).

15 In Australia, see AIATSIS 2011; and in Canada, see McNaughton and Rock 2003.

A more radical stance sometimes emerges. As one non-Indigenous legal academic comments: '[i]t cannot be surprising that many Indigenous Australians believe non-Indigenous researchers should just stay away completely' (Nielsen 2002: 158; see also Smith 1997). Others are calling for a new 'Indigenist' research methodology, by and for Indigenous people, privileging Indigenous voices and grounded within their own way of doing things (Rigney 1999; Martin- Mirraboopa 2003; Foley 2003; Findlay 2000; Ermine 1995). As will become clear, while I am sympathetic to these strategies as reactions to the repressions of colonization, a historical sensibility shows, as Edward Said (1993) argues, that '[p]artly because of empire, all cultures are involved in one another; none is single and pure, all are hybrid, heterogeneous, extraordinarily differentiated, and unmonolithic' (xxv). It is thus not the inclusion of different methods and perspectives that is problematic, but rather the suggestion that these might be pure and untainted, that we can 'stay away' from each other.

Although my initial research questions – testing the propositions of critical, discursive legal pluralism in native title claims – could have envisaged a collaborative endeavour with a specific group of people relating to their law and their perspectives on the native title process, a second approach, influenced by Said's *Culture and Imperialism*, suggested itself: to engage in a critical reflection on the way that racial and cultural difference is constituted in native title. My analysis is largely textual and relies on published materials. However, I have also gained insight from attending mediation sessions of the Australian NNTT, being involved behind the scenes at NSW Native Title Services, and interviewing legal practitioners, NNTT mediators and an Australian Federal Court judge.

The 'stay away' attitude seems to enforce the idea that the cultural or racial components of legal phenomena are necessarily the responsibility only of those who are marked as different, as if 'White' were not a race, as if through being normalized, White were invisible, or as if our understandings of racial difference were not themselves shaped by mainstream legal discourse (Williams 1997: 6). The silence of researchers on these issues may then become complicit in the status quo; it may be an abdication of the responsibility, incurred by privilege, to speak out against oppression (Alcoff 1991/92: 7). In the same way that 'Critical White Studies' turns the lens of race onto the formerly raceless in order to 'unpack the social and normative power of whiteness' (Davies 2002: 281; see also Delgado and Stefancic 2001; Frankenburg: 1997; Nakayama and Martin 1999), legal theory needs to scrutinize the way that the articulation of difference in native title institutes power relations, making some things invisible and others simply normal.

Consequently, the questions of culture, race and 'difference' that generally interest me in native title are how European Australianness emerges as a norm, and how Indigeneity gets produced as different from it. The norm can be invisible – there is just 'law' and 'people', for instance, not Western/state/colonial law or European/settler/non-Indigenous Australians. By using the labels European, Western, White, settler, I try to bring to the fore some of these absent markers of race, culture and origin. The strategy of putting into question those absent markers is part of the 'unlearning of privilege' and the making visible of the investigator that Gayatri

Spivak urges as part of an anti-imperial project: 'to learn to speak to (rather than listen to or speak for) the historically muted subject' (Spivak 1988: 295).

The Native Title Act uses the terminology 'Aboriginal Peoples and Torres Strait Islanders' to distinguish the two groups of people who may potentially claim native title. The current use of 'Indigenous' in academic and administrative discourse in Australia suggests it as a generic descriptor of first Australians, being inclusive of both 'Aboriginal' peoples who live on the mainland and 'Torres Strait Islanders'. There has been an observable historical progression from 'Native', to 'Aborigine' or 'Aboriginal' (also used as a noun), to Indigenous person, where terms have sometimes consciously been adopted at various stages because of different associations that are seen as more respectful or inclusive.

While 'Aboriginal' refers to the fact of coming before, the name itself came after the arrival of Europeans, and so ironically represents an erasure of the languages and identities that came before. As Marcia Langton and William Jonas (1994) comment, 'before the coming of non-Aborigines [e]veryone was simply a person, and each language had its own word for person. Different groups distinguished one another in different contexts by different names (by their language, their country, etc.)' (3). European terms, therefore, are frequently rejected as essentializing, both effacing the many diverse peoples that made up the pre-colonial population of Australia, and silencing peoples' own languages and names for themselves. An alternative practice of naming is to avoid generalizations and use local group names such as Yolngu in Arnhem Land, Nunga in southwestern Western Australia and Koori in the southeastern states, and where my discussion is of particular people I adopt this practice. A further step is to then name the newcomers in local languages: Balanda in Arnhem Land, Kartiya in the Central Desert and Gubba in the Southeast, for instance (Carey 2004; Tilbury 2000). I have occasionally used the Aboriginal-English vernacular of 'Whitefella' and 'Blackfella'. As we shall see below, however, group names are never epistemologically neutral, as they are bound up with ways of understanding human groupings, and a colonial history of demographic disruption and practices of naming.[16]

When the focus of discussion is on national institutions and discourse, however, it makes sense to use the terms employed in those contexts: Indigenous, Aboriginal and Torres Strait Islander. This is also a recognition of the fact that, despite their differences, Indigenous peoples were and are treated as an 'other' to settlers, and all suffered and continue to suffer the impact (although varied and particular) of colonialism. Finally, the word 'native' in 'native title' seems to be an anomaly – maintained by the courts for the legal doctrine of native title when in Australia it sounds pejorative or at least out-dated in reference to human beings. In Canada, on the other hand, where 'native' is still in use in the vernacular as a descriptor of people and culture, the common law recognition of traditional title is known as 'Aboriginal title'.

16 Such as the 'language group' names mapped by Tindale (1974) in the 1930s, and the recent increase in social importance of language groupings.

In that ethics is a 'responsibility to others', my research ethic in preparing this book has been to respond to those that I have met and whose words I have listened to or read, and to take seriously the claims of both Indigenous and non-Indigenous persons. The following section begins to implement this methodology as a crucial component to discursive legal pluralist analysis by engaging critical resources from my own intellectual tradition that have taken to questioning ways of thinking, doing and being, and brings them into dialogue with the traditions of Indigenous Australians.

Critical Resources for Legal Pluralism

An Intercultural Conversation

In making comparisons or finding 'difference', those engaged in intercultural conversations about law discover not only the distinctiveness of others' law but also the particularities of their own. They can thus gain insights with valuable critical traction, should they choose to use them in this way. Indigenous peoples, for their part, have been able to articulate how European ways appear to them at times strange and violent, rather than natural and universal, in contrast to their own. As a number of postcolonial thinkers have argued, the 'cross-pollination' effect of comparison may work to create hybrid epistemes at the same as it articulates the contrasts that allow us to identify cultural and other differences. My purpose in the following section is to develop a critical intercultural conversation, responding to the comments and observations of some Indigenous thinkers with insights from the Western philosophical tradition, in order to draw out some themes for legal pluralism as a hybrid approach.

Why do you Whitefellas always have to know everything?
Galarrwuy Yunupingu's question[17] expresses his frustration with what he takes as the assumption that there might be an 'everything' to know and that we ought to be able to access it. Like Gurukman, the greedy frog in David Gulpillil's story who drank all the water,[18] certain approaches to Western epistemology – we can think of Francis Bacon and the metaphors of taming nature (Graham 2011: 30) – have expressed a desire to explore, uncover and achieve mastery over everything in the universe. This urge is structured by a basic separation between a world 'out there' and a human consciousness that can apprehend it and use it. Knowledge can have an 'everything' if the facts of nature are universal and form a unique whole. The European scientific tradition, and prominent strands of European philosophy,

17 Recounted by Rick Farley in an interview with the author, 3 November 2003.

18 Retold in Watson (1997: 42–4). The other animals, dying of thirst, eventually tickle the frog to make him laugh and release the water.

have traditionally purported to discover principles and facts that transcend their particular context of time and space.

For peoples like the Yolngu in the north or the Arrernte in central Australia, on the other hand, knowledge is intimately related to the land and so is of necessity local. It is also differentiated between individuals or groups because the details of 'country' – knowing the songs and stories that tell how particular places came to be as they are – are the privilege or right only of those who are the custodians of that country. As Deborah Bird Rose (1996a) writes, 'the fact of localised knowledge is itself Law' for many Aboriginal peoples (13). Information is not freely available to all; it is possible that it may only be spoken about in specific places and contexts. It may be gender specific. The language in which it may be spoken about is itself marked with the place in which the language resides. There is not necessarily a single overarching structure into which parts of life fit like a jigsaw.[19] At the same time, the attribution of every geophysical feature and living thing at the local level to the activities of 'Dreaming' ancestors in the beginning, connects the concreteness of the local to the vast scales of infinite time and great power. As a kind of founding philosophy whose stories stretch across the whole of mainland Australia, the Dreaming is both the mythological creation period and a continuing ordering principle. Through birth, individuals may have one, or more, Dreamings that give them a totemic identity with an ancestral Dreaming being, and through that, an association with a set of places, stories, ceremonies and kin. The Dreaming beings 'are just as much alive today as they were in the beginning' (Silas Roberts, quoted in Rose 1996a: 24) and so the Dreaming as a timescape and the source of life and law is an 'everywhen'.[20] As Richard Howitt puts it, the Dreaming provides 'a scale metaphor which encompasses the infinite within the immediate' (Howitt and Suchet-Pearson 2003: 561).

White man got no Dreaming. Him go 'nother way[21]

This statement, from an informant to anthropologist W.E.H. Stanner, contrasts the man's own conceptual universe – the Dreaming – with that of White people, who have their own way of knowing. This very claim to know differently is a critique of the universalist pretensions of the Enlightenment tradition, or at least the vulgarization of 'reason' as empirical certitude and universal knowledge (Saul 1993). In this respect the observation shares the argument of feminist thinkers that one's cultural position (such as gender and other specificities) 'is epistemically salient' (Alcoff 1991/92: 7) or with postcolonialists and poststructuralists who find the Western universal rational subject to be based on 'an ethically unsustainable omission of the Other' (Ghandi 1998: 39) and of an infinite variety of others. In general, the contestation of universalism says that knowledge is socially constructed and depends on the lived experiences of individuals.

19 See Christie and Perrett 1996: 61.

20 W.E.H. Stanner's (1998) famous neologism (228).

21 'Intelligent old man' quoted in Stanner 1998: 227.

Even the stage on which universal facts play out – the stable and linear time and space coordinates of Cartesian geometry and Newtonian physics – has in the West been brought into question by contemporary geographers, who argue that time and space are cultural products (Lefebvre 1991). Quantum physics shows that time and space are qualities relative to each other that cannot be measured accurately simultaneously, and that the act of observation or measurement can never be purged from the experiment: no facts exist without the observer.[22] The conceptual construct of space as linear has visual counterparts in the artistic technique of perspective – in use since the Renaissance – that causes objects to appear further away by making them progressively smaller along lines of sight, thereby tricking the human eye into seeing as if from a particular point in space. One commentator contrasts this technique to central desert Aboriginal painting (the famous 'dot paintings'), in which looking does not place one as an objective observer in space, but rather as someone immersed in proximate and tactile sensual connections (Watson 2003: 50–5).

A boundary is to cross

The Yolngu from the northeast of Australia's Northern Territory have a saying that 'a boundary is to cross'. Through this aphorism they address the ontological problem that one needs categories in order to make sense of the world, but that borders between categories are problematic if treated as a discontinuity or exclusion. The tendency to categorize may well be common to all human systems of thought, and inherent to language (Lakoff 1987; Bowker and Star 1999): if in Western secular thought all matter can be divided into 'animal, vegetable or mineral', the Yolngu divide the things of their world (including words) into one of two moieties, *Dhuwa* or *Yirritja*. And in the central Australian desert, people are allocated to one of eight 'skin' groups, based on birth, and with which Dreamings and places are associated.[23] In modern Western ways of thinking, however, the divisions in language are symptomatic of a particular kind of ontology, in which the categories form constituent, organized parts of a whole. Like atoms, the parts themselves are irreducible, essentially identical to others in the same category and separate from those in other categories. The identity of things is marked then by *essences* and by *discontinuities* (Christie 1994: 24). Identities are often paired in a hierarchical binary such as self/other, mind/matter, man/nature, reason/emotion, civilized/savage, subject/object. Because the second term is effectively designated as an absence of the first term, the apparent dualism is a singularity; it is the 'self' set within a hall of mirrors, the dominant mired in a monologue (Rose 2004: 19–21).

As Michael Christie (1994) discovered when he began to learn the Yolngu Matha language, this atomistic structure does not always hold. Every person, group, place, fish or tree seemed to have a number of different names whose use

22 For example Einstein's Theory of Relativity (a forerunner of quantum theory) and Heisenberg's (1958) uncertainty principle (129). See generally Penrose and Isham 1986.

23 See for instance the Walpiri at Warrabri in Bell 1983: Appendix 2.

depended on the context and the speaker's skill in selecting the most appropriate word when different aspects of life were foregrounded (27). Alternative names associated different sets of connections between people, places, stories, spirits and so on, such that there were no absolute ontological distinctions or 'macro categories' (like plant/animal) (26). Grammatically, says Christie, Yolngu Matha cannot readily be used to make propositional statements about units of reality that persist over time, such as 'the cat is on the mat'. Instead, Yolngu speak aphoristic sentences that evoke human experiences with tropes: catness at matness, for instance. Only the context would indicate whether the speaker had a specific cat in mind (27). Other Indigenous languages are verb rather than noun dominant (like English), so that being or process rather than 'thingness' is evoked. In Cree (northern Canada), for instance, the word for person, *iiyiyuu*, can be glossed as 'he lives' (although there is no gendered pronoun), an animate quality of personhood shared by humans, animals, spirits and geophysical agents (Colin Scott, cited in Howitt and Suchet-Pearson 2003: 562). A verb-based world is always in flux.

The difficulties that anthropologists have had with naming Yolngu social and land tenure groupings seems to have to do with the underlying metaphors of group terminology in English, which 'depend on spatial images of segmentary structure, external boundaries and taxonomic hierarchy', rather than the images of connectedness or junction used in Yolngu Matha, such as parts of the human body or the roots of plants (Keen 1995: 502). A *bundurr* (knee) name called out in ceremonies is the proper name for a human and a spiritual ancestor, a living person and a place, and so links them all like a joint. Yolngu names do not label them as individuals (another atomism) but 'locate them as nodes on a rich network of people and places related through their totemic relationships' (Christie 1994: 29).

Atomism is also endemic to a form of reasoning structured around either/or logic and analytical cognition which reasons by breaking propositions down into constituent parts. As has become obvious in court-room cross-examination where this kind of logic is elevated as the path to truth, Indigenous witnesses may have no problem with avowing two apparently contradictory statements.[24] In other critiques of Western logic, Afrocentric scholars have argued that the diunital reasoning prevalent in African cultures leads to both/and conclusions and does not seek to consider information by organizing it into categories (Myers 1988: 11).

Within recent Western theory, critiques of binaries as constructed and culturally specific, if not simply artificial, are becoming more common. Said (1979), for instance, has shown how the West, or Occident, is a category that was constructed in opposition to the Orient, itself a collection of images built up through the imperial, administrative and scientific practices of Europeans. Similarly, the racial category 'Black' has shifted over centuries to include different peoples depending on economic, social or demographic concerns, and often preceding European contact

24 As anthropologist Nicholas Evans explains in cross-examination in *The Lardil Peoples v State of Queensland* 2004): [81], ('*Lardil Peoples*').

with those societies.[25] European linguistic philosophy, such as that espoused by Ludwig Wittgenstein, argues that it is these loose agglomerations or families of associations that, through practice and over time, give words their meaning, rather than any essential definition or attribution (Wittgenstein 1968: §66–§71).

Deeper semiotic analysis has shown that the work of purification that is necessary to keep categories separate in fact creates efflorescent hybrids.[26] The poststructuralist theory of Jacques Derrida and others demonstrates that categorization depends on qualifying criteria that are neither in nor out of the category, but at the limit, and what is excluded from an essential entity, quality or phenomenon is semantically a part of it.[27] For example, whereas knowledge about the world, and the disciplines of philosophy and science which produce that knowledge, have since the Enlightenment been based on a rationality that banishes imagery and myth in their quest for the purity of fact, many Western scholars are now reclaiming the importance of narrative and imagery in the construction of the world (Cover 1983), arguing that philosophy has its own imagery – particularly one built into the language of foundation and spatial distinction – and that the very pretension to mythlessness is itself a form of mythology (Derrida 1982; Le Dœuff 1990; Fitzpatrick 1992a).

In maintaining that 'a boundary is to cross', the Yolngu treat differentiations made in geographical space that identify distinct 'countries' not as a way to exclude others, but rather as a way to help express an alphabet of relationships between people and country, a system of tenure as it were (Williams 1982: 148). For the people at Yarralin in the Northern Territory, the tracks which Dreaming ancestors followed mark out boundaries, but are also referred to as 'strings' that are webs of connection. A boundary merely means that the world made by the Dreaming is not uniform, and the strings create 'sets of identities that cross-cut each other' (Rose 1992: 55). Karen Martin-Booran Mirraboopa (2003), from Southeast Queensland, also explains her Quandamooka ontology in relational terms; the entities in the Quandamooka universe – men, women, spirits, country, skies and waterways, animals, plants – have their identity in their relation: 'Whilst they are differentiated, these relations are not oppositional, nor binaric, but are inclusive and accepting of diversity. These relations serve to define and unite, not to oppose or alienate' (207).

You've got to get it [the Law] from that ground, to start off with. The grounds always stay: the Law's always there (Guruma Elder, in Brehaut and Vitenburgs 2001: 10)

The characterization of Indigenous legal traditions as oral is a source of doubt on the part of Western officials regarding claims to authenticity and antiquity. To critically approach the contrast to written law, we need to understand the

25 See Jacobson 1999.

26 See Latour (1993) on the categories of human and non-human, (10–12).

27 See Derrida (1976: 30–65) and (1987: Ch II); Lyotard 1984.

relationship of writing to objectivity, continuity and change. Knowledge of a world 'out there' is objective, in Western common sense, both in the sense of treating knowledge as an object with an existence independent of human agents, but also in the sense of being produced by a methodology that guarantees truth by setting aside the personal, the irrational or the artistic. Crucial to objectivism is the idea of language as a medium of representation, itself an arbitrary referent to an exterior objective reality, and a style of speaking that distances speakers from their interested speaking position. From this perspective, the fact that Indigenous cultures had no written language means that the sameness of the present (knowledge, law, practices) with respect to the past cannot be guaranteed. Indeed, claims to continuity are systematically viewed with suspicion because they cannot be proved by writing. This view is shaped by a Western understanding of language as having a purely referential function. The guarantee of sameness depends on transmitting across time accurately the words which tell what used to happen, and which are as corruptible as memory is fallible.

In contrast, one hears time and time again the insistence by Australian Indigenous people that there has only been one Law since the beginning, that they have always followed the same way, and that all knowledge was laid down in the Dreaming. But in contemplating the possibilities of constancy in an oral tradition there are two points to consider. First, for many Indigenous peoples language too is a thing in the world that was left in the land by the ancestors, or borrowed from environmental elements. It has taste, location and power and is not just a means of referring to something else. The second point is that although, in one way, reality or truth is said to abide in language, and although knowledge of law is considered to be singular and unchanging in the sense that 'the ground always stays', in another way, knowledge about law is contextual and openly negotiated. Elisabeth Povinelli (1993) observes that women at Belyuen in the Northern Territory, for instance, continually modify environmental classifications based on their experience of country and their interpretations of events with regard to Dreaming beings – the Dreamings *are* constant, but they might be 'tricky'. Conversely, the women modify their statements of true fact (about the presence of good food or dangerous Dreamings, for instance) with conditionals (maybe, just try, let's see) 'at that moment when it will be acted upon and someone held responsible for that action' (685). Statements of truth are always made in the context of an assessment of the consequences that will arise because that person is part of an ecosystem and part of a community.

In Yolngu ceremonies, the stories, images and connections of the Dreaming can be said to provide a repertoire from which a form of ritual is negotiated, and from which all people present will be able to read off a celebration of the ancestral journey that is specific to their country in a way that also connects them to the other participants. 'At a different place or a different time, with a different group of participants, the configurations of symbols would be very different, and the selection of dances, songs, objects, sculptures, painted designs etc. must reflect these differences' (Christie 1994: 31). The ceremony instantiates the particularities of that event; it is a reading of the local present and not an abstract perspective.

According to Christie (1994), 'Galtha [ceremony] emphasises that knowledge is not constituted by objective facts, but by ongoing negotiation of our various partial perspectives' (33). Thus although the resources for making knowledge are eternal and not of human origin, the specific meaning is explicitly constructed in the particularity of the here and now through physical acts; knowledge is performative.

The overt context and place dependency of Indigenous law and knowledge and the emphasis on relation, negotiation and enacted, rather than essential and universal, qualities in Indigenous philosophy bring Indigenous critiques of Western law close to some currents of contemporary debates in legal theory. In these debates, some argue that law is not the application of rules, but the negotiation of knowledge, the telling of narrative, the exchange of symbols and the enactment of power relations. Taking these qualities on board, however, means that I must recognize my own writing – and my current observation of similarities and differences – as a practice enacting these observations for the particular purpose of critiquing Western law, of inviting the reader to see in a particular way, and not some general truth.

Themes for Legal Pluralism

The preceding set of examples have introduced some themes that are relevant to a critical, discursive legal pluralism because they challenge the universal with the local and particular, the essential and discontinuous with the hybrid and relational, and the objective with the contextual, enacted or negotiated. The themes provide in each instance a plural alternative to the dominant intellectual context for law, because they break into the monopoly of thinking that is assumed to be universal, and because they themselves are always plural qualities: multiple, changing, aspectival. But rather than thinking of these themes as strict alternatives, plural thinking means understanding that whether something is local or universal, continuous or in flux, depends on how one looks at it, such as whether in the archetypal quantum physics experiment one is measuring for waves or for particles.[28] Being able to countenance the both/and *and* the either/or of this situation is to acknowledge the necessarily artificial nature of the boundaries drawn, the alternative truths that are made absent in the process, and the power involved in getting others to accept the distinction as real.

Unsurprisingly, the orthodox understanding of modern law shares many of the Western tropes just identified. Law is assumed to exist as an objective entity – a finite legal system whose components can be fixed and known. Humans, and their world, are prior to law, independent from it; law is applied *to* them. Discontinuous

28 Although in many physics experiments light behaves like a wave – producing interference patterns that resemble ripples on water – in other experiments, it behaves like a discrete particle which is either in one place or another. The conclusion is that light has a dual wave/particle character, and that its behaviour depends on the design of the experiment (see Heisenberg 1958: 13).

at territorial or jurisdictional boundaries, law is considered nonetheless to have constant or universal application within those boundaries. The authority of modern law depends on its separation from politics, its rationality on its separation from art, its functionality on its separation from facts. Legal reasoning is propositional, and language represents, but is distinct from, the law.

Some versions of legal pluralism have engaged with the critiques and alternatives discussed in the previous section. We have seen that the general premise of legal pluralism is that the state does not have a monopoly on law. Other law exists and may be equally or more important in peoples' lives. Once it abandons institutional pedigree as a means of identifying law, legal pluralism must widen its understanding of what law is. Law has many forms. It may be written or unwritten, explicit or implicit. Each community may have its own set of normative rules and practices. As people belong to more than one social grouping and community overlap, so one group's law intersects with the law of others.

When we come to questions of the nature of law and the possibility of intersection, our critical resources become particularly necessary. The idea that there is *the* law of the state and *the* law of different communities posits a reified entity that has a defined content. Often that content, or its function, risks replicating the idea of law as authoritative rules for social order that comes from state legal theory, and risks forgetting the possibility of different kinds of law. This risk can only be averted by maintaining dialogue about the nature of law, but these conversations do not just represent law, they continually reconstitute our understandings of it. This then adds a sense of 'internal' pluralism to law: we do not have one, or even many, fixed entities called law.

Here, our critiques of objectivity would indicate that the importance of interpretation to the meaning, substance and application of law situates it within the local, the particular, and the inter-personal. This challenges the 'view from nowhere' of *the* law and immediately renders law subjective, indeterminate and open to contestation. The local, meanwhile, is but one scale at which law is met. Law's diversity derives in part from the number of different maps we can use to read it (Santos 1987: 298). As for intersection, if one person and her interpretations of the law of the different communities to which she belongs is the site at which laws overlap, then legal systems are separate only to the extent that they are experienced or articulated as such, but will in any case meet in her thoughts and practice and influence each other.

A discursive understanding of legal pluralism suggests that all law's boundaries are transgressed as soon as they are drawn. There are politics, aesthetics and fact in law just as there are laws of politics, art and science. These boundaries are not concrete things with a millennial constancy; rather they are continually and actively created and maintained when we 'do law'. While we ought to see boundaries as necessary to making meaning, we must ask whether particular boundaries are the best ones to maintain, and acknowledge that all boundaries are partial and permeable, that they are links rather than barriers. A critical, discursive legal pluralism thus draws on a range of contemporary theory that focuses on practice, performativity and enacted knowledge rather than objective, representational and propositional knowledge, and looks to the way people practise law, bring it to life and give it embodied meaning, a way that escapes an orthodox account of law as the application of rules.

Here I have begun a preliminary sketch of the version of legal pluralism I am advocating as an epistemology, an ontology and a theory of practice; in other words, a way of thinking, being and doing law. Many of the themes for this version of legal pluralism share a sense of two-way movement and relation. In this book I use three different terms – dialectic, dialogic and discursive – to evoke this, but because – despite coming from the same linguistic root – they have different connotations in philosophy, a brief explanation is required.

Dialectic

In questioning a posited, objective and universal law and promoting a processual, non-essential and relational understanding of law, I draw on principles associated with dialectics, which in classical Greek philosophy was the art of discussion or debate involving the exchange of propositions and counterpropositions, leading to a synthesis of propositions or a to shift in the debate itself. In contemporary philosophy, dialectics has three key tropes.[29] First, reality and history are *dynamic*: what we perceive as stable things or structures do not exist outside of or prior to the processes, flows, and relations that create, sustain, or undermine them. Second, things are not essential or pure, but are internally *heterogeneous* at every level: different elements can be seen depending on the scale at which analysis takes place, and these categories are themselves contingent and provisional. Third, parts and wholes are *mutually constituting*. Often described as a 'dialectic relation', mutual constitution comes about because of the processes that link things rather than as a result of cause and effect. For instance, 'Whitefellas' and 'Blackfellas' constitute one another through processes of relating as raced people, and my body and the surrounding air constitute each other through the process of breathing.[30]

Dialogic

This less 'technical' term still conveys a sense of process and relation, but, in contrast to dialectic, the dialogic has a clearer sense of the human activity of talking or communicating. It is thus particularly useful to a legal pluralism concerned with the human element in law, and with an intercultural ethics in which one is listening and responding. For Hans-Georg Gadamer (1979), for instance, conversation is an activity through which we bring our 'horizon of understanding' into contact with

29 I rely on David Harvey's (1996) useful summary (49–57).

30 Dialectics is also associated with a specific strand of European philosophy through G.W.F. Hegel and Karl Marx. Hegel's thesis/anti-thesis/synthesis in which the preliminary contradiction between thesis and anti-thesis is resolved or overcome is linked to his view of history as a progression towards ever greater completeness and rationality. In Marx there is a similar aspiration to progress (in pitting the proletariat against the bourgeoisie we arrive at a classless society), and a view of history as deterministic, which I do not wish to adopt.

that of another person, developing a new understanding, a new assessment of our own intellectual tradition, in light of the interaction (347). I find the notion of the dialogic especially suited to the theme of call and response that I develop in this book to argue against the foundationalism of modern law.[31]

'Dialogue' is also promoted as a key element in contemporary theories of justice, in which justice is served by deliberative democracy or the inclusion of all 'voices' in public debate and the development of law and policy.[32] While genuinely inclusive dialogue is sometimes held out as an ideal which is unattainable because of the realities of oppression, ignorance and prejudice,[33] the dialogue I am interested in is one which takes place in spite of the non-ideal situatedness of people, and because it is inherent to the sense-making capacity of language.[34]

Discursive

Finally, the possibility that power is a necessary part of communication, and that it is not possible to separate power and rationality, has been taken up in what is known as 'discourse theory'. Discourse, as used by Michel Foucault and others, explicitly addresses the relation of power to speech, and is thus useful to developing legal pluralism in the context of native title. Such phrases as 'legal discourse' or 'feminist discourse', meaning loose collections or conventions of speech, writing and discussion around the relevant topic, imply a concept of power in that such conventions are constraining to those affected by them. In Foucault's sense, we are shaped by the discourses in which we participate, and language – both the said and the unsaid – is the site of struggles of power. Discourse has effects in the real world. Thus 'discursive' describes, like dialectic, the constitutive production of things: reason is constructed by discourses on insanity and fiction, for instance.

It is an appreciation of discursivity – and the relation between power and language – which leads to the observation that, even if language is radically undetermined, the powerful are always trying to fix and determine it. In law, discourse analysis shows the systematic appropriation and privileging of certain meanings and the rejection of others as extrinsic, unauthorized or threatening (Goodrich 1987: 3; Jackson 1995; Cornell 1992). Discourse is thus not only relational and productive. It is meaning grounded in practice and the physical instance, and so does not privilege the abstraction of language, words and text, but entails a comprehensive sense of human communication.

A number of writers have taken up some of these pluralist, critical and discursive themes in analyses of Indigenous rights. Jeremy Webber (1995; 2000) has emphasized interaction and mutual influence, concluding that doctrines of

31 I am indebted to innumerable exchanges with Desmond Manderson on this theme: see, for his part, Manderson 2012: 124, chapter 9.

32 See Fishkin 1992; Sen 2009.

33 Such as the ideal speech situation theory of Jürgen Habermas: see McCarthy 1988: 306–10.

34 See for instance, Bakhtin 1981; Wittgenstein 1968.

native title (and Aboriginal title in Canada) are the mediated result of a 'normative community' between settlers and Indigenous peoples. Stewart Motha (2005) uses native title jurisprudence as the impetus to launch a radical critique of the monopoly of sovereignty using the idea from the work of Jean-Luc Nancy that the singular is already plural. Richard Mohr (2002) provides a finessed semiotic account of how, through aesthetic and discursive practices, Indigenous law and the common law continually 'reframe' each other so as to change the meaning of law. Simon Chesterman (1998) engages more conspicuously in a critical legal pluralism that asks how colonial power relations are constituted in the deployment, by judges in native title cases, of analytical categories (law as behaviour, law as institutionalized norm enforcement) and how some norms thereby become privileged and elevated to the status of law.

The contributions of Indigenous commentators often extend to the form in which the intellectual exploration of pluralism takes place. Irene Watson (1998) analyses colonial law through story-telling and the use of Nunga concepts of *ruwe* and the *Maldarbi*, reversing the process of translation that takes place in native title. John Borrows, an Anishanabek legal scholar from Canada, has a large body of work drawing on his peoples' teachings and stories that collectively argues for an intermingling of Indigenous and Western jurisprudence (2002; 2005; 2010). And Yugambeh scholar Christine Black (2011) offers a theoretical frame worked up from Indigenous texts, stories, contemporary Western jurisprudence on law, film and popular culture and her own travels and experiences of country within which she suggests different Indigenous peoples can explore and consider their own legal regimes.

What this book aims to do, through a thicker description of Indigenous rights claims processes and discourse, is to develop a more consistently critical and discursive legal pluralist narrative of Indigenous rights. It hopes to open up a space of engagement with Indigenous legal traditions as well as turn a critical eye on how it is that state law institutionalizes differences between legal traditions that solidify colonial power relations. In querying the raft of assumptions about law with which decisions about native title are approached by the courts, however, I show that law is already more plural and dialogic than the orthodox theory would lead us to believe. This undermines the court's claim to authority and the 'Just So' story of sovereignty, and engenders a different sort of responsibility for the decisions that are being made.

Chapter 2 (Recognition) takes up the central question of recognition in Indigenous rights, drawing on critiques of the politics of cultural recognition to argue that the key issue is one of sovereignty, not merely in the obvious sense of a political monopoly of control over territory, but in an attempt to masterfully determine meaning in time through the cognitive gaze of recognition. Chapter 3 (Law in Time and Space), extends the problem of recognition to the identification of law as fact, first by considering the failure of the claimants in the Australian case *Members of the Yorta Yorta Aboriginal Community v Victoria* (2002) to establish the contemporary existence of traditional laws and customs in evidence, and second, by questioning the social scientific model for legal pluralism. The spatial and temporal aspects of sovereignty are contrasted with a different configuration of coordinates in Yorta Yorta expressions of belonging to place.

The claim that I lay out in these two chapters for the interdependence between individuals, communities and legal traditions, and between law and its various 'others', is then deepened by examining three specific aspects that are characteristic of the process of claiming Indigenous rights. The first, considered in Chapter 4 (Translation), is the need to translate from Indigenous languages and cultures into the terms of recognition. I argue that the experience of translation – and the impossibility of translation – becomes constitutive of both the claimants' law and the Court's law. The second is the fact that courts' rules of evidence have often had to adapt to novel forms of proof in establishing Indigenous rights. In Chapter 5 (Proof), I analyse the work done by a painting, the *Ngurrara Canvas*, after it was submitted as evidence in a native title claim, arguing that the process of proof becomes a pedagogical one that teaches participants something different about the nature of law, truth and country. Lastly, Chapter 6 (Negotiated Agreements), argues that negotiations between government, industry and claimants in the resolution of claims put into practice a law more fluid and dialogic than can be explained by orthodox legal theory. Translation, proof and negotiation demonstrate the legal pluralism argued for in this book: not a simplistic model of parallel legal orders or overlapping laws contained in a singular space, but a pluralization of the spaces, times, texts, images and processes of law.

Chapter 2
Recognition

> It begins, I think, with the act of recognition. Recognition that it was we who did the dispossessing. We took the traditional lands and smashed the traditional way of life. We brought the disasters. The alcohol. We committed the murders. We took the children from their mothers. We practiced discrimination and exclusion (Keating 1992).

> The tension between recognising the familiar in order to confirm what we already know and listening for the unfamiliar that disrupts what we already know is at the heart of contemporary theories of recognition. How is it possible to recognise the unfamiliar and disruptive? If it is unfamiliar, how can we perceive it or know it or recognise it? (Oliver 2001: 2)

Introduction

This book began with a quote stating that justice is a question of relative identity: who we are to each other and the space we make for each other's universe. In contemporary political philosophy, this question is mostly discussed in terms of recognition. With a debt to G.W.F. Hegel, key theorists such as Axel Honneth and Charles Taylor understand identity as constructed in relation to, and through the recognition of, others. In law, recognition is embedded in the functional grammar of legal rights: it is what courts do to parties' claims to validate them. But lawyerly usage is largely unreflexive, and there is relatively little attempt in legal theory to connect legal recognition to the heavily worked concept in the psychology, philosophy and politics of difference and identity. Recognition is also a key term in legal discourses of Indigenous rights, which cannot help but engage with themes of difference and identity to justify distinctive rights, but I will argue in this chapter that, for the most part, they employ an impoverished concept of recognition that confounds the justice claims of Indigenous peoples.

In the wave of Indigenous rights recognition around the world since the 1970s, national regimes of recognition are often seen as initiating a post-colonial moment of sorts, making a break with a past in which Indigenous peoples were ignored or denigrated, and promising a new footing for future relationships between them and dominant society. The invocation of pre-existing and continuing Indigenous law within the borders of the nation state in regimes of recognition, co-existing with state law, gives us a starting point for exploring a theory of legal pluralism. But unpacking the idea of recognition helps provide a richer account of co-existence, one that develops into a critique of the positivist model of law and a more complex understanding of what I am calling the plurality of law.

An initial set of problems with recognition comes from a tension between its sense as identification and its constructive sense of granting a status. Instead of taking recognition as constitutive of identity, many lawyers assume that law recognizes by attaching legal labels and consequences to the object of recognition, whether that be rights, tribal identity or property relations under traditional laws and customs. Such an approach – an archetypal example of the core legal activity of applying law to facts – suffers from ethnocentricity in the labels used, and, in presuming a pre-existing object, tends to reify an essentialized version of an authentic Indigenous 'culture'. In his extensive critique of the politics of recognition, Patchen Markell (2003: ch 2) considers these first two problems as part of the incoherence of the politics of recognition, combining, as it does, three threads of modernist philosophy identified by Taylor – universalism, authentic cultures and identities, and Hegel's intersubjective recognition – that pull in different directions.

After reviewing the philosophies of recognition that inform contemporary political discourse, this chapter will explore this set of problems with recognition in the jurisprudence of Indigenous rights in Australia and Canada. As common law countries, both have inherited a 'doctrine of recognition'[1] whereby, on the reception of English law in the colonies, the pre-existing property rights of the inhabitants continued until abrogated by the new sovereign, although the doctrine has evolved in locally specific ways. Native or Aboriginal title is described as *sui generis*, since, due to the contribution of Indigenous law, it constitutes a unique form of title that does not fit into pre-existing legal categories. The resulting focus on Indigenous 'difference' means recognition is often approached as a process of translating the nature of Indigenous relations to land into the language of common law rights and interests. Criticisms of state recognition tend to turn around how closely the translation matches Indigenous perspectives. Where it is seen to fail in this task, Indigenous title is recast as partial recognition, or misrecognition, of Indigenous peoples. Further, often there is a baseline built in to the legal system, such as the limited property mandate of the courts, a cultural prejudice against oral histories in evidence, or the doctrine of state sovereignty that excludes the normativity of Indigenous law.

These stopping points are not just related to ignorance. They are symptoms of a third, larger problem with recognition: in the context of a continuing colonial relationship, the systematic treatment of Indigenous ways as inferior or unrecognizable is driven by a desire to maintain non-Indigenous control over the nation and its resources. A basic irony in the paradigm of recognition – in which the act of asking for recognition from a non-Indigenous institution reinforces the subordinate position of Indigenous claimants and the institution's privilege to decide

1 In some accounts, the principle I describe is called the 'doctrine of continuity' while the recognition doctrine refers to the view that only those rights granted formal recognition by the new sovereign can survive the change of sovereignty (for example, McNeil 1989: 165–74). Following Slattery, I also use 'doctrine of recognition' to refer to the automatic survival of pre-existing rights (Slattery 2006: 283–4).

– represents, as Frantz Fanon argued in the 1950s, a kind of pathology of the colonial relationship (1967: 11). Given their lack of control over the terms of recognition, Indigenous peoples may find themselves trapped in a colonial 'hall of mirrors' that leads to a never-ending cycle of failures of, and thus further need for, recognition.

However, while there is a great deal of frustration with regimes of recognition, and scepticism over whether the courts can adequately recognize Indigenous differences in property, law or culture, recognition remains central to many Indigenous claims for justice. A number of authors have attempted to rehabilitate or supplement recognition in a way that is sensitive to issues of power. Some argue for 'transformative' recognition that tackles the structural causes of defective recognition. Others look to the materiality of struggles for freedom, or Indigenous traditions as alternative sources of meaning, to break out of the hall of mirrors. However, Markell's (2003) argument about the incoherence of recognition makes a compelling point about the ways in which the drive for recognition mistakes the basic human condition: in attempting to guarantee that we are effectively represented in social and political life through proper recognition so that we may 'act in accordance with who we are' (12), we forget that the very reason why we need recognition from others is our constitutive vulnerability to them. Rather than being an injustice per se, misrecognition is a symptom of some peoples' pursuit of independent agency at the expense of others (4–5, 10–15).

This re-thinking of recognition complicates the role of law in the process of recognition. Legal positivism assumes a separate world to which law is applied as the deliberate act of will of the exclusive sovereign. But our more complex understanding of recognition argues that legal acts of recognition are constitutive of their objects, undermining the world/law distinction. Neither 'Indigenous peoples' nor their 'law' as such pre-exist the recognition encounter. It also takes recognition as a mutual exchange in which the identities of the recognizers are also involved: although the state might purport to be a neutral medium for interpersonal recognition, the processes by which 'the people' it represents are designated are the same as those that provide the foundations for its sovereignty (Derrida 1986: 11). The state is 'both a participant in and an artifact of the politics of recognition' (Markell 2003: 28). Once we understand recognition in this way, we see that despite its power, the state is not able to constitute itself, and it too remains vulnerable to its interactions with other actors. Re-thinking recognition breaks down the simplistic orthodox picture by acknowledging an intrinsic discursive and relational quality in law that confounds the state's attempts to master the meaning of law. The recognition of Indigenous law is tied up with both the 'external' and 'internal' legal pluralism that this book develops.

Theories of Recognition

In everyday terms, recognition means perceiving something that you already know – a face you have seen before, for example. Or it can infer familiarity with a generic characteristic even if the specific person or thing has never been seen before: we could say of a complete stranger that we recognize that they are upset, or of a meal that it is recognized as being healthy based on certain criteria. Recognition can have the sense of accepting the other person's perspective, a gesture of understanding: I recognize that you are upset, so I don't mind that you yelled at me. Alternatively, there is recognition as acknowledgement, reward, validation: to be recognized for a job well done. Dictionary definitions demonstrate this polysemy in a range of senses from knowledge (to identify, distinguish, perceive, recollect, realize) to acceptance (avowal, admission of truth or validity, submission to authority) and evaluation (appreciation, approval, gratitude) (OED Online 2013).

In an extended analysis of the semantic usages of recognition, Paul Ricoeur (2005) traces a development from a primary sense of intellectual mastery in the active voice (grasping something with the mind) to a passive sense of being recognized by, or seeking recognition from, others. He notes that recognition differs from knowledge in suggesting a hesitation, a difficulty to be overcome in arriving at the truth, whether due to the passage of time or to the uncertainty of identifying common characteristics (7). Markell (2003) sees a tension between recognition as retrospective identification of a pre-existing entity (which entails both a cognitive and evaluative aspect, since recognition often leads to treating persons or things differently) and recognition as a creative act, according a status – to recognized states, for instance – that did not exist prior to the act (39–40).

These different aspects of recognition are explored in a range of academic disciplines, from psychology to political theory, that treat recognition as a bridge between the known and the unknown, or between the self and the other, making it both a 'phenomenology of identity and a theory of knowledge' (Douzinas 2002: 384). Cognitive psychologists have investigated how infants come to 'recognize' their parents – how patterns of visual and other stimuli come to be identified over time as belonging to the same unity separate from that of the infant (Bushnell et al. 1989). This process is seen as key to the formation of peoples' sense of self. On a different scale, 'recognition' has, according to some, become 'the paradigmatic form of political conflict' in the post-socialist era (Fraser 1997: 11).[2] To understand how recognition in these different domains is related and how it explains certain problems in the discourse of Indigenous rights, we need to trace its intellectual inheritance back to the philosophy of G.W.F. Hegel. Hegel was influential in Fanon's accounts of the problems of liberation for colonized peoples (1967) and, more recently, in Charles Taylor's (1992) call for recognizing the worth of diverse cultural traditions in multicultural societies that has become a touchstone in the politics of recognition.

Recognition and Subjectivity

The story of recognition extends back to the *anagnôrisis* of Greek tragic theatre (Markell 2003: ch 3), and variants of it such as acceptance, esteem, and dignity,

2 See also Honneth 2002.

had played a role in political philosophy from the Greek *polis* to the imperative of respect in Kant. Hegel, however, was the key historical figure to put recognition at the core of his ethics. Most famously, he developed a relational idea of the person/subjectivity/self-consciousness that ran counter to the enlightenment paradigm of individualism: 'Self-consciousness exists in and for itself when, and by the fact that, it so exists for another; that is, it exists only in being acknowledged' (Hegel 1977: 111). In other words, unlike theories – such as Descartes's *cogito ergo sum* – in which human self-consciousness is *a priori* or self-subsisting, Hegel's view of self-consciousness is that it emerges first through a process of *negation* – by reference to what it is not – and second through *recognition* (*Anerkennung*) by others.

Hegel (1977) illustrates this process with a parable that has become known as the 'master/slave dialectic'.[3] In the preliminary stages of the dialectic (104–10), it is the experience of a desire for something that is missing (hunger, for example) that makes a person aware of a self that desires (*I* am hungry) relative to the objects that must be mastered in order to satisfy the desire (food) (Kojève 1980: 3–4). The consumption of objects is unsatisfying for the purposes of preserving the 'I', however, because in the moment of mastery that confirms the subject's independence the object is destroyed:

> Desire and the self-certainty obtained in its gratification, are conditioned by the object, for self-certainty comes from superseding this other: in order that this supersession can take place, there must be this other. Thus self-consciousness, by its negative relation to the object, is unable to supersede it; it is really because of that relation that it produces the object again, and the desire as well (Hegel 1977: 109).

Only another subject can satisfy the desire for lasting affirmation of a subject's humanity and agency, because it can continue to exist even as it is 'superseded' or mastered; it can provide ongoing recognition of the self as subject. Self-consciousness results from this innate human need for recognition, through a process which at once allows for socialization through our identification with others, as well as individuation through our awareness of our difference from others.

In Hegel's parable, a 'life-and-death struggle' (114) for recognition ensues, however, because being recognized turns the self into an object for an other and threatens its sovereignty. The struggle ends only when one party 'learns that life is as essential to it as pure self-consciousness' (115) and chooses to become a slave to the other, abandoning their freedom and desire for recognition, rather than be killed. The 'master' has won the battle as the 'slave' is now given over to realizing the desires of the master; the master has proved his freedom by risking death rather than submitting to the other.

---

3 Sometimes translated as lord and bondsman.

This is a temporary resolution of the struggle, however. The slave's recognition of the master's freedom is unsatisfying because it is not the recognition of an equally esteemed other freely given, not the recognition of someone in whom the master can see himself: 'What now really confronts him is not an independent consciousness, but a dependent one. He is, therefore, not certain of *being-for-self* as the truth of himself' (117). The master's recognition of the slave is deficient, too, because she is a non-person in the eyes of the master. On the other hand, the slave comes to realize her own independence through being able to transform the material world into means of sustenance (118). In the end, the dialectic between two selves must come to an equilibrium in which there is a mirroring of recognition. Mutual recognition is Hegel's ideal ethical state.

Hegel has been particularly influential in French existential theory, largely due to the lectures of Alexandre Kojève and Jean Hippolyte on Hegel in the 1930s and 40s. Their students included Jean Paul Sartre, Jacques Lacan, Emmanuel Levinas, Michel Foucault and Jacques Derrida (Peperzak 1993: 11–12; Butler 1999). Through the prominence of the master/slave dialectic in their interpretations of Hegel[4] – the dominant self and the subordinate other – comes the emphasis in later poststructural and postmodern theory on the category of the 'Other' that features in contemporary philosophical discourse on recognition.

Recognition and Legal Rights

The association between self-consciousness and the recognition of legal rights is developed by Hegel in *Philosophy of Right* (1967). The attribution of legal rights mediates the intersubjective dialectic once the subject moves from the primary sphere of the family to the secondary sphere of civic community. While the struggle of individuals to protect the possession of things, necessary to the fulfilment of desire with respect to the material world, is immediate and particular, the mutual recognition of rights to property protects our wants by universalizing them. Rights admit people into a political community, giving them a universal identity as citizens and legal actors above and beyond their varied and embedded local selves: 'What was formerly the simple and abstract realization of my private will becomes, when recognized, a tangible factor of the existing general will and consciousness' (§217). Legal rights represent the ability of the state to overcome the struggle for recognition.

A Hegelian theory of human rights thus depends on mutual recognition between human selves once the master realizes that his self-consciousness is dependent on the recognition of others, and this, as Lewis Hinchman (1984) argues, is coincident with or equivalent to the emergence of a rule-following community: '[a]n individual can only follow a rule if he grasps the idea that his own existence has something important in common with the existence of other people. For the

4 Marx had also taken this, in its guise as class struggle, as the core of human life. See O'Malley 1970.

essence of a rule is that it bind *all* individuals who find themselves in a certain situation' (24). However, modern human rights largely follow a liberal and natural law tradition in which rights expressed and protected immutable characteristics of human nature that pre-existed their transition to civil society – this is what makes them universal and unshakeable. Rights were attached to a *monologic* rather than a *dialogic* subject, an individual whose identity is independent of the world and other people. The dialectic bent that has come to influence psychoanalysis and social theory in the twentieth century has generally had little impact on the discourse of legal rights, and thus western legal theory is still largely 'inhabited' by autonomous individuals.[5]

The Hegelian dependent subject is still pertinent to mainstream approaches to law in two ways, however. First, practically speaking, without the recognition of my rights by others, my unilateral claims or abstract calculations are worthless and unable to be actualized. Second, specific categories of personal rights arising out of contract or property transactions have the effect of creating mutual legal personalities – lessor/lessee, for instance. However, legal recognition is restrained within particular categories of legal identity, through which individuals are simply interpellated by the state (Althusser 1971: 127–88). Costas Douzinas (2002) thus argues that in the context of modern rights, Hegel's parable of recognition has to be supplemented by an idea of subjection to the state (a sense of recognition as acceptance/submission that we noted earlier): '[l]egal and human rights are the institutional tokens of our identity' with which we bargain in our larger negotiations of identity with our social partners, 'always against the monologue of legal subjection' (386). The assumption that state recognition is necessarily one-sided will be challenged below, but questioning the way in which the state participates in the recognition dialectic is an important addition to analyses of the politics of recognition.

Because the range of legally catalogued identities is limited, rights will be experienced by some as being distortions or misrecognitions of their selves-in-progress.[6] In fleshing out a theoretical foundation for a contemporary politics of recognition based on Hegel's master/slave dialectic, Axel Honneth (1995) claimed that the injury of misrecognition, whether inflicted by other individuals, or by the law, belongs on the list of basic human wrongs (131–4). Douzinas (2002) thinks the emergence of new rights claims themselves can be matched directly to 'inadequate or defective recognition' (391). But whereas the original dialectic

---

5 For example, John Locke's account of property grounds it in an innate right to property in our own body and labour (1764: §27), while John Rawls's theory of rights depends on what individuals in the 'original position' would devise prior to joining society and taking up their lot in life (1971: 11–12).

6 Hegel himself thought that the abstract universalism of legal recognition would be supplemented by honour gained through membership of associations (such as guilds and professions), which would be based on the particular achievements and capacities of each individual (1967: §205).

giving rise to self-consciousness is between individuals, and in the second sphere the state mediates the relationships between individuals through legal rights, many contemporary rights claims are made on the basis of group identity.

Group Identity and the Politics of Recognition

As many observers have noted, recognition emerged as a keyword in collective justice claims towards the end of the 1980s, with the waning of the more redistributive concerns of socialist class conflict and welfare politics (Tully 1995: 1–4; Fraser 1997: 11; Taylor 1992: 25–6). Nationalist movements following the breakup of the USSR and Yugoslavia, and the rise of Indigenism, multiculturalism and feminism all offer examples of the use of recognition to articulate struggles over identity and difference, leading to a 'politics of recognition'. There are two ways in which recognition is a group concern. The first is that oppression due to misrecognition or the denial of recognition is often experienced along group lines, on the basis of shared characteristics such as skin colour or sex, for instance, or of a collective identity such as race, gender, religion or class.[7] The second is that the same Hegelian dialectic source of individual self-consciousness can be seen playing out at the level of groups or cultures, wherein a group's identity is created through recursive interactions with other groups. We claim aspects of our identity based on membership of collectives, and because these locate us in social and moral space – providing a larger framework for thought, evaluation, communication and action, a 'horizon within which things can take on a stable significance' (Taylor 1989: 27–8) – a misrecognition based on a demeaning version of group identity by others can be crippling. Crucially, in the influential work of theorists like Taylor and Honneth, it is the Hegelian dialectic understanding of self-consciousness in the second point that explains the experience of oppression in the first.

In his essay, 'The Politics of Recognition' (1992), Taylor explains the current potency of recognition discourse as resulting from its combination of two ideas with their origins in Enlightenment ideals that have 'burrowed very deep into modern consciousness': universal equality and individual authenticity (30). Combined with the Hegelian notion that we depend on others for our construction of self, these ideas ground the modern politics of recognition that this section will develop. However, as the sections following this one will detail, Markell (2003) argues that there is an ontological error in the partial way that Hegel has been taken on in the politics of recognition, evident in a certain tension in my previous paragraph. A group's identity is 'created' through interactions with other groups, yet the injustices we are interested in are often described in terms of misrecognition – the reflection back of a demeaning version as measured against some other,

7 'Indigenous people share a cultural heritage but they also share the experience of colonisation. These shared experiences (socialisation, heritage, history) validate and provide an enclave of inclusion and solidarity, detached from the wider community' (Larissa Behrendt 2003: 79).

internal, antecedent or true, version of identity.[8] According to Markell, the idea of accurate perception of identity, who people really are, is necessary 'in order to hold out the prospect of a *successful* regime of mutual recognition' (57) which is the endpoint of Taylor's essay, just as it was for Hegel. But how can that identity exist apart from these intersubjective movements? The error identified by Markell is found in the characterization of the original injustice in the master/slave scenario – not that there is unequal recognition brought on by the master's failure to see and respect the identity of the slave, but that one party has failed 'to acknowledge its own fundamental condition of dependence and to abandon its impossible quest for sovereign agency' (124). The error is deeply tied to the tension between the cognitive and creative aspects of recognition that we noted earlier.

At the time when the 'The Rights of Man' replaced the preferential system of feudal Europe with the ideals of universal dignity that demanded respect for what is innately human in all of us, the 'universe' was limited to European men of property. But the idea of equality was soon deployed to expand the civic rights of Europe's Jewish population and remove repressive measures against them (Markell 2003: 131–8). Nineteenth- and twentieth-century struggles by women, African Americans and Indigenous peoples also demanded formal legal and political equality on the basis that these immutable characteristics of humanity give rise to rights that exist in all people. Laws that prevented some people from voting or owning property, or worse, that made them into the property of others, were, in this lens of universality, considered a non-recognition of their status as human beings.

But, as Taylor (1992) notes, the breakdown of social hierarchies and the fixed roles that went with them led to a more individualized and subjective notion of identity than had previously been held. Through Rousseau we have inherited the idea that morality is a question of following our authentic inner voice, and from Herder, that we each have an original way of being human, that each *Volk* has its own authentic culture that it should look to and fulfil (29–30). In this lens, assimilation to the majority identity is 'the cardinal sin against the ideal of authenticity' (38) and leads to claims, like those coming from what Catherine Mackinnon (1987) dubs 'difference feminism', that what is unique to that group of people should be equally valued (33). For example, Carol Gilligan (1982) argued that women have differently structured moral reason to men, and that psychological theories of development should take account of these differences rather than treat women as defective men.

But universal dignity and authenticity alone cannot explain the pull towards recognition without some sense that they are not things we can generate on our own. Thus it is what Taylor (1992) calls the 'fundamentally dialogic character' of human life, rendered 'almost invisible [in] mainstream modern philosophy' that makes recognition by others so essential: 'We become full human agents, capable of understanding ourselves, and hence of defining our identity, through

8 See also Fraser 2000: 112.

our acquisition of rich human languages of expression ... always in dialogue with, sometimes in struggle against, the things our significant others want to see in us' (32–3). Hegel is implicit here, but is invoked more directly by Taylor when 'equal recognition [as] the appropriate model for a healthy democratic society' (36) echoes his later mention of Hegel's 'regime of reciprocal recognition among equals' (50).

The politics of recognition thus embodies a tension between sameness (equality, universality) and difference (identity, specificity) born out in interpersonal exchanges. It is precisely the dyad of sameness and difference that drives claims for recognition where some special characteristics are to be taken into account in the name of a shared one – the universal human agency that entails the freedom to choose one's form of life, the inherent capacity of all peoples to hold property, or simply the equal worth of all cultures. As Taylor (1992) points out, the two are organically linked because the principal that everyone has a universal quality of human dignity implies, when viewed through the second lens of authenticity, that it is each individual in their uniqueness that demands equal respect (39–41). Equality then requires the equality of our differences.

The Problems with Recognition

Of course, there is a philosophical tension, even a tautology, in the 'equality of our differences'. Because of this, one particular problem that has plagued the politics of recognition through the dyad of sameness and difference is that of assimilation, or ethnocentrism: the differences, the uniqueness, of the other can only be recognized in terms of the self. Stewart Motha (1998) argues that in any liberal humanist attempt to recognize difference, 'a universal is being smuggled in' (79, 85). Even when the stopping point is nothing smaller than humanity, the other is always being reduced to the terms of the self: they are human, like us. Difference is erased 'by the very gesture that purports to recognise it' (86).

In the passage quoted in the epigraph, Kelly Oliver characterizes this as a cognitive problem – how can we re-cognize that of which we have no cognition? The cognitive gaze calls up the sense of recognition as mastery that we noted earlier, which tends to objectify the other by rendering her 'known, understood, interpretable ... [robbing] her of her alterity' (Yar 2001: 62). The counter-strategies of subjugated groups include aiming to strengthen group members' senses of self through 'consciousness raising', and seeking to replace the assimilative criteria for judgment anchored in dominant perspectives with evaluation 'on our terms'. But for those seeking just relations with others outside their group, the dilemma appears still: to try to understand the other and close them within the terms of recognition, or to eschew the terms of recognition with the risk that we then 'become indifferent to the other's form of life' (Schaap 2005: 54).

One valuable contribution of Taylor's (1992) essay is his response to the problem of ethnocentricity in the terms of recognition, as well as to what he sees as an inappropriate premise in the counter demand for equal recognition: 'that we owe equal respect to all cultures' (66) as an automatic judgment of worth. Taking equal worth as an *a priori* aspect of cultures, he argues, would turn recognition into a condescending platitude rather than an act of respect, and presumes we already have the standards against which the judgment could be made (66–73). Taylor suggests, then, that recognition must always involve a process of enquiry that begins with the presumption that cultures are *capable* of being of equal worth but then tries to learn what it is about the other culture that demands respect. Crucially, the enquiry can never be merely about the *content* of another culture, and must inevitably involve (Taylor borrows the term from Gadamer's hermeneutics[9]) a 'fusion of horizons' in which the standards of judgment themselves come into dialogue with those of other peoples in order to develop new terms of comparison. The result is that: '[i]f and when we ultimately find substantive support for our initial presumption [of worth], it is on the basis of an understanding of what constitutes worth that we couldn't possibly have had at the beginning. We have reached the judgment partly through transforming our own standards' (67).

The 'fusion of horizons' approach brings Hegel's intersubjective dialectic into the realm of cognition to quash both the presumption that we can recognize without knowing the Other, and that knowledge relevant to recognition can pre-exist dialogue with others. With this move, Taylor addresses a second problem with the politics of recognition, namely the reification of an essential identity. There is a tension between the belief in an authentic individual self, and by extension, authentic cultures, and the need for both of these to be actualized through the recognition of others because of the essentially dialogic nature of human existence. The problem of reification has arisen largely because the 'authenticity' aspect of the philosophical inheritance of recognition has eclipsed that of the dialogic subject. In Taylor's example above, the demand for cultural recognition 'on our terms' is problematic because it fails to see that any engagement with value judgments can proceed meaningfully only through dialogue.

Another example of the tension lies in the reification of identity in identity/difference politics, where there is pressure to mobilize around one aspect of identity as if it speaks for the whole self so that, for example, race or gender becomes one's defining characteristic to the exclusion of the experience of hybrid identities (and multiple oppressions) (see hooks 1981). And then, because the heterogeneity of peoples' selves is reduced to generalizations in order to crowd

9 There is a certain inconsistency between Taylor's theory of mutual recognition which comes from Hegel, and his invocation of a Gadamerian dialogue as the way to arrive at a fused horizon of understanding that will form the basis of judgments of worth in the process of recognition, given that Gadamer seems to have abandoned the latter term as irrelevant to dialogue (Vessey 2011: 143). However, Gadamer's use of *Annerkennung* to refer to the acceptance of another's authority as a condition of dialogue, based on, as Vessey puts it, 'the awareness of our own finitude, the awareness of the need for language for any understanding, and the awareness that the meanings in language always go beyond our control' (149) gels with Markell's (2003) rereading of Hegel (103–8).

around a unified claim on behalf of groups, this in turn can have the effect of prescribing an essential identity for members of the group: the replacement of one tyranny with another (Appiah 1994: 163; Fraser 2002: 24; Wolfe 1999: 179–83).

Taylor has not escaped the contradiction between demands for recognition based on a distinct identity, and the admission that recognition is necessary because identity is a work in progress created intersubjectively, as several critics have noted (Oliver 2001: 45; Schaap 2005: 44; Markell 2003: 40). Although, as Andrew Schaap says, he 'glosses over the essentialism inherent in the ethic of authenticity by arguing that its emergence reflects the fact that … identity can no longer be taken for granted but must be struggled for', he nevertheless condemns misrecognition 'because it fails to see the other as she really is' (Schaap 2005: 44).[10] Fixing an authentic group identity as a measure of proper recognition denies the flux of identity produced in relation to others through the very process of recognition itself.

But where those relations are oppressive and the selves created are unhealthy, how are individuals and groups to escape the terms in which their intersubjective recognition takes place? Here we come to a critical third problem in the idea of recognition that, following Oliver, I will call its pathology, and which the work of Fanon (1967), one of the first thinkers to bring the psychoanalytic theories of Freud and Lacan on child development to the experience of 'black' people as a colonized group, illustrates in a nutshell. First, we have his diagnosis of the psychological effects on individual children of their upbringing as members of a maligned group. Conventional psychoanalytic explanations for neuroses – rooted in childhood and the family – were, he thought, less relevant for his fellow Africans than the trauma of being black in a culture defined by whites. Antillean children were socialized through games and French language children's literature in which, quite unsurprisingly, they identified with the white heroes fighting the forces of evil in the guise of 'injuns' or 'savages' (145–6).

On discovering that they were in fact 'black', a kind of mirror neurosis set in: they valued themselves to the extent that they were white, and yet despise themselves because they were and always would be black. The suffering of being robbed of all worth or individuality produces the perverse impulse: 'I will quite simply try to make myself white: that is I will compel the white man to *acknowledge* that I am human' (Fanon 1967: 98).[11] But the struggle for recognition in the actual workings of colonial slavery does not, as in Hegel's dialectic, result in equilibrium and mutual recognition: after all, the colonist wants not recognition from the slave, but work. Meanwhile, says Fanon, unlike Hegel's slave, the negro does not find independence through labour, but strives to *be* like the master (98).

---

10 As Markell (2003) notes (60), Taylor sees the problem in using an unstable, indeterminate and incomplete identity as the grounds for agency (and thus a criteria for recognition), but tries to rescue it by claiming that our best projection of a self-narrative into the future based on our 'sense of what we have become' will do the job (Taylor 1989: 47–8).

11 Emphasis added.

Consequently, since most situations in which the politics of recognition are deployed result from oppression, there is an imbalance in the apparent need for recognition. Oppressed peoples need recognition from the very group responsible for oppressing them; moreover, the selves that seek recognition have been shaped by the oppressive relationship. In this way, the act of recognition merely repeats the colonial hierarchy that gave rise to oppression in the first place: in Kelly Oliver's (2001) take on Fanon, 'recognition itself is part of the pathology of oppression and domination' (23). Fanon alternates between two solutions: one of violent revolution as the way to undo the violence of the original subjugation (2004: 1–62), the other involving replacing the 'alienating mirror' of racist socialization with a progressive one in an effort to expose the ways in which one's own attempts toward liberation are complicit with one's oppression and to address the structural source of that oppression (1967: 168).

Challenging the structures of domination is also the focus of radical feminists such as Mackinnon, for whom the differences between men and women as we know them are produced by gendered relations of power. She argues that women's reality has been shaped by life under patriarchy, such that the female voice touted by Gilligan – the ethic of care, a concern with relationships rather than rights – is just a reflection of what men want women to be (1987: 38–9). Likewise, Nancy Fraser's preference for transformative over affirmative remedies for misrecognition supports the need to destabilize the production of identities related to material inequalities rather than merely revalue them (1997: 24, 30). From this perspective, Taylor's investigative model seems uninflected by concerns about power, even in its attempts to redress ethnocentricity. As Oliver (2001) writes, his theory assumes one person taking 'the position of the judge of others who confers or withholds recognition' and 'does not take into account the effects of Western culture on those whom we [those in power] choose to study, nor does it allow that the one-way gaze of the judging subject is reversible' (46).

But ethnocentricity, reification and domination still do not get us to the bottom of the ontological problem with recognition, embodied in the tension between its cognitive and creative senses. In German there are two words: *Wiedererkennung* approximates the first epistemic sense of re-identification, while Hegel's term *Anerkennung* covers the practical sense of granting a certain status.[12] The first sense suggests mastery and is backwards looking to what is. The second sense contains the relational element of recognition and is forward looking to what is enabled. For Markell (2003), the key to understanding the problems with recognition is the temporality of the combined English term that 'links an agent's past and present to her future' (10), as opposed to the largely spatial imagination that most thinking about injustice as either exclusion or assimilation has involved. In particular, taking identity as an antecedent set of facts which, given successful recognition, can empower our future actions, promotes a view of a sovereign self (12–13). When proper recognition is said to be 'founded on accurate mutual knowledge'

12 See Translator's Note, Honneth 1995: viii.

(40), it expresses this sovereign mastery, although anchored in knowledge rather than the more familiar liberal terrain of choice or dominion (11). However, this view of agency disavows what Markell calls human finitude, our 'constitutive vulnerability to the unpredictable reactions and responses of others' (36), and contains the basic ontological error in recognition discourse.

The ontological error leads to a misapprehension of the underlying injustice in the master/slave dialectic. When Honneth, Taylor and others characterize misrecognition as a harm suffered by its victims to be righted by a better form of recognition, they not only obscure the relational character of acts of recognition, they also turn towards the consequences of misrecognition rather than its source. In a careful re-reading of Hegel, Markell (2003) argues that the source of oppressive practices is 'the desire for sovereign agency' which drives both the master and the slave to risk life in the struggle for recognition (22). However, what produces the inequality of the outcome is not the asymmetry of recognition, but the slave's realization that 'life is as essential to it as pure self-consciousness', that the original desire is impossible to fulfil because of our finitude. The master, on the other hand, has used the slave's labour to insulate him from his own dependence in a simulation of sovereignty that leaves the other 'to bear a disproportionate share of the costs and burdens involved in social life' (22). In attempting to assure ourselves of a stable identity over time, our spatial solutions have been either to exclude or assimilate different others, or to include differences in a way that allocates bearers of difference specific social roles within a unified polity, both containing and managing them as a legible, 'orderly catalog of identities' (25).

This more general understanding of sovereignty as mistaken independence also has a bearing on the usual sense of sovereignty associated with law and the state. In the usual view of Hegel's *Philosophy of Right*, the state represents a resolution to the struggle for recognition not just because it formalizes individual identities in legal rights, but because it expresses the mutual dependence of selves through membership in a political community (Markell 2003: 125). Markell questions the state as this site of reconciliation that transcends the struggle for recognition. As one of the 'central objects of identification onto which persons displace, and through which they pursue, the desire for independent and masterful agency' (28), it, too, is engaged in a struggle for recognition. Rules about citizenship and other rights and entitlements help create differentiated identities between people, while they allow the state to pursue its own project of sovereignty by creating forms of political identification and allegiance and asserting an authoritative position in social life (26–7).

In sum, if the initial problems with the recognition of difference turn on the assimilative terms of recognition *as* something, the solution does not lie in choosing a different set of terms ('ours' rather than 'yours') because of the risk of reification and essentialism that come with 'authenticity'. Recovering the dialogic, constitutive aspects of the terms of recognition, as Taylor's 'fusion of horizons' tries to do, is an important rejoinder to ethnocentrism and reification, but it takes insufficient notice of the lop-sided dynamics of oppression. Deconstructing the production of identity through relations of power is a necessary salve to the pathology of recognition. Importantly, though, the solution is not *more* recognition from those who have withheld it, but an acceptance of the terms of our dependent human condition,[13] what Markell (2003) calls a politics of acknowledgement (35). Striving for sovereign independence is untenable and its appearance always comes at the expense of others.

The following two parts will show how these problems play out in both the orthodox legal construction of *sui generis* rights and the complaints of misrecognition. A monologic view of the individual, and a reified understanding of culture, combine with a positivist model of law such that – at its most impoverished – recognition is simply a label granted or withheld by legal institutions. What a return to the roots of the idea of recognition can help to achieve is a more subtle reading of what the process of recognition in Indigenous rights is doing, namely effecting the mutually dependent development of cultural, political and legal entities. With this understanding, the court cannot place itself outside of judgments of authenticity and continuity, nor proclaim its own autonomy. Finally, the critiques we have engaged in suggest that recognition in itself is problematic as a means to address the injustices of colonial law.

Recognition and Indigenous Rights

Even a cursory history of Indigenous rights shows that there has been an interdependent relationship between colonial experience and the refinement of modern ideas of property, rights and law. In the early sixteenth century, Bartolomé de las Casas argued vehemently against the Spanish conquest on the basis that '[a]ll the races of humankind are one' and worthy of Christian love and brotherly kindness. In doing so he revived the flagging tradition of natural rights by arguing that each 'Indian' had a right to liberty, property and self-government that could not be overridden by the consent of a majority (Tierney 2004: 10–11). Vitoria and Grotius followed by articulating a *jus gentium* that extended to Indians the presumption that they owned the lands they occupied, although their theories of just war justified taking these lands without consent for conduct contrary to the natural law which binds all humans. Thomas Hobbes, John Locke and others who laid the ground for liberal thought took Indigenous peoples in the Americas as representative of a preliminary stage in human social evolution – the 'state of nature' – and used them as a foil for identifying rights accruing naturally as compared to those that necessarily depended on an organized government to enforce them. Locke defined property in a way that treated European-style agriculture and the market exchange of land as giving superior status to the natural

13 The reference to Hannah Arendt's *The Human Condition* (1958: 179) is deliberate, and Markell draws inspiration from her picture of the 'non-sovereign' character of human action (2003: 13–14).

rights of use and possession that he saw in Indigenous peoples' customary use of land (Tully 1993: 138).

Seventeenth-century English discourses of conquest tended to presume the infidel status of Indigenous peoples as justification for conquest. Defenders of the new colony in Virginia incorporated the presumption of England's Lord Chief Justice Coke in *Calvin's Case* (1608) that, unlike the situation of a Christian kingdom, any laws or rights that infidels may have had were abrogated on conquest, as they were presumed contrary to the laws of God and nature (Williams 1990: 199–202). Other cases of the time rejected Coke's opinion, holding that all pre-existing laws would continue unless repugnant to the common law (McHugh 2011: 289–90). Whatever the official view, however, when Indigenous nations were strong and the strategic interests of the English lay in maintaining peaceful relations, either to avoid costly wars or facilitate trade, there was a need to gain consent for the extension of settlement into Indigenous territories. According to Robert Williams, this led to a compromised policy of recognition in the early days of the Virginia Company's settlement in Jamestown: while still in effective possession, Indigenous peoples' claims to land would be accepted (and deeds at the time took Aboriginal nations as 'true, sole and lawful owners' capable of passing a valid interest in land to purchasers (Jennings 1975: 143) but their consent could not be acknowledged as an exercise of sovereignty, for only Christian Kings could legitimately exercise that power bestowed on them by God (Williams 1990: 215–16).

English colonial law of the eighteenth century, developed by the Privy Council in respect of all British colonies, continued to separate the question of the acquisition of sovereignty from the recognition of pre-existing property rights. Mirroring the three principle international law justifications of territorial acquisition – cession, conquest and the occupation of vacant lands (*terra nullius*) – colonial law maintained a distinction between ceded or conquered colonies, and those considered unoccupied. According to the commentaries of William Blackstone (1800), published 20 years before British colonization of Australia, different consequences obtain in the two categories of colony for the laws which will be in force:

> … if an uninhabited country be discovered and planted by English subjects, all the English laws are immediately there in force … But in conquered or ceded countries that have already laws of their own, the King may indeed alter and change those laws; but, till he does actually change them, the ancient laws of the country remain, unless such as are against the law of God, as in the case of an infidel country (106–7).

This recognition principle is known as the 'doctrine of continuity': the British Crown acquired sovereignty and introduced the common law, but pre-existing titles to land survived to be recognized by that law.

In British North American colonies, the *Royal Proclamation of 1763* 'reserved to the … Indians' lands possessed by them as their 'hunting grounds' and asserted a royal prerogative right to treat with Indigenous peoples for the cession of their lands. Following the American War of Independence that ended in 1783, the rejection of many aspects of British common law in the US, Westward expansion with attendant speculation in unceded land, and power struggles between the states and the federal government produced a variety of competing theories of the status of Indigenous property. These included a sovereign title or fee simple ownership of the soil with governments having only a right of first purchase, outright non-ownership, or a mere right of occupancy that burdened the underlying ultimate title of the governments (Banner 2005: 150–90). A series of cases heard by the Marshall Supreme Court settled on the last theory, characterizing Indigenous peoples as 'domestic dependent nations' with limited sovereignty within the United States. The core of American federal Indian law from that era on has been the recognition or 'acknowledgement' of Indian tribes as a distinct community from historical times, and on which treaty, Indian title and self-government rights depend (Goldberg et al 2010: 127–32).

However, crucial to recognition in the doctrine of continuity is that hesitation noted by Ricoeur, in which that which lies on the borderline of the known is assessed. In the doctrine of continuity, the matter of which countries already had 'laws of their own' was ambiguous. There was a problematic 'enlarged' version of *terra nullius* that included lands inhabited by peoples that were, according to Europeans, so 'low in the scale of social organisation' that they were not considered to have recognizable government, laws or property rights (*In Re Southern Rhodesia* 1919: 233; and see Ritter 1996). Australia was treated as a settled colony under this view, as were, arguably, parts of North America, while other parts were considered conquered or ceded. A more charitable attitude to colonized peoples prevailed in a Privy Council decision concerning Nigeria two years later, in which Viscount Haldane warned against using English legal conceptions as the standard in recognizing native title (*Amodu Tijani* 1921: 3–4). As we will see, tensions between a humanity that we share and differences in religious beliefs or social organization, or between the universal application of criteria for property such as occupation and the distinctive forms of Indigenous property, persist in contemporary expressions of Indigenous rights.

Australian Native Title: The Equality of our Differences

In the first 200 years since British colonization in 1788, a handful of cases had classed Australia as a settled colony for the preliminary question of the reception of English law, but did not concern Indigenous peoples directly. Until the *Mabo* case in 1992, Indigenous claims to land in Australia had only been directly considered once, in the *Milirrpum* case decided in 1971. In its result, the Yolngu claimants failed to convince a trial judge both that they owned the land and that the common law recognized Aboriginal title in Australia. The Federal government's refusal to discuss land rights following the decision prompted a series of protests and strikes. After appointing a Royal Commission, a new government led by

Gough Whitlam adopted the Aboriginal Land Rights Act 1976 to allow land in the Northern Territory to be claimed by groups 'entitled under Aboriginal traditions to the use or occupation of the land' (s. 4(1)). Other Australian jurisdictions, such as Queensland, failed to follow this example, and in 1982, Eddie Koiki Mabo, a Meriam man from the Murray Islands in the Torres Strait between Australia and Papua New Guinea, launched a case to gain legal recognition of his traditional ownership, which ended with a High Court judgment in favour of the Meriam peoples on 3 June 1992.

The Murray Islands had not been annexed to Queensland until 1879, and the Islander peoples there, with a strong sense of distinctness from mainland Aboriginal peoples,[14] had been left comparatively to themselves. As portrayed in the trial judge's findings of fact, the Meriam Islanders used their land in almost paradigmatically English ways – they lived in villages, cultivated gardens, and, as was noted as early as 1886, had a system of tenure in which every acre was likely to have a 'legitimate hereditary owner' (*Mabo* 1992: [15]). The question before the High Court was, as Justice Brennan put it in his leading opinion with which the majority of judges concurred, whether by the islands' annexation by Queensland on 1 August 1879, the Queen disentitled the Islanders, without their knowledge, from occupying lands on which they had lived for centuries past (*Mabo* 1992: [23]). His answer was no, as was the answer of Justices Deane and Gaudron, and Justice Toohey in two separate opinions, giving rise to the first articulation of common law native title accepted in Australian law. His decision that 'the common law … recognizes a form of native title which … where it has not been extinguished, reflects the entitlement of the indigenous inhabitants, in accordance with their laws or customs, to their traditional lands', now forms the basis of the statutory definition of native title (Native Title Act 1993: s. 223).

Unsurprisingly, recognition and its cognates are used frequently in the text of the decisions. 'Annexation', or the settlement of land considered uninhabited, was in the past *recognized* by international law as a valid method of acquiring sovereignty, for instance (*Mabo* 1992, Brennan J: [31], [77], Deane and Gaudron JJ [2]). The Indigenous inhabitants had no sovereign *recognized* by European nations (Brennan J: [36]). The concern of the common law for British settlers in foreign parts led to the *recognition* that such settlers should be regarded as living under the law of England if the local law was unsuitable for Christian Europeans (Brennan J: [35]). Most central is the question of the recognition of the 'rights and interests' of the Meriam appellants as native title (Brennan J: [28], Deane and Gaudron JJ: [11]).

Out of the polysemy we noted in the previous part, these uses fall, unsurprisingly enough, within the second set of senses of accepting something as true or valid, which includes the juridical sense. But when we read between the lines some of the other senses come into play. Let us consider the object of recognition. It is 'rights

14 On the question of cultural differences between mainland indigenous peoples and Torres Strait Islanders, see Beckett 1994: 7–10.

and interests' that will be recognized as native title. If some other phenomena lie behind these rights – ways of living on the land, Indigenous laws or beliefs – it is always at one remove: the common law 'recognizes a form of native title which … reflects the entitlement of the indigenous inhabitants, in accordance with their laws or customs' (*Mabo* 1992, Mason CJ and McHugh J: [2]). Thus the content of native title is to be 'determined by reference to the pre-existing native law' (Deane and Gaudron JJ: [19]). Although Aboriginal law is never the direct grammatical object of recognition itself, it is evidence of laws and customs that must support a claim for the existence of recognizable rights and interests and that will become the object of juridical knowledge practices that identify, distinguish and name them.

The cognitive and backwards-looking recognition of a pre-existing source of native title rights and interests is combined with the creative forward-looking act of granting legal status as native title in a series of comments in the majority judgments. Toohey J considers that recognition gives traditional title a 'common law existence' by protecting 'that which already exists traditionally' ([36]). Deane and Gaudron JJ articulate this ontological creation as an act of translation: 'pre-existing native claims … [are] translated into or recognized as estates, rights or other interests' ([8]). All three concurring judgments cite Viscount Haldane on 'the inappropriateness of forcing the native title to conform to traditional common law concepts', accepting that Indigenous claims to land are *sui generis* and unique (Deane and Gaudron JJ: [22]).[15] But the hesitation or difficulty that must be overcome in order to recognize is not far off, as when Brennan J suggests that '[i]f it be necessary to categorize an interest in land as proprietary in order that it survive a change in sovereignty, the interest possessed by a community that is in exclusive possession of land falls into that category ([53])'.

That the juridical and evaluative sense of recognition as accepting claims as valid is entwined in these comments with the epistemological process of identification and distinction is of course unsurprising to lawyers: it is the ubiquitous activity of applying law to the facts. In this case, however, the hesitation or difficulty is something that weighs on Toohey J's mind because of the risk of ethnocentric judgment: 'the use of the term 'title' is artificial and capable of misleading. The rights claimed … do not correspond to the concept of ownership as understood by the land law of England' ([9]). He almost appears to eschew any kind of translation: the 'nature of traditional title' is irrelevant to the question of whether it has survived the assumption of Crown sovereignty as a recognizable interest. The threshold question is simply whether 'reasonably coherent rights and duties were, and are, exercised in an area of land' ([36]). Making native title conform to English property law would 'defeat the purpose of recognition' (Toohey J: [36]).

It is in the purpose of recognition that we start unpacking some of the broader political resonances of recognition discussed in the previous part. In the judgments of Brennan J and Deane and Gaudron JJ in particular, the decision heralds a transitional moment for Australian law away from a past governed by the unjust

15 See also *Mabo* 1992, Deane and Gaudron JJ: [13], Toohey J: [32].

non- or misrecognition of *terra nullius* in which Indigenous interests, claims and perspectives were 'denigrated' or not taken into account. Under the principle of enlarged *terra nullius* as described in the judgments (Brennan J: [33]–[34]; Deane and Gaudron JJ: [46]; Toohey J: [14]–[18]), the original population of Australia was literally equated with an absence of people; they were so 'low on the scale of social organization' that their presence could be ignored in parcelling out titles in the colony (Brennan J: [38]–[41]). The difference of Indigenous peoples was also identified, but then subordinated to a European sense of what was proper. This past is rejected in powerful terms as a 'discriminatory denigration' (Brennan J: [39]), 'a national legacy of unutterable shame', and 'the darkest aspect of the history of this nation' (Deane and Gaudron JJ: [50], [56]).

The recognition of native title, in contrast, represents a new era of justice and respect for human rights, especially concerning equality before the law (Brennan J: [29]). The judges note that both ideas of racial equality and anthropological knowledge have advanced since the nineteenth century. International conventions signed by Australia demonstrate the nation's commitment to universal human rights, including the International Convention on the Elimination of All Forms of Racial Discrimination (ICERD), art. 5 of which requires non-discrimination in the right to own and inherit property. Anthropological evidence, such as that in the *Milirrpum* case, now shows a 'subtle and elaborate' system of law. There is no warrant for treating peoples as 'too low in the scale of social organization to be acknowledged as possessing rights and interests in land' (Brennan J: [63]). Consequently, to avoid ethnocentrism, it is Indigenous peoples' *own* forms of property that should be equally respected.

That equality was such a concern, at least in this ground-laying case, makes Australian native title unique compared to the more historically grounded approaches in Canada, the US and New Zealand. To a great extent, the parameters of native title's equality jurisprudence were set by the earlier case *Mabo (No.1)* (1988)[16] in which Eddie Mabo challenged the Queensland government's attempt to extinguish, by legislation, any potential native title in the Murray Islands as contrary to the Racial Discrimination Act 1975 (Cth), s. 10 of which prohibits legislation the effect of which is that one racial group does not enjoy rights enjoyed by another. Queensland had argued that native title rights, if they existed, were not held by any racial group other than Aborigines and Torres Strait Islanders, so the legislation was not depriving them of rights enjoyed by others (Wilson J: [19], Dawson J: [29]–[30]).

A slim majority of the High Court in *Mabo (No.1)* held that because s. 10 implemented ICERD, the traditional rights that were extinguished by the Queensland legislation and the Crown derived rights that were left unimpaired were comparable under a more general human right not to be arbitrarily deprived of property. Deane J, for instance, stressed the relevant right as 'a moral entitlement to be treated in accordance with standards dictated by the fundamental notions of

16 Thanks to Alexander Reilly for this observation.

human dignity and essential equality which underlie the international recognition of human rights' ([20]). By extension, the ability to enjoy rights inherited under their own traditions was thus crucial to equal treatment of Indigenous peoples.

The implicit politics of recognition that emerges in Australian native title jurisprudence is that all peoples have the *prima facie* capacity to hold rights in land, and those held by Indigenous peoples should not be limited by judgments made with European precepts in mind but are *sui generis* rights 'ascertained according to the laws and customs of the indigenous people who, by those laws and customs, have a connection with the land' (*Mabo* 1992, Brennan J: [83]). Without limiting native title by analogy to the common law, however, some translations have to be made in order to gain the protection of the common law. The occupation of territory by a group, for instance, must be characterized as proprietary in order to survive the assertion of sovereignty. Practices and beliefs must be rendered as rights and interests. Further, locating the source of native title in Indigenous 'laws and customs' leads to the possibility of extinguishment if these laws are no longer acknowledged, such that proof is required that traditional laws and customs continue to provide people with their connection to the land (Brennan J: [83]), a matter to which I will return in the next chapter.

Canadian Aboriginal Rights: Intersocietal Law

The genesis of Aboriginal rights in Canada is more diffuse and therefore more complicated to trace. A history of trade and military alliances in Canada's eastern regions gave way to more formalized land cession treaties in the Great Lakes region and prairie provinces after the end of the war between Britain and France and the passage of the *Royal Proclamation 1763*, which 'reserved to the … Indians' lands possessed by them as their 'hunting grounds'. While the *St. Catherine's Milling* (1888) decision by the Privy Council held that Indian title to land, a 'mere burden' on the full proprietary estate of the Crown, was derived from the provisions of the Royal Proclamation (54, 58), later cases emphasized pre-existing Indigenous occupation, combined with customary law, as the basis of title, drawing on both the US Marshall decisions and the colonial common law of continuity (*Calder* 1973: 380–5; *Delgamuukw* 1997: [114)). But the crux of a contemporary jurisprudence of recognition is s. 35 of the Constitution, introduced along with a Charter of Rights and Freedoms in 1982, in which 'existing Aboriginal and treaty rights are hereby recognized and affirmed'.

For our purposes, the Canadian jurisprudence is interesting because it offers an alternative to equality as the frame for recognition, and thus struggles with the question of cultural difference and Indigenous identity in a different way. The first Supreme Court decision to consider the significance of constitutional 'recognition and affirmation' was *R v Sparrow* (1990). In elucidating the purpose of s. 35, the unified court compares the original British policy of 'respect for [Aboriginal peoples'] right to occupy their traditional lands' with a history of those rights being downplayed, dishonoured and ignored, and, in light of this history, interprets recent political events such as the 1973 Comprehensive Land Claims policy and the inclusion of s. 35 as an expression of government responsibility – an historic 'fiduciary duty' – associated with federal jurisdiction under s. 91(24) of the Constitution over 'Indians, and the lands reserved for Indians'. The implication of constitutional protection is that rights may no longer be unilaterally extinguished. But the court also finds that 'rights that are recognised and affirmed are not absolute'; rather, '"recognition and affirmation" incorporate the fiduciary relationship' such that 'federal power must be reconciled with federal duty' ([49]–[62]). The court consequently requires that any regulatory infringements of Aboriginal rights or title pass a justificatory test to ensure that the objective is valid and consistent with the overall honour of the Crown, that impacts are minimized and that those affected are consulted ([67]–[83]). Thus the idea of an historic relationship between the Canadian Crown and Aboriginal peoples that imposes restraint on government power, rather than equality of property rights, is the operative interpretive principle in Canadian Aboriginal rights law.

It was not until cases addressing what kinds of contemporary activities would gain constitutional protection that the Supreme Court espoused an explicit view on the object of s. 35 recognition. In the first of these, *R v. Van Der Peet* (1996), the majority opinion by Chief Justice Lamer makes the word 'Aboriginal' do the work of determining whether Sto:lo woman Dorothy Van Der Peet, in selling fish caught under a restrictive Indian food fish licence, was immune from prosecution under provincial fisheries regulation. While individual rights are said to be defined according to liberal enlightenment precepts as 'held by all people in society because each person is entitled to dignity and respect' ([18]) in a way that is not applicable to Aboriginal rights, Lamer CJ struggles to supply an alternative basis for them: 'they arise from the fact that aboriginal people are *aboriginal*' ([19]). Any definition must 'capture *both* the aboriginal and the rights in aboriginal rights' ([20]). The principle distinguishing factor of Aboriginal peoples is that they were living in North America prior to the arrival of Europeans, occupying the land and 'participating in distinctive cultures' ([30]). Citing with approval the definition of native title in *Mabo* that locates its origin in traditional laws and customs, Lamer CJ defines Aboriginal rights in terms of 'practices, customs and traditions that are integral to the distinctive aboriginal cultures' of pre-existing societies ([45]). The reference point is the time of first contact with European colonists, since this is the point beyond which, presumably, one can be sure that practices are distinctively Aboriginal. As Ms Van Der Peet found, it has been very difficult to get the court to accept that commercial activities were 'Aboriginal' in this sense ([85]–[91]).

The role of Aboriginal law in Canadian Aboriginal rights is perhaps more subtle than in Australian native title. The *sui generis* character of native title comes from the fact that it is rights and interests held under traditional laws and customs that are being recognized by – and translated into – the common law. For Canadian Aboriginal rights, however, in cases beginning with *Guerin v The Queen* and developed in *Sparrow*, *Van Der Peet* and the Aboriginal title case *Delgamuukw*, the *sui generis* character is said to be located in the collection of principles that emerged in historic practices of treaty making in North America and in the courts' interpretation of those practices. As Brian Slattery puts it, the law of Aboriginal rights 'is a form of intersocietal law that evolved from long-standing practices linking the various communities' (Slattery 1992: 120–21).[17] As the definition of rights is an ongoing project, courts are to 'take into account' or 'be sensitive' to the perspective of Aboriginal peoples on the meaning of the rights claimed, although this 'must be framed in terms cognizable to the Canadian legal and constitutional structure' (*Van der Peet* 1996: [49]). From *Van Der Peet* onwards, the purpose of s. 35 is framed as the reconciliation of the fact of Aboriginal peoples' prior presence with the assertion of Crown sovereignty, and the definition of rights framed as the reconciliation of perspectives.

Although Aboriginal title is considered to be a 'species of Aboriginal right', it is not defined in terms of specific practices on the land, but rather as arising from exclusive occupation of traditional territories prior to the assertion of British sovereignty. However, this source represents the reconciliation principle referred to above: physical occupation is relevant because of the common law principle that occupation is *prima facie* proof of legal possession, but the prior presence of Aboriginal peoples implies a title originating in their pre-existing systems of law (*Delgamuukw* 1997: [114]). Consequently, both factual occupation and Aboriginal law should be taken into account in proving occupancy ([147]). Further, given the importance of Aboriginal law as a source, Aboriginal title cannot sustain uses that would be irreconcilable with 'the nature of the occupation of that land and the relationship that the particular group has had with the land which together have given rise to aboriginal title in the first place'. This places an 'inherent limit' on uses that would destroy the value of the land in terms of the significance it originally had ([128]).

In contrast to the *Mabo* decision, contemporary Canadian jurisprudence on Aboriginal rights is not couched in revolutionary language and is presented more in terms of continuity with older principles. Nevertheless, the references in *Sparrow* and other cases to past injustices and discrimination, to the 'biases and prejudices of another era' (*Simon v The Queen* 1985: [21]), and the reading of s. 35 as the promise of a 'just settlement' with Aboriginal peoples (*Sparrow* 1990: [54]), lend themselves to an interpretation of this jurisprudence as 'redemptive constitutionalism' as Mark Walters (2006) has done (495), and similarly mark a certain post-colonial desire.

Out of our three historic antecedents to the politics of recognition, the principle of universal dignity features overtly only in Australian native title, while the principle of authenticity ends up being crucial in the enunciation both of native title and of Aboriginal rights. It is taken for granted that recognition by others, via the courts, is necessary to sustain both universal dignity and Indigenous identity. But the subtleties of the concept of recognition are missing. This approach to recognition through the courts' orthodox legal theory renders identity static and

17 Cited with approval by Lamer CJ, *Van Der Peet* 1996: [42].

pre-existent, defined by its difference from non-Aboriginality and according to a European sense of Indigenous authenticity. Indigenous 'difference' becomes a fixed measure that then explicitly permits judgments of extinguishment or non-authenticity.

Misrecognition

In this part I assess the paradigm of recognition implicit in the critical literature on Indigenous rights through three main themes: equality, difference and translation. For example, courts are criticized for treating non-Indigenous property rights preferentially, for assessing Indigenous 'tradition' through European lenses, or for translating Indigenous laws and customs in ways that do not reflect the way Indigenous peoples think – for 'misrecognizing' them. However, where critiques of the court's recognition consider native title as a failure to reflect a true Indigenous identity or culture, they repeat the ontological error of the court in treating difference as static and pre-ordained. The problem with seeing recognition in this way in terms of accurate or inaccurate labelling, as some critics do, is, first, that a particular account of Indigenous difference risks being objectified as the essential *sui generis* account of native title, and second, that the source of injustice is misidentified. I finish by considering ways to think beyond recognition.

Equality

Arguments based in equality have informed both detractors and supporters of Indigenous rights. First, Australian critics of *Mabo*, adhering to a formal version of equality, felt the decision threatened the liberal principle of the equality of all citizens and their equal treatment in law, and consequently misrecognized the essential sameness of Indigenous and non-Indigenous peoples regarding property rights (Cooray 1994).[18] In Canada, preferential schemes for Aboriginal fishers responding to the *Sparrow* decision were attacked in the *R v Kapp* (2008) litigation as a breach of the equality provisions of the Canadian Charter of Rights and Freedoms ([2]) according to which 'every individual… has the right to the… equal benefit of the law without discrimination' (s.15, Constitution Act 1982). The court declined to analyse the equality implications on Aboriginal rights *per se*, but concluded that the preferential scheme was protected by s. 15(2) of the Charter as a programme directed towards substantive equality, or the 'amelioration of conditions of disadvantaged individuals or groups' ([61]). Similarly, certain Canadian theorists such as Will Kymlicka and Patrick Macklem have defended the protection of Aboriginal cultural practices through constitutional rights in terms of this substantive version of equality as distributive justice: while cultures provide the necessary context for meaningful decision-making, history has placed

18 And see generally Cowlishaw 1995: 43–64.

Indigenous peoples at a systemic disadvantage in the 'cultural market place' that rights protection redresses (Kymlicka 1995: 113; Macklem 2001: 71–4). Finally, many other commentators, like the *Mabo* judgments themselves, go beyond the idea of Indigenous rights as a 'special measure' and justify them in terms of equal respect for cultural or proprietary distinctiveness (for example, Jonas 2001: 60–62).

Whether seen in terms of redressing disadvantage or more generally as a question of equal treatment or respect on principle, equality arguments for Indigenous rights cannot get very far without considering, as in Aristotle's original formula, what is to be treated alike and what is to be treated as unlike. In *Mabo*, the 'differences' of native title (such as its communal character, or its source outside the common law and in oral traditions) have to be taken into account so that, as a form of property, it may be treated the same as non-native title. In Canada, and despite the general absence of equality discourse in the courts' jurisprudence, Aboriginal title is defended as the formal equal application of the common law principle of the superiority of prior title and the emphasis on occupancy as the basis of title, as long as occupancy is not judged only in terms familiar to Europeans (Macklem 2001: 78–85). Going beyond property, Andrew Lokan (1999) considers that giving effect to Aboriginal law and custom is necessary for its own sake because equality is about the equality in the status of Aboriginal and European law (83). Patrick Macklem (2001) supplements his arguments about the constitutional significance of Aboriginal cultural difference and prior occupation with one based in the original formal equality of self-governing peoples (119–28).[19] Michael Detmold (1993) puts it more strongly, arguing that by defining native title rights by reference to Indigenous custom and law, the common law approaches the highest form of ontological equality because it has the effect of seeing claimants fully as subjects; it is a recognition of the other as 'conceiver and perceiver … [as] a second and different end-point of perception and desire' (41).

However, Detmold, Lokan and many others argue that this vision of equality has not manifested in the details of Indigenous rights regimes. For example, following Brennan J's ruling in *Mabo* that existing non-Indigenous property holdings would be undisturbed by native title recognition so as not to threaten the 'skeleton of principle' underpinning Australian property law, the Native Title Act 1993 retrospectively validated all interests granted prior to *Mabo*, making native title what Noel Pearson (1995) called a 'remnant title', subordinate to other interests (95).[20] Contrary to s. 51 (xxxi) of the Australian Constitution which requires 'just terms' (that is, just compensation) for the government's acquisition of property, no compensation is available for past extinguishment of native title (Bartlett 2000: 70; Pearson 1993: 83–5). A growing judicial discourse of the inherent 'weakness' or 'fragility' of native title led to decisions that even a temporary grant of freehold, never taken up physically and later resumed by the Crown, would permanently

19 See also generally Hoehn 2012.

20 See also Hunter 1997; McNeil 2001–2002; Bartlett 1997: 47–8.

extinguish native title. In the words of High Court judge Kirby J, 'the grant of such an interest, without more, "blows away" the native title forever' (*Fejo* 1998: [112]).

Parity in treatment of property is also a concern in Canada. In *Delgamuukw*, Lamer CJ indicated that, although Aboriginal title is constitutionally protected, the application of the *Sparrow* test would allow it to be infringed for a range of purposes, including 'the development of agriculture, forestry, mining, and hydroelectric power, the general economic development of the interior of British Columbia, protection of the environment or endangered species, the building of infrastructure and the settlement of foreign populations to support those aims' ([165]). Kent McNeil (2000) argues that the purposes listed by Lamer CJ, some of which entertain the taking of Aboriginal title lands for private enterprise, far outstrip the narrow 'public purposes' for which ordinary private property may be expropriated under governing statute, and seriously undermine the strength of constitutional protection for Aboriginal title (55–75).

More significantly, the regimes of recognition are condemned for the persistence of an unequal burden even in the gestures towards the recognition of difference. Shaping the possible uses of traditional lands by reference to pre-colonial laws, customs and practices, as is mandated by the definition of native title, the 'inherent limit' in Aboriginal title and the protection of pre-contact practices as Aboriginal rights, reduces the potential for Indigenous peoples to engage in economic development whereas non-Aboriginal peoples are subject to no such restrictions on their use of land (Morris 2012: 1; Borrows 2002: 64). The highly fact-specific nature of Indigenous rights means that claimants are required to procure archaeological, anthropological, linguistic and historical evidence of continuity in traditional laws and customs over centuries (O'Hair 1993: 70–71; Brennan 2004: 37–9).[21] The Australian Human Rights and Equal Opportunity Commission's report on Native Title in 1994 stated that 'to require the proving of biological descent back to [1788] is an absurd and discriminatory requirement. No other title holder has to establish this and would not be likely to satisfy this requirement if they had to' (Aboriginal and Torres Strait Islander Justice Commissioner 1994). In both Canada and Australia, the onus lies with Indigenous claimants to establish continuity between past and present occupation, practices or laws and customs, seemingly on the basis of a presumption of underlying Crown title (McNeil 1999: 778–9). This is in contrast to New Zealand, which has recently enacted a rebuttable presumption in favour of the non-extinguishment of customary interests (Marine and Coastal Area (Takutai Moana) Act 2011, s. 106).

This onus of proof is part of a larger problem of one-sidedness that John Borrows has vehemently argued against in the Canadian context. In *Sparrow* the court assumes that 'there was from the outset never any doubt that sovereignty and legislative power, and indeed the underlying title, to such lands vested in

21 Richard Bartlett (2003) points out that existing common law and international law principles on recognition do not require that traditional laws continue to be acknowledged in the present day. Neither is this an explicit requirement of the Native Title Act, s. 223 (41).

the Crown' ([49]). *Van Der Peet* takes the purpose of Aboriginal rights to be the reconciliation of the fact of Aboriginal peoples' prior presence with the sovereignty of the Crown (also a fact?) ([31]), while its companion case *R v Gladstone* (1996) justifies limitations on rights because Aboriginal societies are subsumed within a 'broader social, political and economic community' in whose interests the Crown must act ([73]).[22] In *Delgamuukw*, the openness to Aboriginal perspectives on evidence does not extend to Aboriginal perspectives on the Crown's assertion of sovereignty; they must not 'strain the "Canadian legal and constitutional structure"' (Borrows 1999: 556–7).[23] Inequitably, the degree of scrutiny to which the claims of Aboriginal peoples are subject is simply not required for Crown sovereignty or title, something Borrows (2002) argues offends the basic principles of the rule of law against the arbitrary exercise of power (111–37). Similarly, in *Mabo*, the Crown's assertion of sovereignty, plausibly rendered illegitimate with the Court's rejection of *terra nullius*, was held to be an 'act of State' beyond the purview of the court. The door onto the survival of Indigenous sovereignty or jurisdiction would remain firmly shut in the eyes of the common law.[24]

Detmold argues that the concept of equality between Indigenous and non-Indigenous peoples as equality before the law is spurious when, as he perceives the case in native title, they are not treated equally 'in the matter of the *law before which* they are treated equally' (Detmold 1993: 43). He thereby highlights one of the flaws of a paradigm of recognition by law that has, as he calls them, 'stopping points'. Whenever there is a stopping point such as property, the sovereign right to extinguish, or the act of State, there is a denial of fundamental equality, which is 'that your difference is of equal status to my own' (43).

Difference: Ethnocentricity, Reification and Essentialism

To the extent that equality in the above commentary is the equality of differences, a separate set of critiques emerges around the way in which Indigenous practices and understandings are assessed by courts, which largely map onto the critiques of ethnocentricity, reification and essentialism in identity politics discussed above. As we have seen, Indigenous rights take Indigenous difference into account by couching definitions in terms of traditional laws, customs and practices, or by including the 'Aboriginal perspective' on both the definition of rights and the ways in which they may be proved. Courts are instructed to accept alternative forms

---

22 See also Ladner and McCrossan 2009: 272.

23 See also *Mitchell v MNR* (2001) at [153]–[154] where Aboriginal practices must be compatible with Crown sovereignty in order to be recognised as Aboriginal rights.

24 See Reynolds 1996; Nettheim 1993: 108–9; Nettheim 1997: 495; Pether 1998: 125; and Simpson 1993: 208–9. The suggestion that *Mabo* implicitly recognized Aboriginal jurisdiction over criminal matters was tested in *R v Archie Glass* (Unreported, Sully J, 22 January 1993) and *The Crown v Leeton James Jacky* (Unreported, Campbell J, 10 June 1993) and flatly rejected in both: see Flood 1993.

of evidence – such as oral histories, songs, dances, regalia and paintings – as well as to be respectful of Indigenous protocols concerning privacy, taboo and the secret/sacred aspects of knowledge (Australian Federal Court Rules, Order 78 s. 4; *Delgamuukw* 1997: [84]–[88]; Anderson 2003).

The Canadian Supreme Court's definition of Aboriginal rights as 'practices, customs and traditions integral to the distinctive cultures of aboriginal peoples' (*Van der Peet* 1996: [48]) at the time of European contact has been subject to trenchant criticism, essentially on the basis that it freezes Aboriginality in the past and in terms of a stereotyped catalogue of practices (Cheng 1997; Otis 1997). For some critics, the problem is that the wrong set of practices is being identified, at the wrong level of generality (the right to fish for specific species rather than to procure a livelihood from traditional territories or to be self-governing, for instance) (Borrows 2002: 63) and in a way that misrecognizes innovation in response to new circumstances as something other than a cultural trait (Niezen 2003: 1). For others, the model of culture as an object rather than as a process or an adjective (Appadurai 1996: 13), one that can be ascertained in definitive terms from the outside rather than being inherently perspectival, ignores half a century of anthropological thought, and has the effect of reifying Aboriginal culture through the court's inquiry (Asch 2000: 129–31). According to Gordon Christie (1998), this happens particularly because of the focus on practices rather than the intellectual aspects of culture – values, principles and beliefs – that make them meaningful and constitute what is valuable to Aboriginal peoples in their cultures (449–50). Taking the Aboriginal perspective on this definition into account produces the observation that 'the concept of "culture" is inherently cultural' (Barsh and Henderson 1997: 1002).

The Supreme Court took these criticisms on board to some extent in the more recent decisions of *R v Sappier; R v Gray* (2006), broadening the characterization of relevant activities away from the specific uses of resources towards an understanding of how it supported a particular way of life – protecting 'the forest, not just individual trees' (MacIntosh 2007: 32; Charlton 2007/08) – and acknowledging the relative and subjective nature of identifying what is distinctive in a culture (*R v. Sappier; R v. Gray* 2006: [45]). But the problem of locating Aboriginal culture in an untouched past remains, reflecting 'a careful attempt to define the terms of protecting Aboriginal culture in a way that does not threaten Canadian sovereignty over Aboriginal people' (Isenberg 2007: 91. See also Dick 2009: 973; Asch 2000: 133–7).

The dominant position of the Canadian state is more generally visible in the way the 'reconciliation of perspectives' has been framed: the Aboriginal perspective must be expressed in terms cognizable to Canadian law. In the 2005 *Marshall* decision on Aboriginal title, Chief Justice McLachlin wrote that reconciliation in this sense involved examining 'the pre-sovereignty aboriginal practice and translat[ing] that practice, as faithfully and objectively as it can, into a modern legal right' ([48]). The import of that approach for the Aboriginal title claim of the Mi'kmaq defendants in the case was that title could not be defined in any other way than in the core terms of English title: exclusive possession. Similarly, the Australian High Court has characterized the recognition of native title in terms of translation, frankly admitting that the way the court's task is framed is a denaturing process:

> The spiritual or religious is translated into the legal. This requires the fragmentation of an integrated view of the ordering of affairs into rights and interests which are considered apart from the duties and obligations which go with them (*Western Australia v. Ward* 2002: [14]).

To address some of these stopping points, Borrows recommends a return in Canadian jurisprudence to Aboriginal ancestral laws and customs as the source of Aboriginal rights, and more will be said about this below (Borrows 1997/98: 56–7). On its own, locating Indigenous rights in traditional laws and customs does not dislodge the problems of ethnocentrism, reification or essentialism, however, since parallel criticisms are made of the way Indigenous laws and customs are approached in Australian native title jurisprudence. As we will see in the next chapter, the *Yorta Yorta* (2008) case identifies the relevant legal system from which native title rights derive as the system existing in 1788, with continuity up to the present day, such that, as Michael Dodson (1996a) complains, native title claimants must associate themselves with 'a pristine and inaccessible past' (5). As with the *Van der Peet* culture model, the criteria for identifying the factual existence of laws and customs remain firmly occidental, and treat Indigenous law, in positivist fashion, as a fact, an object with a quantifiable existence. The original 'respect for difference' in Indigenous rights has become an *expectation* of difference; what is *sui generis* and unique to Indigenous peoples has become fixed as a standard that must be met.

Translation

Whether through the lens of equality or that of respect for difference, the recognition of Indigenous rights is frequently taken to necessitate translation. Particularly where this is understood as a process of choosing 'terms' to represent an 'original', translation points us back to the ontological concerns with recognition we raised earlier. Justice French (2002) of the Australian Federal Court describes the legal act of recognition as reflective of the human cognitive act: 'It translates the old into the new. It conveys the reconstruction of understanding – the shock of awareness – the new realisation of what we had passed over unseen' (130). The work done by lawyers, anthropologists and other experts to describe and interpret the relationships between a claimant group and the land yields a title which can only ever be 'a poor reflection of the full cultural, historical and human reality from which that title is derived' (148). Translation is 'a mapping from one set comprising traditional laws and customs onto the other comprising the Australian legal system' (French and Lane 2002: 28), but is always, as in French's comment, a poor rendering of the 'original'.

As with the difficulty of capturing 'culture' in Aboriginal rights, Australian courts readily admit that translation of native title rights and interests from Indigenous reality is an imperfect project, a 'problem of considerable difficulty' (*Mabo* 1992, Brennan J: [64]). Patricia Lane (2000a) gives a number of reasons why defining the nature of native title is difficult. Firstly, Aboriginal laws relating to land are intensely local and thus diverse across Australia, and they are continually in evolution. Secondly, defining a 'property right' rather than, for example, a 'religious obligation' begs the question of the conceptual nature of property in non-Indigenous law, a matter which is far from settled in western jurisprudence (11–14).[25] Choosing appropriate words and concepts with which to integrate native title into the mainstream property system carries outcomes of practical and symbolic significance. For example, if property is characterized, after W.N. Hohfeld, as a 'bundle of rights' (Penner 1996: 724), it makes it easier to conceive of title as a list of separate rights which can be permanently extinguished, one by one, by inconsistent interests (*Ward* 2000, Beaumont and Von Doussa JJ: [109]). If, in contrast, property consists of an underlying relationship with the land, Crown grants would lead to a suspension of inconsistent rights but not a permanent destruction of property (*Ward* 2000, North J: [763]).

Consequently, critics have taken issue with choices about the terms of translation that they argue unnecessarily limit or weaken native title with respect to the interests of non-Indigenous peoples, and take insufficient account of an Indigenous perspective on the meaning of laws and customs. The choice to call native title 'inherently fragile',[26] because of the proposition in *Mabo* that native title could be extinguished by inconsistent Crown grant, becomes a self-fulfilling characterization that works to push uncertain instances of extinguishment towards a *fait accompli*, as Alexander Reilly (2002) argues ([44]–[51]). The 'bundle of rights' analogy fails to address the central role played by the maintenance of cultural heritage in native title claims, because it ignores the possibility that there is an underlying unity to the rights, a unity often expressed as a cultural connection to the land (Strelein 2001: 103–24).[27]

Commentators defending the extension of native title to art, cultural expressions or 'whatever is regarded in Aboriginal law as part of land ownership'

25 See for example Gray and Gray 1998. Native title cases have provoked some discussions about the nature of property in western law – see Gleeson CJ, Gaudron, Kirby and Hayne JJ, *Yanner v Eaton* (1999) 166 ALR 259: 8; Beaumont and Von Doussa JJ, *Ward* 2000: [100]–[102].

26 Deane and Gaudron JJ posit the 'vulnerability' of native title to extinguishment in *Mabo* 1992: [112]; Kirby in *Wik* (1996) rejected the inherent fragility of native title [10], but then suggested the fragility of rights derived outside the common law as the basis for extinguishment in *Fejo* (1998: [151]); in *Ward* (2000), 'inherent fragility' appears as an established characterization: [39] (Gleeson CJ, Gaudron, Gummow and Hayne JJ), [156] (McHugh J), [280] (Callinan J).

27 See also Barnett 2000 on this point.

(Gray 1993: 10) argue on the basis that Australian law should seriously engage with 'Indigenous conceptualisation[s] of the nature of the relationship between people and objects or between people and place' (Pannel 1994: 33). And Dodson, as Aboriginal Social Justice Commissioner for the Human Rights and Equal Opportunity Commission, claimed that determinations of native title purporting to recognize traditional laws have to take into account the full networks of social, political, economic and religious systems to which it is related, and crucially, the meanings it has to Aboriginal peoples. 'To "recognise" native title on any other criteria is not recognition, but a distortion effecting a form of legal assimilation' (Aboriginal and Torres Strait Islander Justice Commissioner 1994). Beyond the terms themselves is the courts approach to translation, which treats terminology (such as the bundle of rights) as axiomatic rather than an approximation that should flexibly meet the overarching *purpose* of recognition (Strelein 2001: 105).

In Canada, McLachlin CJ's turn to translation in *Marshall* and *Bernard* (2005) is seen as an entirely different model from the traditional *sui generis* one (Slattery 2006: 279–81) (and the latter term does not appear in her judgment). Although most criticisms target this rather specific understanding of the translation task (requiring that practices 'fit' within the scope of a modern legal right) they show up what is endemic in a wider understanding of recognition as cognitive translation, and that is its one-sidedness. The common law is a fixed reality to which Aboriginal rights must conform (Walters 2006: 502; Banks 2006: 127): it is always the translator and never the translated. In contrast, Justice LeBel, in his minority opinion, cautioned that the role of Aboriginal perspectives is not just to assist in interpreting Aboriginal practices to see if they fit common law categories, but to 'shape … the very concept of Aboriginal title' ([130]). Although Brian Slattery (2006) emphatically announces that '[n]o translation is needed' in the *sui generis*, intersocietal version of Aboriginal rights that bridges Indigenous and European-based land systems (280–81), clearly any kind of inter-cultural or linguistic dialogue happens through translation. What he appears to be rejecting, instead, is the one-way translation where common law categories are not vulnerable to change.

Beyond Recognition

Caught within the politics of recognition as a translation model, we are instinctively drawn to criticizing Indigenous rights on the grounds that there are better terms of recognition, associated with an authentic 'original'. As I will argue in Chapter 4, contemporary perspectives from literature and anthropology complicate the simplistic idea of an objective original that I have left untouched for the moment. Suffice it to say for now that the search for the authentic terms of translation may be futile if we understand recognition as the problematic cognitive exercise referred to by Oliver. Canadian authors Henderson, Benson and Findlay (2000) note that Aboriginal forms of tenure are embedded in Aboriginal knowledges and the languages in which they are expressed, which suggests that it is not possible to arrive at the *sui generis* conception even through an infinite regression of terms that starts with property and goes back to land, belonging and being – the 'full networks of social, political, economic and religious systems'. Each such category expresses a distinctive non-Indigenous vision of the world that would constitute a 'foreign imposition' – a smuggled universal – for Aboriginal peoples. Justice in Canadian law, they argue, is conditioned by the possibility of addressing Aboriginal tenure in Aboriginal languages (401).

Although Henderson, Benson and Findlay at times appear to suggest that Indigenous and non-Indigenous perspectives are incommensurable, they obviously want courts and lawyers to struggle with Indigenous languages and traditions as part of the 'intersocietal' approach. Similarly, Motha's solution to the persistent and fatal universal term of liberal humanism is dialogue about the terms of recognition, and he himself takes 'capacity for meaningful dialogue' as a universal human given (1998: 88). So for some, the way out of one-sided recognition is to engage in cross-cultural theorizing about Aboriginal rights, leading to a Tayloresque dialogue about our horizons of evaluation (Newman 2007). In the influential work of James Tully, the constitution itself is an activity of inter-cultural dialogue 'in which the culturally diverse sovereign citizens of contemporary societies negotiate agreements on their forms of association over time' (Tully 1995: 30). Constitutive dialogue seems to be what Borrows has in mind when he makes a case for the recognition of Indigenous law, rather than the labelling process of the Australian cases that takes Indigenous laws and customs as facts, since his examples of the possibilities of recognition drawing on Anishnabek law show a fusion or, to use a very Canadian term, *métissage*, of Indigenous and non-Indigenous forms of law.[28]

Given that legal decision-making is dominated by the cognitive sense of recognition through the process of 'fact-finding' and structured by the imbalance of the court as recognizer, it may not be the best forum for inter-cultural dialogue. For this and other reasons, the courts themselves have pushed parties towards the political process and negotiated agreements as the preferred forum for resolving Indigenous claims. In Canada, the general settlement of unresolved Aboriginal title claims are dealt with in the Federal Comprehensive Land Claim or British Columbia Treaty Commission processes, while smaller scale interim negotiations are anticipated around development projects that affect Aboriginal rights prior to any formal recognition under the doctrine of the Crown's 'duty to consult' (*Haida Nation* 2004: [10]). In Australia, negotiations are built into the Native Title Act as the first mandatory stage of a native title claim, while the 'right to negotiate' over specific development acts is a rough equivalent of the duty to consult. Chapter 6 will consider in greater detail the relevance of negotiated agreements to legal pluralism and the recognition of Indigenous law. For now I will note that in reality, the terms of political recognition are often as little open to the shifting of horizons as the

28 For example, a traditional story that explains why Anishnabek should respect the deer is told in case-law format with facts, issues and reasons in Borrows 1996: 649–52. On the *métis* identity of Canada and Canadian law in particular, see Saul 2008.

legal ones. Government parties use their own (unscrutinized) version of the court's identification criteria in order for parties to be considered eligible for the process. The language of the agreements, while sometimes introducing local Indigenous terminology,[29] is deeply shaped by models of exploitative property, and the process is often presented as a take-it-or leave it proposition by the governments (Raybould 2007).

In addition, the fusion of horizons might be just a fancy way of searching for better terms in a process of one-way recognition if it is still something 'granted' by agents of the state. Taking up Fanon's concern for the pathology of oppression, Glen Coulthard (2007) argues that even when the object of recognition shifts from culture to nationhood and self-determination, the politics of recognition have little potential to transform the colonial relationship because they leave intact the legal, political and socio-economic structures that work *with* cultural misrecognition to subordinate Indigenous peoples (451–2). As we noted above, the conditions of mutual dependence that provide the impetus towards the equilibrium of mutual recognition in Hegel do not exist for colonial states, which either require colonized peoples to work, or to disappear, so that they can use their land and resources.

One way to move beyond the pathology of recognition suggested by Fanon involves a turn away from the master and towards the liberating praxis of the slave. The solution in his early work was for colonized peoples to develop a 'progressive' mirror born out of self-affirmation and a struggle for freedom on their own terms, as distinct from a demand for *recognition* (1967: 222). Further, although as Edward Said (1993) has noted, the reclamation of tradition has had essentialist and fundamentalist tendencies in several anti-colonial nationalist movements (xiii), the turn to Indigenous languages, law and political traditions – and a set of internal recognition relations that complicate Hegel's master/slave binary – has enabled distinctive anti-colonial critiques to emerge (Coulthard 2007: 454). The progressive mirror has been an important tool in exposing the ways in which people's own attempts toward liberation are complicit with their oppression, and to address the structural sources of that oppression.

A turn to the role of body in Hegel's dialectic, and in particular its 'spatial and temporal instability', allows Brenna Bhandar (2011) to recuperate the 'emancipatory purchase' that recognition seems to hold given its persistence in political claims: the body and its desires cannot be captured by the always-already categories of recognition (230). To the materiality of the body we could add the materiality of the land, with which Indigenous law and identity are often connected, as holding out promise for decolonization beyond the endless mirrors of representation. The materiality of places prescribes the limits of sustainable activities on the land in a very real way as a source of law (Graham 2011: 198–200; Black 2011: 31–3; Sheridan and Longboat 2006: 374), and although these prescriptions have been woven into Indigenous law, mythology and imagination in a variety of ways, their specificities will always outrun any representational category.

29 See Nisga'a Final Agreement 1999.

In Markell's alternative 'politics of acknowledgement', his term 'finitude' expresses the limits of our ability to ground our actions in identity, given its dependence on our unpredictable interactions with others. While we traced the principle of human interdependence to Hegel because of the importance of Hegelian recognition in contemporary political discourse, we should nevertheless be circumspect about adopting a theory that assigned stages in the development of human consciousness to different races of people, and (colonial) history as the self-justificatory unfolding of progress (see Tebebu 2010: xi–xiv and passim). But we do not have to look to Hegel for an understanding of human finitude in this sense. We might also find an abdication of our 'claim to absolute independence' (Markell 2003: 107), in the holism expressed in the Algonquin prayer 'All my relations' (Henderson and McCaslin 2005: 7), in Cree rituals of gratitude that acknowledge the success of the hunter to lie with the gift of the animal (Nadasdy 2007), in the Yolngu naming ceremonies discussed in Chapter 1 that highlight connections through 'joint' metaphors even as they name distinctions, or in the Ngarinyin 'law of relationship' in which everything in existence is patterned into two parts that are interdependent (Bell 1998: 18).

While Markell focuses on finitude in terms of human relations rather than the more usual sense of mortality (107), the physical limits of existence are a crucial aspect of the colonial context. For if mastery over meaning is an impossible project, dominion over property – which is the other aspect of the sovereign self and the sovereign state – is an unsustainable one, and will eventually have to contend with the interdependence of all living things. The final chapter of Borrows's book *Recovering Canada* (2002), from which this book has borrowed its title – '"Landed" Citizenship: An Indigenous Declaration of Interdependence' – encapsulates these two forms of finitude that Borrows discusses in terms of environmental stewardship, responsibility and civic-mindedness, and contingent and mutually interconnected cultures (144–50).

Conclusion

The promise of recognition through Indigenous rights is, in various measures, that Indigenous peoples will gain equal respect as property holders, that their human dignity as practitioners of distinctive cultures will be upheld and those cultures protected from encroachment, and that they will be accepted by the dominant society for 'who they really are'. It is no surprise, however, that Indigenous rights raise the familiar critiques of identity politics. Particularly when recognition is seen as a translation or mapping exercise emphasizing a cognitive activity, equality and justice in the recognition regimes is pursued as the seemingly unattainable quest for the 'Indigenous perspective'. Translations relating to land use always retain the cultural associations of the broader legal and economic system in which the courts operate, and produce reified and essentialist versions of Indigenous identity, culture and law. In the guise of recognizing difference, the process of adjudication asks Indigenous peoples to be themselves, but retains the power to determine what and who is authentic. Deborah Bird Rose (1996b) writes that it is 'difficult to conceive of a more cruel and elegant expression of cultural domination' (35).

As Coulthard (2007) has noted, the limits of recognition are propped up by the 'background legal, political and economic framework of the colonial relationship itself' suggesting that decolonization must run on two fronts: Indigenous peoples must look towards their own traditions to ground their practices of freedom and combat the internalization of colonial modes of recognition, and all of us must endeavour to address the 'structural impediments to participatory parity' (451). The most important kind of recognition may well be that expressed by former Australian Prime Minister Paul Keating in the epigraph, one that holds a mirror to the colonial self. Conversely, the kinds of dialogue suggested by Taylor and Tully offer one way in which Indigenous peoples can be respected as having something to contribute to the standards of normative evaluation rather than being 'recognized'. The prospect that all participants are liable to experience a shift in their horizons means that even those 'stopping points' like property or sovereignty are potentially unstable.

In writing of native title in Australia, Justice French (2002) calls recognition 'the human experience of seeing each other anew' (129) but the cognitive act that this involves, the one that moves the legal system to make new rules, does not go far enough. In working through theories of recognition, we have seen that recognition is not just the accretion of new knowledge about others, but the disruption of the old self and the creation of a new one that the shift in our cognitive horizons entails. In this creative act, the very idea of an objective self is undone. Regimes of recognition can be said to collaborate in discursively producing 'Aboriginality' as an object of knowledge, paired in perpetual subordinate status to its other, 'Australian' or 'Canadian', as a way of maintaining control over the nation and its resources.[30] Exposing this knowledge-making for what it is gives us at least a first step in addressing the pathology of recognition.

The diagnosis of the ontological problem with recognition that we are led to by Markell allows us to finesse some of these critiques and solutions. Reification and essentialism are problematic partially because cultures and identities (and, I will add, law) are, in reality, multiple, overlapping, contingent and continually in flux. But the solution is not a more complex and accurate recognition map, for these aspects of human existence are also temporally 'finite' in Markell's sense. This urges caution on those who seek recognition: not only is recognition incoherent in that it depends on the involvement of others in the construction of identity but claims another 'true' identity as the measure of recognition, but it also only matters because of a misplaced aspiration to sovereignty, an attempt to master our future by grounding action in who we really are (Markell 2003: 12–13). We can further diagnose the condition of those who are cast as recognizers: the state and dominant

30 See the analysis of the *Yorta Yorta* decision in these terms in Golder 2004.

society are similarly subject to the condition of human finitude and their pursuit of sovereignty is at best an approximation that comes at the expense of others.

In one sense the problems with recognition in Indigenous rights are just raw politics, a 'pragmatic compromise' between different claims over the same land. In the contemporary political climate of nations such as Canada and Australia, it is not surprising that this compromise favours dominant interests and groups. The limitations of recognition go beyond mere political or legal will, however, because they are built into the institutions, processes and concepts of Western law and government. In fact, the orthodox positivist model of law bears the perfect imprint of the ontological error in the politics of recognition. The fact/law distinction eschews the constructivist version of recognition in favour of the cognitive one, which allows state law to pursue its independence from the social, and its sovereignty over meaning.

Despite their dominance in a political sense, however, court decisions, legislative processes and official discourse do not have a monopoly on meaning-making. The recognition of an 'other' law outside of the state law shores up its borders through the assertion of sovereignty, but that outside is perennially threatening and destabilizing to the inside. That constitutive recognition is a two-way affair does not mean that it is fair, balanced or respectful. The representatives of state law may not knowingly seek recognition from Indigenous participants in processing rights claims. But in their translations their own horizons of judgment cannot help but change. Again, this change may not mean common law becomes more open, less doctrinal or less authoritarian. Its response may well be to assert sovereignty more vehemently or return to dogmatic articulations of foundational principles of western property. But the fact that recognition implicates interdependence has already undermined some of the autonomy declared in those statements. Law, property, rights (and selves) exist in conditions of finitude, and as the unstable, indeterminate products of encounter, speech and action. The following chapter will show how this is a central theme of legal pluralism.

Chapter 3

Law in Time and Space: Dimensions of Legal Pluralism

> There is but one law applicable to, and binding upon, all the people of Australia. The content of the law may occasionally be in doubt. It may sometimes require the application of legal reasoning to discover the rule to be observed and to exclude laws that are invalid. But, ultimately, a single governing law is discoverable and enforceable, if necessary, in this Court. (Justice Michael Kirby)[1]

> That rule of Dreamtime, when Dreamtime give us them rule, that's why we're doing it. We follow one law all the time. Every hour, every day and every year and every month. All follow that law, only one. Some pass away, some born, they still same, following one law. (Jackie Holmes Akemarr)[2]

Introduction

Time has passed. The people are still here. They know who they are, although names get put to this use, or that. Yorta Yorta, Moira tribes, Bangerang. The people know where they belong. *Dhungula*, the river etched in dirt by the digging stick of the woman sent from the hills by *Biami*, the creator. A big Murray River cod, *burnanga*. An extended family of 4,000.

Yorta Yorta woka deyawin! Ngunuk bga loatbaty!

(Yorta Yorta land this one here! I am talking to you!)[3]

Time has passed. The law has been unsettled, changed, decided, resettled. What follows is 'the adjustment of the law', the continued 'process of elucidation of the law ... the construction of the provisions of applicable legislation ... and the extension, by analogical reasoning into new factual and legal situations, of the basic principles stated in *Mabo [No2]*' (Kirby J, *Yarmirr* 2001: [241]).

In the throes of this adjustment, the people must lift one foot, and then the other, and begin to dance through an intricately spun web. Now as a clan or group substantially maintaining a traditional connection to the lands of their ancestors (*Yorta Yorta* 1998). Now as a community living under traditional laws and

---

1 *Commonwealth v Yarmirr* (2001) 208 CLR 1, 115 ('*Yarmirr*').

2 Jackie Homes Akemarr, native title claimant quoted in *The Alyawarr, Kaytetye, Warumungu, Wakay Native Title Claim Group v Northern Territory* [2004] FCA 472 (Unreported, Mansfield J, 23 April 2004): [137].

3 Adaptation from the transcript of the trial, testimony of Lesley Shadrach James, from the play *Yanagai! Yanagai!* by James 2003: 25.

customs (*Yorta Yorta* 2001, Branson and Katz JJ: [108]). Now as the inheritors of a normative system, intact and continuous since White people first came to their country (*Yorta Yorta* 2002, Gleeson CJ, Gummow and Hayne JJ: [38]). And because native title is traced to what was earlier ignored, misunderstood, erased – shall we call it the vitality of Indigenous law? – then (the common law is settling into concrete) vital Indigenous law there must and shall be! Norms not habits! Continuity not revival! One two, one two!

* * *

The previous chapter argued that the failure of the recognition of Indigenous rights as a postcolonial moment turned on the problem of sovereignty, not simply in terms of a restricted object of recognition that excludes Indigenous sovereignty to the advantage of the Crown's dominion over land, but in terms of a futile desire to exercise sovereign agency as mastery over meaning. This chapter will show how the same patterns of dominion and mastery are found in orthodox theories of law, and will seek to articulate a pluralistic legal theory that reflects the alternatives to recognition suggested previously: a turn to Indigenous knowledges and the law of places, a concern with the way structures of difference are created and hierarchialized, and an acknowledgement of our 'finitude': our constitutive vulnerability to, and dependence on, the speech and actions of others.

To do these things requires moving away from the more abstract and general register of the previous chapter to a more specific example grounded in a particular place, in this instance to the case *Members of the Yorta Yorta Aboriginal Community v Victoria*, and the floodplains of the Murray River (*Dhungula*) that were under claim. The decision, upheld on appeal to the High Court of Australia (2002), denied native title to the claimant community because the trial judge held that they and their ancestors had not continuously maintained their system of laws and customs. By investigating closely the object of recognition that failed to appear in this case, it will become apparent that the courts are relying on a specific ontology of law as a body of rules with an objective existence in time and space. Translated into strictures on spatial sovereignty and temporal change, this ontology resulted in a rejection of the Yorta Yorta Aboriginal Community's claim to traditional law.

As in other Australian decisions, the *Yorta Yorta* judges speak the language of a kind of legal pluralism: Indigenous laws and customs are recognized by the common law. Empirical proof of the existence of contemporary Indigenous laws and customs is required for a successful claim. Recognition is even characterized as the intersection of the common law with Indigenous laws and customs. The law of Kirby J's court co-exists with the law of Jackie Holmes Akemarr's Dreamtime.

But the idea of co-existence is immediately undone by the language of totality: there is only one Australian law. The court resolves the apparent paradox of legal pluralism by adopting the cognitive mode of recognition and categorically separating the common law and Indigenous law: only the former is true law – the latter is mere social fact to be identified and assessed by law's agents. Further, the intersection is imagined as located at the moment that the British claimed sovereignty so that the rights recognized are those that existed at that point in time. Rights generated later would infringe the principle of the monopoly of state sovereignty and cannot be recognized by the common law. The intersection is a one-off historical event rather than an ongoing process.

Beginning with an analysis of the *Yorta Yorta* case, this chapter will examine the idea of intersection as it was adopted in the majority opinion of the High Court, and spell out the threshold forensic question that claimants must address in proving the existence of traditional laws and customs, a question that holds to implicit social-scientific criteria for the existence of law. Although the court disclaims the relevance of Western legal theory to any characterization of Indigenous law, their analysis is heavily reliant on a presumptive theory that distinguishes between 'normative rules' and 'habits' or 'mere knowledge'. In this chapter, I will tease out some of the theoretical assumptions behind these distinctions and argue that they misunderstand the relationship between law, practice and narrative.

These assumptions form part of the deeper ontology of Western law that works to exclude claims like that of the Yorta Yorta Aboriginal Community. The two quotes in the epigraph, when considered together, give a powerful illustration of this ontology and its persistent misreading of Indigenous law. In Kirby J's statement, a claim to the one-ness of law in *space* is read in terms of territory, sovereignty and exclusion. As space in modern European thought is boundaried and uniform, so law's domain is exclusive and can admit to no multiplicity. Like many other Australian Indigenous law men and women, Akemarr also makes a claim for the one-ness of law, but unity in *time* is read in native title jurisprudence as stasis, a hangover from earlier theories of Indigenous peoples' traditions as a primitive law that is incapable of change. Both these readings are the result of the reification of law. Within its space/time configuration, the court reads the Yorta Yorta Aboriginal Community's claim to law spatially as a challenge to sovereignty, which it must reject as law. Similarly, it reads a claim to law over time as mandating constancy of a legal object, which in this case it rejects as fact.

An alternative reading can be made by looking to two important sources of Indigenous law: stories and the physical landscape, both of which 'engage multiple time-spaces' through the representation and embodiment of different time and space scales simultaneously (Wilcock and Brierley 2012: 2). Yorta Yorta narratives account for landscape in terms of the deep time of creation as well as engaging current-day concerns with environmental damage. Their bodily metaphors for the health-maintaining cycles of the river system give sentience to the landscape and identify the people in and with the land; space is variegated, in flux, and personal.

As mentioned in the brief account I gave in Chapter 1, many legal pluralist theories have explicitly set themselves against the monopoly of the state over law and the ethnocentrism of presuming that Western concepts of law are universal. However, there has also been a pervasive reliance in these theories on a kind of empiricism that treats all law as objective fact, reproducing the problems of recognition-as-identification that were examined in Chapter 2. In contrast, some theorists have highlighted the role that language and practice play, in representing and enacting law, as a site for the production of law and normativity, deeply questioning the objectivist accounts of law. These theories will be brought into conversation with Yorta Yorta narratives of place so as to understand their native title case as a claim to belonging, to identity in place. The continuity of belonging over time is then something of which the claim itself is a manifestation and which is continually constructed in the present.

The Yorta Yorta Case

Fighting for Revival

From its source in the Australian Alps, the Murray River, *Dhungula*, feeds the flood plains of southern New South Wales and Northern Victoria that the Yorta Yorta Aboriginal Community call home and ends, 2,375 kilometres further, in South Australia, seriously depleted due to heavy use of its water for agricultural irrigation upstream. Yorta Yorta historian Wayne Atkinson estimates that since 1860 when his ancestors demanded a ten pound tax on paddle-steamers to compensate disruption to their fishing, around 17 separate attempts have been made by the Yorta Yorta to claim land or compensation (1996: 285). When the Native Title Act came into effect in 1994, they were one of the first groups to lodge a claim. Covering an area that saw European settlement with the first squatters venturing out from the colony at Melbourne in the 1830s, their claim was destined to be a kind of test case for how native title doctrine would treat the impact of colonization. Unlike the Murray Islanders in *Mabo*, the Yorta Yorta had not been 'left to their own devices', and, because of the disruption of White settlement and policies such as assimilation, did not fit the stereotype of a 'traditional' community – read untouched and unchanging – as easily. What was the limit at which the court would consider the rights claimed to have no foundation? What would it mean for the Yorta Yorta to continue to 'acknowledge traditional laws' and 'observe traditional customs', or to maintain a connection to the land, as the Act required?

Before Olney J in the Federal Court, the Yorta Yorta Aboriginal Community submitted that they had inherited native title rights to the area from their ancestors, and had enjoyed those rights through the generations, first by maintaining continuing, uninterrupted occupation in the majority of the claim area, and (even where this had not been the case) by maintaining a traditional connection with the area. It was argued that the community members continued to exercise customs, inherited from their ancestors, 'in adapted form', which in their 'essential features' were continuous with the system of custom and tradition existing in 1788. Amongst the historical evidence submitted were two works (1883, 1886) by one of the early English pioneers in the region, Edward Curr, which described, in the manner of a Victorian travel diary, his meetings with and observations of the local 'Bangerang Blacks' and their neighbours.

In oral testimony, the Yorta Yorta witnesses gave evidence about their family trees, their relationship to the land, and their continuing practice of adapted forms of custom: camping, gathering 'bush tucker' and fishing, looking after sacred sites such as middens and scarred trees used by their ancestors to make bark canoes, conservation of timber and water resources, and the reburial of remains returned from museums. Several witnesses spoke of Yorta Yorta culture as undergoing a renaissance after a long history of attempts to suppress it: '[i]t is like a jigsaw puzzle that has been destroyed and we are now in the process of putting it all back' (Colin Walker, *Yorta Yorta* 2001: [199]);'[o]ur culture's been asleep and [now] it's been awakened' (Frances Mathyssen, *Yorta Yorta* 2001: [200]). Counsel for the respondents, on the other hand, tried to establish that the Yorta Yorta Aboriginal Community could not claim a connection to the land as a 'traditional community living under their laws and customs'[4] if they only recently identified themselves as Yorta Yorta per se, and if they had only begun to renew their interest in traditional culture in the preceding 10 or 15 years ([200]).

Olney J found that the accounts given of *contemporary* community practices and values could not be regarded as matters relating to the observance of *traditional* laws and customs as documented by the pioneer Curr, whom he regarded as the best source of evidence for the laws and customs existing at the time sovereignty was claimed. In fact, he held, even from the 1860s, the evidence showed substantial dispossession of the claimants' ancestors and gave no indication that they continued to observe 'those aspects of traditional lifestyle' noted by Curr 30 years earlier (*Yorta Yorta* 1998: [118]). For instance, a petition from residents at the Maloga mission in 1881, which stated that the signatories found their old mode of life not in keeping with their aspirations to settle down and farm the land, was held to provide a further indication of the abandonment of traditional ways ([120]). The Native Title Act required, Olney J said, a 'continuous link back to the laws and customs of the original inhabitants' of the area ([128]). The language of the witnesses backfired on them: resurrection is not the sign of survival but of prior death. In this case, the 'tide of history ha[d] washed away any real acknowledgment of traditional law' ([3]).[5]

Voluminous criticism of the decision ensued. In looking for a match between the past and the present, Olney J was said to have required Yorta Yorta culture to be 'frozen in time', something both impossible and unreasonable given the impact of colonization on Indigenous lives, and a requirement expressly excluded in Brennan J's definition of native title as adaptable to changing circumstances. The 'tide of history' was condemned as a metaphor implicitly removing agency from settler Australians and absolving present law of any responsibility for the lack of recognition (Kerruish and Perrin 1999: 7; Ritter 2004: 117).[6]

---

4 A phrase from Brennan J's *Mabo* judgment.

5 Quoting Brennan J in *Mabo*, regarding circumstances in which native title would be extinguished.

6 And see generally Case 1998/9; Pitty 2000, Clarkson 2001, Cockayne 2001, Reilly 2001;Weiner 2002; Bartlett 2003; Harris 2003; Young 2008: 351–77.

On appeal, the claimants pushed the fallacy of the 'frozen in time' approach. They argued that attempting to create an account of Yorta Yorta culture prior to the arrival of Europeans, and to take it as a starting point to which the judge then compared current beliefs and practices, led Olney J to overemphasize differences with their contemporary way of life and failed to allow for the ability of traditional laws and customs to evolve over time.[7] The Full Federal Court, however, rejected the appeal on the basis that the evidence before Olney J was more than sufficient to support a finding that, at some point between the beginning of colonization and the date of the native title claim, the community had 'lost its character as a traditional community' (*Yorta Yorta* 2001: [194]).[8] 'Traditional', they held, required an objective assessment that 'the law or custom has in substance been handed down from generation to generation' ([127]).

On their final appeal before the High Court, the Yorta Yorta Aboriginal Community shifted their argument once more: both Olney J and the Full Federal Court had essentially required proof positive of continuous historical acknowledgement of traditional law, even though the language of the Native Title Act was in the present tense. This was incorrect, they argued, because what mattered were the rights and interests held under traditional laws *presently* acknowledged. It was thus not fatal to their claim to have a break in the acknowledgement of the laws, or if the laws were seen as being 'revived' rather than continuously observed.[9] The majority of Gleeson, Gummow and Hayne JJ agreed that the wording of the Act was all important, but found that the conjunction of the definition in s. 223(1)(a) in the present tense with the qualifier 'traditional', required continuity. Revival would fail the test. Why does 'traditional' not mean, as Kirby and Gaudron JJ in the minority argue, simply those aspects of culture which 'have their origins in the past'? (*Yorta Yorta* 2002: [114]). The majority created a conceptual geometry of intersection for native title based on the spatiality of sovereignty, the temporal constancy of law, and some socio-legal theory, to arrive at their conclusion.

The Limiting Work of 'Intersection'

Although native title has its origins in traditional laws and customs, s. 223(1)(c) of the Act requires that it be *recognized* by the common law. The High Court had

7 Between the trial and the appeal, there had been a High Court decision accepting that the use of modern methods of hunting were consistent with traditional customs: *Yanner v Eaton* (1999) 166 ALR 259, 277 (Gummow J).

8 This was an expression from Brennan J's *Mabo* judgment which the Full Federal Court majority reasoned was incorporated into the statutory definition by way of the requirement in s. 223(1)(c) that native title rights and interests be 'recognised by the common law of Australia'.

9 See Transcript of Proceedings, *Members of the Yorta Yorta Aboriginal Community v Victoria* (High Court, 23 May 2002) at http://www.austlii.edu.au/au/other/HCATrans/2002/251.html (accessed 1 May 2014).

earlier described native title rights – neither 'creatures of the common law' (*Fejo* 1998: [53]) nor a purely Indigenous phenomenon – as 'an intersection of traditional laws and customs with the common law' ([46]). In *Commonwealth v Yarmirr* (2001), 'intersection' was then used as a heuristic for resolving the inconsistency of a distinction between land and sea which existed in the common law but not in the traditions of the Croker Island clans, and allowed non-exclusive native title over the sea (Gleeson CJ, Gaudron, Gummow and Hayne JJ: [37]–[38], Kirby J: [244]). Similarly, in *WA v Ward* (2002) the idea of intersection provided a general framework or starting point in which the translation from the content of traditional laws and customs to the language of statute and common law was configured ([85]).

In *Yorta Yorta*, the conceptual geometry of intersection has three parts. First, the intersection of two normative orders gets mapped onto spatial and temporal coordinates. The temporal location of intersection, say the majority, is determined by the consequence of the Crown's acquisition of sovereignty and it fixes *what* is to be recognized. Prior to the date of the Crown's acquisition of sovereignty, Indigenous societies had sovereignty and held rights over the land that were eligible to be recognized by the common law; after that date, however, the doctrine of sole sovereignty mandates that there can be no other legitimate source of rights and interests than the Crown within the spatial borders of Australia, 'no parallel law-making system' (*Yorta Yorta* 2002: [44]). When, through the vehicle of native title, the new legal order recognizes traditional rights to land, it can only be recognizing the rights and interests that existed at the time sovereignty was claimed.

Second, there is the normative aspect of law. Native title is not the recognition of any random aspect of traditional law, since the Native Title Act recognizes only *rights and interests* possessed under traditional laws acknowledged and traditional customs observed by the claimants. The Court considers this to mean that the Act requires a body of laws and customs consisting of rules with a *normative* content: 'without that quality, there may be observable patterns of behaviour but not rights or interests in relation to land or waters' (*Yorta Yorta* 2002: [42]). The judgment makes a brief reference to the way that English legal theorists John Austin and HLA Hart have defined law and legal rules. Their theories are not pursued because they 'may or may not be fruitful' in this context ([41]), although, as we shall see, they are implicit in the Court's assumptions about law.

'Normative' is not defined in the decision, but a few clues to what it might mean are given in the Court's assessment of whether there has been an interruption in the acknowledgement of traditional law. On the one hand, the *exercise* of the rights or the practice of laws is not crucial to the continued *possession* of rights and interests. In many successful native title claims, the exercise of traditional rights was made impossible through the intervention of colonial settlement, the dislocation of communities and the banning of traditional practices;[10] it is

10 Such as initiation ceremonies, speaking traditional languages, and 'skin'-based marriages. In many parts of Australia, people are required to marry only from certain groups identified by their totem or 'skin' within the kinship system. See for example Sackett 1976.

inconsistent rights that extinguish native title, not inconsistent use (Gleeson CJ, Gaudron, Gummow and Hayne JJ, *Ward* 2002: [215]). Normative rules do not necessarily have to be carried out to exist.

On the other hand, the Court finds that the Yorta Yorta underwent a period in which 'the content of the laws and customs is passed on from individual to individual' even though it is not practised, and suggests that during this time there might have been only 'knowledge' rather than 'observance and acknowledgement' of laws and customs (*Yorta Yorta* 2002: [51]–[52]). The distinctions between knowledge, acknowledgement and practice seem to suggest that the rules that count in native title – the normative ones – are neither simply those that 'exist' as abstract propositional statements of which one has 'mere knowledge', nor necessarily those that are followed in practice. What is left between cognition and action is feeling or attitude, so normative rules that are acknowledged must be those that summon in claimants a sense of 'must' or obligation.

But what if 'knowledge' of the law is like a seed which, when conditions are right, springs once more into the fullness of acknowledgement: the 'revival' argued by the witnesses? Here, there is one final conceptual *coup de grace*: the third aspect of intersection that is the 'inextricable link between a society and its laws and customs' (*Yorta Yorta* 2002: [48]). The passage introducing this final point is worth quoting in full.

> Laws and customs do not exist in a vacuum. They are, in Professor Julius Stone's words, 'socially derivative and non-autonomous'. As Professor Honoré has pointed out, it is axiomatic that 'all laws are laws of a society or group'. Or as was said earlier, in Paton's Jurisprudence, 'law is but a result of all the forces that go to make society'. Law and custom arise out of and, in important respects, go to define a particular society. In this context, 'society' is to be understood as a body of persons united in and by its acknowledgement and observance of a body of laws and customs ([49]).

With this series of socio-legal truisms, the court achieves something ingenious. If a society ceases to acknowledge its laws (normatively), then the particular society defined by acknowledgement of those laws ceases to exist. Should a descendent group of people later revive what has been passed on to them via oral tradition as knowledge only, this is then necessarily a *new* society with *new* laws. And new laws, as we saw in the first step, infringe the doctrine of sovereignty and cannot be recognized by the Crown as native title. The combination of these three points providing a restricted version of intersection – rendering Indigenous law legible as fact and preventing any recognizable new rights – can easily be seen, in terms of the recognition paradigm, as an attempt by the state to make finite the potential boundlessness and perennial unpredictability of Indigenous claims to law.[11]

---

11 Markell sees the same objective behind the deployment of bounded cultures to justify multicultural recognition (2003: 165–71).

In the minority judgments in both appeal courts – Black CJ in the Federal Court and Gaudron and Kirby JJ in the High Court – the trial judge's assessment of the evidence is criticized. His focus on the pre-contact society is said to have reduced any need to seriously assess contemporary laws and customs; the judge's attention was drawn to the dislocation of the Yorta Yorta Community and the abandonment of a traditional *lifestyle*, rather than the possibility of adaptation (Black CJ) or whether current laws and customs were traditional by virtue of having their origins in the past (Gaudron and Kirby JJ). There is reliance by the minorities on the ordinary meaning of tradition as that which is handed down from 'generation to generation, often by word of mouth', rather than a 'rigid adherence to past practices' (*Yorta Yorta* 2002: [112]). To the extent that laws and customs 'differ from past practices, the differences should constitute adaptations ... made in accordance with the shared values or the customs and practices of the people who acknowledge and observe those laws and customs' (*Yorta Yorta* 2002: [114]).

The emphasis of the minorities on this sense of tradition mitigates the empirically difficult task of assessing the laws and customs of another era, and starts from the perspective of the people who practise laws and customs today. Further, it might have avoided what Simon Young complains of as the 'over-specificity' of native title claims that works against a presumption of full legal title in favour of specific incidents of use, and contributes to an inability to accommodate change and permit contemporary economic use of the land (Young 2008: 355–8, 406–12). Nevertheless, although their tests are not bound to the conceptual geometry of intersection that those of the majorities' are, the same distinctions are assumed in other ways: the existence of laws and customs with their origins in the past is still a matter for empirical enquiry, and they do not exist on the same plane as the 'one Australian law'. The following part explores the grounds of the Court's proposed forensic enquiry by situating it with respect to the legal theory implicit in the case.

Law in the *Yorta Yorta* Case

The Court's Legal Theory

The High Court judges' understanding of their own law follows an orthodoxy that can be unravelled from the basic question that they face as an appeal court: What is the law to be applied? All members of the Court agree that the words of the statute are determinant as to the law, although they disagree on their interpretation and the use of interpretive aids such as dictionaries, the Native Title Act Preamble and ministerial statements.[12] If pressed as to why this is, they would probably answer with reference to the historical victory of parliament over the courts which

12 For instance, to show whether Parliament intended s. 223 (1)(c) to incorporate the developing common law. See *Yorta Yorta* 2002, McHugh J: [129]–[134].

led to the superior role of the legislature as law maker, supreme on all but the constitutional validity of laws.[13]

The words of the Native Title Act hold such significance because they are meant to express Parliament's intention. This rationale reflects in a superficial way the theoretical tradition of Thomas Hobbes (1996: 175) and John Austin, who defined law as the general commands – intentional, communicated, and attended by sanction – of a sovereign, the sovereign being the person or institution with the de facto power to make the law or which the people habitually obey, and not itself subject to a superior authority (Austin 1954: 18–30). Statutes are the command of the sovereign parliament as an expression of its will. Although this definition has been much criticized, not least because many laws do not take the form of a command or entail sanctions, but rather confer rights or powers (Hart 1961: 27–8), the idea of the authorial will remains and can be seen in the importance of 'intention' in statutory interpretation.

As rules authored by an identifiable human source, such laws are said to be posited, and the theory which takes human acts of authorship (although qualified in various ways) to be the source of, or criterion for, the existence of law is positivism. Framing authorship as a matter of laying down rules for legal subjects by legal agents is coined as prescriptivism, and both are key elements of orthodox legal theory (Macdonald 2011: 309). Further, while classic common law theory saw judges as 'discoverers' rather than authors of the law (Blackstone 1800: 68–70; Postema 1989: 4–13), contemporary common law theory has been made largely compatible with the sources thesis of positivism, as well as prescriptivism, by conceiving of the common law as a system of rules laid down by competent authorities: judges are in the position of legislator and decided cases are statutory decrees (Hobbes 2005: 27; Simpson 1986: 10–13; Conklin 2001: 6).

Legal orthodoxy also entails three aspects reflective of the spatial and temporal ontology that underlies the Yorta Yorta case: the unity of law and its monopoly by the state, law's autonomy or distinctiveness, and its reified character as an object. Despite the multitude of judges and legislators making law, Kirby J maintains that there is only 'one law'. Law entails a hierarchy of authority that can always provide a single answer to the question 'what is the law?', an instinct which can be traced back to Jean Bodin and Hobbes, and to the fear that without a supreme power, the natural state of humans would be a 'war of every man against every man' (Hobbes 1996: 85). The capacity to produce a single answer gives the impression that laws have a certain and finite meaning.

The unity or monism of law supposes the territorial exclusivity of the sovereign, a way of thinking made possible by the conflation of sovereign power with territorial jurisdiction dating from the seventeenth century. While the advent of cartographic technology turned unique local places into uniform

13 As does Dawson J in *Kable v Director of Public Prosecutions* (1996) 189 CLR 51 at [13]: 'there can be no doubt that parliamentary supremacy is a basic principle of the legal system which has been inherited in this country from the United Kingdom'.

spaces, rational humanism as a way of perceiving government sought to transcend local differences in order to achieve the equal application of the law to everyone (Ford 1999: 866–87). More broadly, legal monism reflects a pattern of thinking, or an aesthetic, which tends to see the world in terms of a coherent system or hierarchy, ordered by a single principle (Davies 2005: 88). The pattern extends from the monotheistic religions that arguably have left residues in the secular political notion of sovereignty (Fitzpatrick 2007), to the scientific epistemology that favours totalizing explanations and single objective truths.

The second aspect is law's distinctiveness. The answer to the question 'what is the law in this case?' requires an implicit threshold question to sort out the law from the non-law. Echoes of this threshold process are heard in the majority's reference to Austin and Hart in their attempt to put their finger on what will differentiate the source of native title rights and interests as opposed to some other phenomenon. In positivism, the threshold question for law is determined by the social facts of its creation – its pedigree or source (Raz 2009: 47)[14] – such as Austin's commands of the sovereign backed by force. Determining the existence of law by its authoritative provenance was historically an important riposte to the theories of natural law which held true law to be that which was in accordance with universal principles (of nature, god, morality, justice or 'right reason'): according to positivists, 'the existence of law is one thing, its merit or demerit is another' (Austin 1954: 184).

Hart (1961), the most influential English-speaking positivist of the twentieth century, replaced Austin's 'command theory' with the idea of law as essentially a system of authoritative rules. The command theory, he argued, could not explain certain things, such as the diversity in kinds of laws which do more than forbid or enjoin action, or the fact that the law makers themselves were bound by law. He sought to distinguish law from non-law – such as the command of the gunman or the habit of going weekly to the cinema – by paying close attention to how people speak of these situations, and deduced that in the case of law, we consider that we have an obligation to obey, and use the language 'ought', 'must' and 'should' which, he says, carry an implicit reference to the notion of a rule (9).

Hart's method here is influenced by the linguistic philosophy of Ludwig Wittgenstein (1968), who argued that the meaning of words like 'law' is not to be found in an essential set of criteria but through the way they are used in ordinary language: meaning is not inherent but attributed through convention. Since language in use is a series of analogies and associations, when we look for meaning in use we will find only 'family resemblances' rather than an essential definition (31). Listening for usage, Hart (1961) observes that 'obligation' is not captured by the existence of a punishment or a personal motive to obey, but rather that the language of obligation is used when people adopt a reflective attitude to the rules and consider them as *reasons* for their behaviour or for the application

14 See the nuance brought to this by Scott Shapiro (2007), distinguishing between 'hard' positivists like Raz and 'soft' positivists who hold simply that the existence of law is attributable to social, rather than moral, facts (31–5).

of sanctions (82). Likewise, merely habitual behaviour can be distinguished from following rules as it does not provoke the same language games, in which 'lapses or faults [are] open to criticism', on deviation (54). It is this 'internal aspect' that Hart associates with rules of obligation (10).

However, when it comes to distinguishing legal from other rules, Hart abandons the conventionalism of linguistic philosophy, and slips into asserting an essential identity for law in order to establish the positivist threshold. In the central and undisputed case we refer to when using the word 'law', he argues, the primary obligatory rules of behaviour (which might otherwise be merely moral or social) are joined by secondary rules that provide authoritative ways to identify primary rules (via the rule of recognition) but also to change and administer them (Hart 1961: 79–96). The rule that native title can be recognized, for instance, would be law because there is a rule of recognition that says 'what parliament enacts, and what the courts from time to time declare, is law'. Such rules may be stated in foundational documents like constitutions, or may be implicit in the way legal officials identify primary rules in practice. In a modern legal system, Hart adds, it is only officials who need hold the internal perspective, taking the rule of recognition as a reason for their actions, as long as private citizens generally obey the valid primary rules of obligation (113).

In Hart's theory, the rule of recognition constitutes the origin of the authority of legal rules, unifies them into a system by means of rational cohesion, and separates them from facts of behaviour or from moral beliefs (93). The key role of officials in identifying law guarantees law's distinctiveness with respect to the diverse phenomena of people's behaviour, attitudes and discourse that might otherwise have been introduced by the internal perspective, and qualifies them as 'facts'. The fact-law distinction structures everything in the common law court process: from the role of trial judges and juries as finders of fact and the limitation of appeals to errors of law, to rules of evidence and the logic of precedent, law and fact seem to inhabit separate planes of existence. Matters of fact seem particular and idiosyncratic, rooted in individual disputes; matters of law can transcend the decisions in which they are articulated and express universal standards for other like cases (Scheppele 1991: 42–4). The fact-law distinction allows some sense to be made of the paradox of declaring there to be only one Australian law and no parallel law-making power while at the same time requiring operational laws and customs as part of the proof of native title. From the perspective of the state legal system, Indigenous laws may be normative, but they are facts rather than 'the law binding upon all the people of Australia' because they have no legal pedigree according to the one sovereign.[15] The two legal systems no longer intersect because they do not exist on the same plane.

Finally, Kirby J's assurance that 'ultimately, a single governing law is discoverable' speaks to the third aspect we are considering, the determinate or

15 The distinction may also be usefully thought of in terms of the problems with recognition.

object-like nature of legal rules. It suggests that law's expressive form will mostly dictate a clear answer, and that its content will be only occasionally in doubt, in which case 'legal reasoning' will discover a single answer. Mainstream legal theorists disagree about whether decisions in these 'hard cases' are to be explained as the application of legal or non-legal principles that judges consider binding, or, as for Hart, as judicial legislation that is necessary because of the limited ability of legal language to cover every eventuality (Dworkin 1975; Schauer 1988: 514–20). Nevertheless, there is widespread acceptance of the idea that, in Hart's (1961) terms, there are usually core, undisputed meanings to rules, and only a penumbra of uncertainty caused by a 'crisis in communication' in the use of general terms (123). In this view, rules then appear to have an existence that is independent from acts of interpretation and that can be empirically demonstrated; reified, they endure solidly over time.

We thus have a picture of the Court's legal theory. Reflecting what Roderick Macdonald calls the 'republican consensus' (Macdonald 2003: 87–9), it consists of positivism (the source of law in social fact distinguished by analytical criteria), centralism and monism (locating law in a single set of (state) institutions) and prescriptivism and chirographism (law consists of rules articulated – and able to be expressed in written form – by legal agents and received by legal subjects) (Macdonald 2011: 309). The unity and autonomy of law captured in writing tend to objectify law as a thing separate from human activity. Here, law's 'thingness' can be seen to extend out into the two axes of space and time: one through the territorial unity of sovereignty, the other through the solidity of law over time, enabled through acts of will, but otherwise stable. These ideas seem to be somewhat undermined by the second set of theorists invoked by the majority when they argue for the 'inextricable link' between law and society. However, the mutual implication of law and society is rather selectively and superficially deployed in the *Yorta Yorta* reasoning, and the judges do not use it to question the autonomy of their own law.

Consequences of Legal Theory for the Yorta Yorta Claim

Gleeson, Gummow and Hayne JJ in the *Yorta Yorta* High Court majority know that they cannot expect Indigenous law to carry the hallmarks of law identified by Western legal theory. Applying the theories of Austin and Hart may or may not be productive. Neither written nor institutionalized, Indigenous law is unlikely to be characterized by sovereign command, to use a rule of recognition, or to give two figs for the difference between law and custom. And yet… As we shall see, the court's relativist stance towards Indigenous law is compromised by the ontological assumptions about law that we have just discussed.

Beginning with s. 223 of the Native Title Act, the court elaborates what it means to possess native title rights and interests under traditional laws acknowledged and traditional customs observed. The judges stress that they are not purporting to define law, Indigenous or otherwise. If they are led to discuss 'law-making systems' or 'rules having normative content' it is not so as to identify the inherent nature of Indigenous legality, but rather to address the 'fundamental premise [in *Mabo*] that the laws and customs of the Indigenous peoples of this country constituted bodies of normative rules which … had in fact given rise to rights and interests in relation to land or waters', and the premise in the Native Title Act that such rights and interests can be possessed under traditional laws and customs (*Yorta Yorta* 2002: [40]).

With deference to the potential inadequacy of Western legal perspectives to describe Indigenous law,[16] the court observes (with an echo of Hart's linguistic method) that rights and interests belonging to a normative system can be identified:

> Of course, those rights and interests may not, and often will not, correspond with rights and interests in land familiar to the Anglo-Australian property lawyer. The rights and interests under traditional laws and customs will often reflect a different conception of 'property' or 'belonging'. But none of those considerations denies the normative quality of the laws and customs of the Indigenous societies. It is only if the rich complexity of Indigenous society is denied that reference to traditional laws and customs as a normative system jars the ear of the listener (*Yorta Yorta* 2002: [40]).

The Court asserts that the jurisprudential questions (Austin, Hart) are not important for 'present purposes'. What concerns them is the question of whether 'the rights and interests concerned originate in a *normative* system' that has existed since the change in sovereignty ([43]).[17] However, jurisprudential questions are already assumed in the geometry of intersection, with its temporal location and the requirement of normative rules, and they map onto the three aspects of legal orthodoxy discussed above: monopoly, autonomy and reification.

First, the proposition that after the Crown acquired sovereignty, 'the normative or law-making system which then existed could not thereafter validly create new rights, duties, or interests' is an example of the territorial exclusivity or monopoly of the state over law. It relies on the theory that rules are valid solely if given validity according to some founding principle such as Austin's sovereign command or Hart's rule of recognition. The legal foundations of Crown sovereignty can be traced back to the 'act of state' that in *Mabo* (1992) is put beyond question as a matter of domestic law (Brennan J: [31]). In that case, sovereignty was held to have been extended over the Murray Islands by the exercise of the Crown's prerogative of annexation evidenced simply by Letters Patent issued by Queen Victoria. In contrast, international law generally required physical occupation to 'perfect'

16 'System' for instance should not be taken to be confined only to a 'developed European body of written laws', they say, quoting Charles Sampford (*Yorta Yorta* 2002: [39]) (who, ironically, would even deny the systematic character of European law (1984: 179–86)).

17 Emphasis in original.

the inchoate title achieved by taking symbolic possession (through planting flags, for instance) (von der Heydte 1935: 457–62), which sounds somewhat akin to Austin's ascription of sovereignty according to *de facto* control or power to make law. Further, jurisdiction, or the law-making power of the Crown, in colonial Australia was asserted over larger territories than had been seen, let alone occupied, by the newcomers. On these bases, we thus either have a 'Just So' story of legal validity (Dorsett and McVeigh 2002) – a paper empire made of puffery – or we have a foundation in the progressive physical control over territory that, given the often violent nature of the colonial frontier, grounds legal validity in Australia in brute force or conquest (Simpson 1993: 198–202).

Alternatively, we could locate legal validity in the rule of recognition that, according to Hart, exists in the practice of legal officials. Taking judicial practice as exemplary, legal validity then depends upon that which the parliament decrees, together with what the courts from time to time determine, consistent with the exclusivity of the above proposition. However, there is a circularity here which has often been noted: if it is the practice of legal officials that reveals the rule of recognition that in turn supports the legal system, how do we first ascertain which people are legal officials?[18] One might want to ask in this context why we should not look also to the practices of Indigenous law men and women in order to ascertain alternative rules of recognition in Australia. Indeed, the majority suggests that

> so far as it is useful to analyse the problem in the jurisprudential terms of the legal positivist, the relevant rule of recognition of a traditional law or custom is a rule of recognition found in the social structures of the relevant Indigenous society as those structures existed at sovereignty (*Yorta Yorta* 2002: [54]).

But this would then beg the question of why only the court's rule of recognition was currently determinative of legal validity rather than the criteria that are used by Indigenous law men and women.

Hart's move from the populist and democratic focus of linguistic philosophy and the internal perspective, to the essential concept of law centred around the rule of recognition and official practice, can be read as a mythological 'primal scene' for modern law, as Peter Fitzpatrick has done (1992a: 192). In Hart's account of this scene, a 'simple tribal society', with only primary rules of obligation, will run into trouble because they have no way to identify, change or efficiently adjudicate breaches of rules (Hart 1961: 78–93). In adopting secondary rules to fulfil these functions, the society moves from the pre- or primitively legal to the fully legal (Hart 1961: 244). Modern law is thereby constructed against – a negation of –

18 See, for instance, Matthew Kramer 1998. Jeremy Waldron (2010: 140) and Brian Tamanaha (2001: 139) also observe that while Hart's theory is focused on official rather than popular practice, it does not specify *state* officials and so becomes open to accommodating legal pluralism.

the projected primitivism of the 'savage state', with the same characteristics of simplicity, uncertainty, stasis and inefficiency as justified the imposition of colonial rule by the official (Fitzpatrick 1992a: 202–3).[19] The containment of legal pluralism in the fact-law distinction can be similarly understood as mythological, in that the source of legal validity that separates Indigenous law-fact from State law-law, in Hart as in the entire canon of modern legal theory,[20] relies on primal stories of origin told about Indigenous peoples.

According to Fitzpatrick, the slip from linguistic philosophy in Hart is explained by the fact that colonized people spoke no language that could be understood so as to contribute to 'linguistic use': they 'had to be spoken for' (202). Similarly, although the Yorta Yorta claimants are asked to speak of their laws and customs under the laws of native title, the rule of recognition 'blind spot' – the Indigenous law-defining practices that the Court's structural assumptions do not permit them to see when they look in their theoretical rear-view mirror – means the court cannot take into account Yorta Yorta understandings of what law is, but can only ask them to produce evidence of normative rules.

This relates to the second aspect of positivist ontology at stake in the *Yorta Yorta* case, the distinctiveness of law from other phenomena. The stance of cultural relativity leads the majority to equivocate on the relevance of Hart's distinction between 'merely convergent habitual behaviour' and legal rules (*Yorta Yorta* 2002: [41]). Nevertheless, it is hard to make sense of the distinction that the Court maintains between 'observable patterns of behaviour' and 'rules having normative content' ([42]) that give rise to rights and interests without reference to Hart.

Hart argues that habits may be observed by an outsider as a mere generality of behaviour, but the key to the existence of a rule-following society lies in the 'internal point of view' of participants. Recall that this was where rules are taken as reasons for 'criticism (including self-criticism), demands for conformity, and … acknowledgements that such criticisms and demands are justified, all of which find their characteristic expression in the normative terminology of "ought", "must", and "should", "right" and "wrong"' (Hart 1961: 57). And yet the internal aspect is decidedly missing from Olney J's analysis in the *Yorta Yorta* trial. There is an emphasis on lifestyle and discrete practices: burials, food consumption, punishment. A superficial comparison of external appearances highlights the differences between now and then.[21]

On appeal, the claimants had argued that the test for whether or not laws and customs were traditional should be based on whether 'those who currently acknowledge a law or observe a custom regard their practice of so doing as

19 Note, however, that Hart acknowledges that the transition to the legal could have negative aspects, such as the abuse of the rules by a centrally organized power: Green 1996: 1698.

20 See Fitzpatrick 1992a: Chapters 3 and 4.

21 Gaudron and Kirby JJ in the minority arrive at a similar conclusion by taking traditions as practices which 'have their origins in the past': *Yorta Yorta* 2002: [114].

traditional' (*Yorta Yorta* 2001: [126]). The Federal Court majority speculated that while this may be a necessary condition, it was not sufficient, and held that the test was an objective one of 'whether the law or custom has in substance been handed down from generation to generation' ([127]). Similarly, the High Court held that the acknowledgement and observance of laws and customs 'must have continued substantially uninterrupted' (*Yorta Yorta* 2002: [87]). Although subjective and objective do not line up completely with internal and external perspectives on behaviour – the former pair concerning the universal reasonableness of an assessment, the latter concerning being a participant as opposed to an observer – and the test here is for the traditional character, rather than the existence, of law, the attitudes of Yorta Yorta members to their behaviour that in Hart's view would constitute normativity are crucial to understanding continuity at the level of norms. Had some effort been made to enunciate a rule as reason for the behaviour, then, for instance, it might have been found that the apparent lack of foresight in food practices observed by Curr – that 'they never abstained from eating the whole of any food they had got with a view to the wants of tomorrow' (*Yorta Yorta* 1998: [115]) – was consistent with contemporary fishing and hunting practices if both are considered with respect to a rule or principle of immediate consumption (Kerruish and Perrin 1999: 6). In contrast, Black CJ's dissent in the Federal Court appeal stressed the limitations of external accounts of Indigenous law, and argued for the need to take the claimants' oral traditions seriously, particularly as a reflection of the evolution of traditional laws and customs over a long time frame (*Yorta Yorta* 2001: [55]–[60]).

In Black CJ's dissent we have a sense that the Hartian focus on rules as *reasons*, both critical and justificatory, is not simply a matter of subjective attitude: taking a rule as a reason is different from merely having a psychological inclination to act in a certain way. As Hart (1961) puts it, '*if* our behaviour is challenged we are disposed to justify it by reference to the rule', and because if, before we had complied with the rule, 'we had been asked to say what the right thing to do was and why, we would, if honest, have cited the rule in reply' (136–7). Rules are thus *inter*-subjective or social rather than subjective or individual (reflecting at the level of discourse the mutual recognition in Hegel's shift to a legal community from Chapter 2). And, importantly for my argument, rules are drawn forth and articulated in the question-and-answer exchanges that Hart describes. In the language of recognition we pursued earlier, this makes discourse a site for the productive recognition of law-as-rules rather than the passive identification or re-presentation of a pre-existing entity.

However, as we saw above, Hart's larger positivist project does not understand rules in this way, and assumes that they have a core of determinate meaning that gives them an objective existence. This third aspect of legal orthodoxy is reflected in the court's search for continuous normativity in the Yorta Yorta Aboriginal Community. Importantly, while the majority seems to accept that 'knowledge of the traditional ways' has been maintained, this is distinguished from the existence of law. As Callinan J puts it in his concurring opinion, '[t]radition, myth and legend are often indistinguishable, but the mere existence of either of the latter, in the sense of a fictitious narrative, or an unauthentic or non-historical story, however venerated by repetition, will not suffice of itself to establish native title rights and interests' (*Yorta Yorta* 2002: [185]).

In orthodox legal theory, the identification of a fact as positing law depends on its legal significance, and it is this that continues through time. Creating legal rules or obligations doesn't just depend on a physical fact – raising hands in Parliament or signing a paper – but in the interpretation that is placed on it: passing legislation or making a will (Kelsen 1967: 477–8). Likewise, the content of laws, rights and obligations thus created – their meaning in terms of how they will be applied – is determined by the plain or undisputed sense of the words used.

Hart's claim that there is a 'core' of certainty in the application of the law had been intended as a response to the legal realist critique of the ability of legal language to impose formal constraints on judicial discretion, with him accepting that law was significantly indeterminate, but only in marginal cases (Schauer 2008: 1109). This position has likewise been subject to criticism, not least because it flies in the face of Hart's own initial subscription to Wittgensteinian linguistic philosophy. Lon Fuller, for instance, argues that 'core' and 'penumbra' are not functions of words, but of the intention of the utterer; certainty felt in the application of the rule is due to certainty felt as to its purpose (Fuller 1957/8: 661–9). In his example, the reason why a homeless person who lies down on a railway station bench falls foul of a rule prohibiting sleeping in the station, while a businessman who nods off while waiting for his train does not, lies not in core definitions of sleeping (a psychological state, lying down, upright), but in the intention of the regulation (to prevent pre-meditated use of the station as a place for sleeping) (664). Further, argues Fuller, meaning is not a property of singular words but is the result of our interpretations, both synchronically – in the context of sentences, paragraphs and so on – and diachronically, becoming apparent to us over time as we test our presumptions of purpose against examples.[22] The susceptibility of law to being drawn out dialogically makes it subject to what we earlier called finitude in the context of human identity, a constitutive dependence on the outcomes of exchanges with others.

Bernard Jackson takes this argument further by pointing out that 'intention' is not the only context in which general words must be assessed, because the terms of a rule – and any interpretive discussion of them – evoke narrative images that give the real clues as to a match between the 'case' and the 'rule' (Jackson 1996: 194–7). The reason why we know 'clearly' how the rule is to be applied in Fuller's example is because the case narrative presents a normative opposition between

22 Fuller (1956) cites the famous passage from Wittgenstein on the meaning of 'game': 'Someone says to me: "Show the children a game". I teach them gaming with dice and the other says "I did not mean that sort of game"' to make the point that purpose is only be drawn out retrospectively (700). Although Hart (1958) did not concede the significance of this point for the separation between law and morality, he did agree that purpose may only become apparent in the reiteration of the rule (628).

businessmen and homeless people through 'an image of respectability on the one hand and deviance on the other' (Fuller 1957/8: 195). While the larger argument from critical legal studies about the radical indeterminacy of the law – whether due to pervasive inconsistencies in the legal rules in any given field and in the ideological commitments animating them (Kennedy 1976; 1983; Tushnet 1984), or because language is infinitely malleable (Unger 1976: 92–4) – is not at stake here, the point I wish to make is that the only interesting sense of what a law 'is' in order to exist as law relates to what it says or means, and that this does not, even in apparently clear cases, stand apart from the human activity of interpretation or the need to enmesh our decisions in larger narratives that help us to understand their significance. Narrative and its imaginative commitments are crucial to our capacity to adjudicate, make distinctions, justify decisions, punish and so on in the name of the law.

This profound connection between law and narrative has been famously articulated by Robert Cover (1983): the difference between 'having a snack and desecrating the fast of Yom Kippur' (8) is not merely because the same act is differently meaningful as judged against a particular rule, but also because each rule is embedded in a vast universe of narrative which makes such actions ways to communicate with others, to claim belonging or distinctness, to 'submit, rejoice, struggle, pervert, mock, disgrace, humiliate or dignify' (8). Narratives are not just what might sometimes explain the particular application of a rule, then, but the very glue of law, and 'no set of legal institutions or prescriptions exists apart from the narratives that locate it and give it meaning' (4).

Cover's principal argument is that this 'world of narrative' – or *nomos* – is the source of legal meaning and is produced through a collective social process. It is thus groups, associations and communities of people that are the site for 'jurisgenesis' – the creation of legal meaning. And even though state law might provide for authoritative precepts and texts, the patterns of narrative which make them meaningful, and which 'give rise to effective or ineffective social control' are uncontrolled, diverse and contested (17). Unlike Ronald Dworkin's (1986) interpretive theory whereby there are merely multiple interpretive attitudes *to* law that don't become law until subjected to the integrity test of fit and justification by a judge (225–38), for Cover these attitudes *are* law because they arise out of a communal commitment to a *nomos* which provides a lexicon for moving between the ideal and the real, and vice versa (9).[23] A court decision does not create law but chooses one among these competing *nomoi* in a *jurispathic* – or law killing – act.

In contrast to the distinction between hearing stories and normatively acknowledging laws and customs in the *Yorta Yorta* case, Cover would say that it is community narratives that create normativity. Given the primacy of normativity in the court's definition of native title, it makes no sense for them to fix a cut-off point (sovereignty) after which laws acknowledged by an Indigenous community can be normative without the capacity for the community to be jurisgenerative.

23 See also Melissaris 2009: 52–3.

Law-sustaining narratives *are* law-creating narratives, because narrative is recursive and the tradition that it embodies can only exist in attempts to re-interpret that tradition.

Assuming that the narratives in question were, for some period, stories about 'what the old people used to do', these accounts continue to be normative because they become analogous to constitutional texts for the 'us' of the Yorta Yorta Community and provide the 'legal DNA' for the interpretation of contemporary practices and commitments. Just as the practice of law may adapt to introduced technologies or demographic situations, so the narration of law adapts to the imposition of the status of colonized minority. Cover writes, '[f]or a group to live its law in the face of the predictable employment of violence against it requires a new elaboration of "law" – the development of an understanding of what is right and just in the violent contexts that the group will encounter' (49). The responsiveness of law to changed social situations does not indicate a break in normativity but its preservation.

Counsel for the Yorta Yorta claimants made an analogy, in oral submissions before the High Court, to Jews during the holocaust or Christians in ancient Rome who were prohibited from practising the requirements of their religion for a period and then continued afterwards, but this assessment of the impact of change does not go far enough. For the new conditions alter the ways in which the content of tradition makes sense: the idea of the promised land, and the observance of particular rituals, sustained the Jewish diaspora in ways that weren't relevant when their ancestors lived in Israel, and yet they are 'Jewish traditions'. As James Weiner (2002) argues, 'diasporic native title claim groups' understandings of their connection to traditional law must be considered as a variety of the contemporary exercise of Indigenous rights in country' (8).

At trial, Olney J held evidence of contemporary beliefs and practices to be essentially irrelevant to the claim, since he had found that there was no positive evidence of the continuance of traditional life in the 1860s in the face of evidence of extensive dispossession, and the suggestive statements of the petition. This document might easily be read as a strategic claim rather than as a cessation of tradition, and physical dispossession is not a bar to recognition. Witnesses gave oral evidence that they had seen their grandparents and great-grandparents speaking the Yorta Yorta language, singing songs and performing dances, and had learnt about laws and customs from them as children (*Yorta Yorta* 2001: [81]). In the face of such evidence of twentieth-century 'acknowledgement of traditional law', Olney J's theory of abandonment needs to be rescued in order to apply here, and it is rescued by the High Court's distinction between knowledge and normativity that turns current practice into revival.

The difference between continuity in practice and continuity in narrative was brought out during the cross-examination of Alfred Turner as to the significance of middens found at old camp sites:

> *Michael Wright*: Now, are all those sites sacred?

Alfred Turner: They are to us.

Michael Wright: Are you permitted to use them?

Alfred Turner: No, no. We would never camp on a site like that … We wish other people would observe that, too.

Michael Wright: Well can you tell me what – when it is that a midden becomes sacred? Is it immediately that it's been used as a campsite, or at some other time?

Alfred Turner: It's sacred to us today because we believe that our forefathers and foremothers used those sites.

Michael Wright: Yes. Well, is a camping site sacred if Yorta Yorta people for example used it last weekend?

Alfred Turner: I wouldn't say that, no.

Michael Wright: I'm just trying to establish at what point of time a campsite becomes a sacred site. Can you help me there?

Alfred Turner: I would say sacred site would be 150 – 200 years.

Michael Wright: So it is a question of antiquity, is it? It has to achieve a certain age before it becomes sacred.

Alfred Turner: No, it doesn't have to achieve a certain age. It's just something that was put there by our people.[24]

In the narrative of sacredness pursued by the cross-examining counsel, it is the age of the specific object (the midden) which is brought into focus rather than the continuity of the veneration of ancestors or the belief in the sacred itself. But Yorta Yorta narratives highlight a different locus of continuity. In a play by Yorta Yorta playwright Andrea James that rakes over the court decision, there is a mantra that sustains the entire action and narrative of the play: 'we are here' (James 2003: 1, 4, 34, 43, 54). The stories on which she draws – of *Biami*, *Dhungula* and *burnanga*, and of Curr and the court process – allow the people to know who they are and where they belong.

But in the Federal Court of Appeal, because senior community members had not 'learnt any Yorta Yorta dance steps', been through initiation ceremonies, or

24 Edited transcript as re-enacted in 'Background Briefing', ABC Radio National Transcripts (11 May 1997). Available at: <http://www.abc.net.au/radionational/programs/backgroundbriefing/yorta-yorta/3563904> ('Background Briefing').

learnt the laws of descent, because Yorta Yorta culture 'is like a jigsaw puzzle that has been destroyed' and is being put back together, then according to the Court, the community has ceased to acknowledge traditional laws (*Yorta Yorta* 2001: [199]).[25] The problem with this and the High Court's insistence on normativity as a 'body of law and customs' that existed continuously since sovereignty (*Yorta Yorta* 2002: [87]) is that it imagines an object – or rather, several discrete objects[26] – that is concrete and external to context and discourse.[27] In my reading, the narrative of destruction and revival is not proof of *expiry*, but rather the new vehicle for belonging, the new articulation of identity to place. It is arguably this broader sense of 'connection' that is required by s. 223(1)(b) of the Native Title Act, not a catalogue of practices (Young 2008: 401–6).

Yorta Yorta Law

If the above analysis of the Yorta Yorta case suggests that we look for a communities' normative connection with the land in their narratives, this section draws on the words and practices of Yorta Yorta Community members to understand that narrative. In particular, I wish to highlight here the way that the land, or 'country', in Yorta Yorta narratives provides an alternative way of configuring the time and space of law. As will be developed more fully in the part that follows, this alternative also challenges us to think about law in a more plural, relational way. Finally, although aspects of the stories are particular to the Yorta Yorta, others resonate more broadly across Australia, and with accounts of Indigenous law in many other places (Borrows 2010: 28–35; Basso 1996: 59–65; Baird 2013: 329).

Let's start with the all important river, *Dhungula*, the 'spiritual and economic' lifeblood of Yorta Yorta country (Atkinson 2008: 187). Yorta Yorta histories understand the natural and cultural features of the land to have been created by the deeds of the spirit ancestor Biami: he sent his woman and a snake down from the high country, who gouged out the shape of the river on their way, and then spoke in thunder that brought rain to fill the tracks made (Atkinson 2008: 186). The creation of landscape features in the distant past is part of the 'Dreaming' complex

---

25 More accurately, it was held that these pieces of evidence supported Olney's finding to that effect.

26 See Simon Young's (2008) argument that the Australian test for Native Title has been overly particular, and that focusing on specific laws and customs rather than an overall connection magnifies findings of change and interruption in processes of proof (351–77).

27 In addition, the focus on change brought about by the *Yorta Yorta* majority's denial of 'significant adaptation' as parallel law-making rather than the focus on continuity in *Mabo*'s 'substantially maintained' test, was shown up in the fact that they have produced opposite results in decisions on what were substantially similar facts in *Jango* (2006) and *Griffiths* (2006), namely, a change in the claimant communities since settlement from a patrilineal to a cognatic descent system. See Howard Highland 2007: 366–8.

or *nomos* that extends across Australia, stories that also tell how peoples, and laws, were placed in the land by Beings who, in their travels, created a network of Dreaming tracks or 'songlines' across the continent (Rumsey 2001: 22–4). Monica Morgan testified before Olney J about these connections:

> We have obligations as the people from this country. We believe that we were placed here, that we come from this country and we have obligations to look after it and be a part of it; and obligations to – when you see that something's depleting, or things are happening, then to modify your activities and your way of life to be able to meet the needs of that country (Background Briefing 1997).

The Murray and Lower Darling Rivers Indigenous Nations (MLDRIN), a 'confederation' the Yorta Yorta have formed with other Indigenous peoples from the river system, state that 'in traditional law, owners are associated with particular places, and through ancestors, an extended landscape' (Weir 2009: 131).

Prior to modern irrigation management, the river was subject to seasonal flows: low in summer, it would often break its banks with winter rains, feeding the plains with water (Weir 2009: 54–6). Nowadays, dams and weirs control the flow, which is drawn off for crops, adding to water table levels and rising salination, or released when there is surplus, causing unseasonal flooding into wetlands (Weir 2009: 55). In contributing to river management, MLDRIN delegates insist that decisions to release water for the purposes of ecological health also take into account 'cultural flows' that return water to areas of cultural significance; for instance, sites of Dreaming stories or medicinal plants (Weir 2009: 112).

Yorta Yorta narratives often use body metaphors to talk about the river. In Uncle Colin Walker's account:

> The old people reckoned it [the river] was a living thing, because when you get fresh water comin' down, the water's goin' down into those little creeks, purifying the kidneys, like our body. If we had no blood runnin' into our kidneys and that, then we'd die – we'd get very sick. So they run out [the water channels onto the floodplain] – they run out and purify it. And that's why the lakes were *clean*. Those lakes [are now] in a mess … you have to look after the other parts. … if you don't look after it, you're not gonna look after yourself are you? (Wilcock and Brierley 2012: 12).

Others talk of weirs on the river as blood clots (Somerville 2013: 181). Jessica Weir (2009) comments that the merging of bodies and the river in Yorta Yorta narratives also arise out of knowing the river as an embodied experience of sensory encounters: seeing, smelling, touching, eating and drinking it (72). Loss of species is thus also the 'extinction of experience' with those species (Pyle 2011: 130). The Dreaming connections create what Aileen Moreton-Robinson (2004) calls an 'inter-substantiation of humans, ancestral beings and land' ([12]). If the land is a body, the bodies of Yorta Yorta people also carry title to the land: 'the physicality of Indigenous people is testimony to the existence of particular tracts of country' (Moreton-Robinson 2004: [12]).

The sense of space produced by experiential knowledge emphasizes the deep links between space and time, and at different scales. For instance, the flooding cycles of *Dhungula* lend themselves to thinking about the river in terms of action over time rather than location, as well as in terms of the succession of life cycles, big and small, that depend on periodic water flows. This is not the abstract river that forms the boundary between New South Wales and Victoria or delivers cubic meters of water. Places are linked by the experiences of moving between them for particular purposes. These lifetime events are also co-present with the deep time events of geological creation that are in evidence in the landscape and told through Dreaming stories: 'Yorta Yorta narratives engage with multiple pasts, presents and futures as they interweave creation stories, cultural health and the "right now" of looking after Country' (Wilcock and Brierley 2012: 13). The space of country is not the uniform space of sovereignty but the variegated space creating by the Dreaming.

I suggested above that in Western legal traditions, writing, and a belief in the fixed meaning of words, produced the effect of the constancy of laws over time. However, historical – that is, linear and irreversible – time is also a contingent factor in this arrangement. In contrast, for many Indigenous Australians, Dreaming law is constant because it is inscribed in the connections laid down in the beginning, which themselves are placed in the land. Dreaming time was both 'in the beginning' and is 'everywhen' (Stanner 1998: 228), the cosmological time that underlies and is within the present (Elkin 1969: 88, 93; Morphy 1999: 265).

One example of continuity in this timescape comes from comparing Indigenous and positivist histories, the latter of which has a similar reliance on writing as a means of fixing the past. Indigenous peoples around Australia tell a narrative of colonization called collectively the 'Captain Cook sagas'. The general shape of the stories is that Captain Cook comes from the sea, kills and oppresses the local people, and takes their land without asking, his 'book law' covering the truth that Aboriginal people own the land (Rose 1984: 31–2). In one version told on the south coast of NSW by Percy Mumbulla in the 1950s, a woman called Tungeei was sitting on 'The Point' telling Mumbulla's father about 'the big ship that came and anchored out at Snapper Island ... ':

> When he landed he gave the Kurris clothes an' them big sea biscuits. Terrible hard biscuits they was. When they was pullin' away to go back to the ship, them wild Kurris were runnin' out of the scrub. They'd stripped right off again. They was throwin' the clothes an' biscuits back at Captain Cook as his men was pullin' away in the boat (Healy 1997: 53).

Many of these sagas are apocryphal, in that Captain Cook did not visit the locations of the stories; however they *are* accurate histories of the general shape of colonial relations, where Captain Cook is the metaphor for the White settlers and their law. A more radical take is suggested by Chris Healy (1997), however, who argues that the sagas involve a different set of distinctions than the categorical one between past and present of positivist history: not between the savage past and the civilized future as in European historiography, but a spatial difference between a law that is immoral and comes from the sea, and the true law, eternal because it comes from the land, moral because it is eternal (58). In Mumbulla's version, the gifts from the sea are explicitly rejected as being without worth – 'terrible hard biscuits'. The evidential systems in use are not those of citation and source materials used in Western historiography. Instead, the lineage of guardians of social memory – from Percy Mumbulla to his father to the woman Tungeei – and the continuity of place – 'The Point' – are present both in the event, and the telling of the event, thus resolving the tension between reality and representation that European history resolves through the continuity of archival sources and academic objectivity (55–7). The indices of truth in these histories are the identity of people and place.

The law that Yorta Yorta Aboriginal Community members tried to articulate for the court is one that ties people to place by being a manifestation of the experience of life in country. The deep identification expressed in pervasive bodily metaphors is testament to a basic ethic of connectivity that situates people in the natural world and underscores the interdependence of all species 'across multiple spatial and temporal scales' (Weir 2009: 68). These are the enduring ontological foundations of law, regardless of how they are expressed. Attempting to see things from a Yorta Yorta perspective, I doubt that they could be displaced other than through the total destruction of life in country (see Weir 2009: 80–81). Connectivity confounds the uniform space of sovereignty through which modern law seeks to exercise dominion, and provides a different set of reference points for constancy over time, rather than an objectified set of rules. The following section explores the challenges of Indigenous law to these dimensions of sovereignty as well as the ways in which it might be possible to build a legal theory around an experience of interdependence.

Legal Pluralism and the Laws of Interdependence

The recognition of Indigenous law by the state adopts the bare bones of a legally pluralist vision: the co-existence in one territory of Indigenous law and state law. Through the *Yorta Yorta* case we have seen that, from the Australian courts' perspective, co-existence is fashioned into a discontinuity between the domains of the factual and the legal. The spatial and temporal aspects of the courts' understanding of law exclude the possibility of 'parallel law-making' in Australia's territory and anticipate the continuity of legal objects over time. In the courts' distinguishing criteria for 'real' law, based on something like Hart's rule of recognition, we see a blind spot that denies a more robust spatial aspect of pluralism: whose practices give rise to the criteria for law? To correct that blind spot, and turn to the discursive practices of participants, we challenge another aspect of sovereignty, that of mastery over the meaning of law, because in discourse law and legal rules are articulated and drawn out, in dialogue with others, over time. This is a temporal aspect of pluralism akin to Markell's concept of finitude in human identity that we used to complicate the politics of recognition in Chapter 2.

Listening to Yorta Yorta people, and, indeed, to other Indigenous people, we hear that law is located in stories, very often those of creation times, that law comes from the land and from lived knowledge of species, geoforms and weather, and that law is spoken by those who know both stories and places, who have a responsibility to tend them. The ethic of connectivity is expressed variously, for example, as kinship, through totemic identification and belief in consubstantiation, in moieties and other social structures, through gift-giving protocols and as the 'law of relationship' (Black 2011:15–16). This ethic challenges not only the republican consensus, but also much of the analytical, fact-based legal pluralism that has dominated social-scientific approaches to law. In this section, I examine these and other pluralist accounts of law in order to seek out ways in which Western legal theory has already engaged, and might better engage, with interdependence. I argue that the shift from thinking of law in functional terms to thinking of it as a discourse is productive for postcolonial jurisprudence in that it turns us away from 'universal' attributes of law that are derived from only certain peoples' experiences with law, and towards the linguistic worlds – the ethos – of peoples who live their law. Nevertheless, there is a tendency in discursive approaches to focus on the masterful individual as a source of law that may not provide the appropriate terms with which to articulate a declaration of interdependence.

Law as Function, Law as Discourse

From the early twentieth century, the dominant approach in academic discourse to talking about legal pluralism, and indeed, about law other than state law, has come from the social sciences. Broad definitions of law – for example, as obligatory social norms (Malinowski 1926), or the way in which a group deals with 'trouble' (Hoebel and Lewellyn 1941: 21) – allowed empirical researchers to identify legal norms, processes and institutions in everything from the rule-making and disciplinary procedures of corporations, universities and sports leagues, the creeds of religious and cultural minorities (Ehrlich 1975; Weyrauch 2001), and neighbourhood dispute resolution,[28] to the behavioural norms of trade networks,[29] social clubs and families.

28 On the resolution of property disputes in an 'illegal' slum see Santos 1977; on fencing disputes and cattle trespass see Ellickson 1991, although note he assumes that in applying their own norms, the farmers and cattlemen 'got the law wrong'; and see generally Galanter 1981.

29 Such as the study of the garment industry in New York City by Moore (1978), although note she differentiates between 'the law' and non-legal or illegal pressures, customs, mores, rules and sanctions: (61–5).

The conflict or overlap between inconsistent and diverse legal orders within the same social group subsequently observed by such empirical researchers is what anthropologist John Griffiths characterized as being representative of legal reality in his seminal text on legal pluralism (Griffiths 1986: 4). In contrast, Griffiths considers the picture of a unified law defined by its necessary connection to the state as purely a product of ideology, one which effectively supports the aspirations of the modern state to exclusive dominion in law and ultimate political hegemony (3). Even the institutional arrangements in which states recognize, codify or administer Indigenous legal traditions (see generally Hooker 1975) are considered by Griffith to be merely 'weak' legal pluralism in contrast to the 'strong' empirical version, since they maintain the notion that the state is the central, overarching and unifying source of law.[30] Recognition 'is justified as a technique of governance on pragmatic grounds' (Griffiths 1986: 5) rather than as a fundamental commitment to diversity in law.

The empirical approach brings us somewhat beyond the limited account of 'intersection' in the *Yorta Yorta* case in order to consider the impact and even constitutive effects of contact between legal orders. For example, pioneer studies of colonial law observed that the process of documentation, interpretation and application of 'customary law' by colonial administrators effectively created a new body of law by distorting local legal notions (Benda-Beckman 1984: 29). Although not supplanting local law, colonial interpretations could orient people differently towards it, for example, as court decisions became the 'object of negotiation and manipulation at the village level' (Benda-Beckman 1984: 30) or as the attribution of an authority to pre-colonial customary law had the effect of empowering certain Indigenous leaders who themselves then claimed as 'tradition' that which served their political aspirations (Fitzpatrick 1984b: 21). In addition, pre-colonial laws take on a different identity in a new context, such as a cash economy, capitalist modes of production or hierarchialized gender relations.[31]

Conversely, the existence of local norms helps explain why reform of state law often brings unanticipated results. In Sally Falk Moore's (1978) study of the New York garment district, a standard union contract governed working conditions in the garment industry, but the seasonal nature of the fashion world where jobs come in waves meant that rules regarding maximum hours were broken during the rush. Between the contractor and the union representative, it was understood that the latter would turn a blind eye to contraventions, while the former gave favours and gifts to the workers and to the union representative. Moore shows how the garment industry is a 'semi-autonomous' field, generating rules, customs

30 See the similar distinction between 'state law pluralism' and 'deep legal pluralism' in Woodman 1999: 5.

31 Something of a parallel argument, using 'culture' rather than 'law' as its example of pre-colonial traits made unrecognizable, is made in the Australian context by Peter Sutton (2001).

and symbols internally, but 'also vulnerable to rules and decisions and other forces emanating from the larger world by which it is surrounded' (55).[32]

In our case, the rights and obligations announced through the Native Title Act can be seen to interact with a tangle of other norms in play in Indigenous resource management. For instance, although the result of the case was that the Yorta Yorta had no surviving native title rights and consequently had no legislative right to negotiate on development under the Native Title Act, the outcome spurred community members to find alternative ways of having a voice in relation to their traditional country. Through MLDRIN, the Yorta Yorta have now signed agreements both with government agencies and non-governmental organizations acknowledging them as traditional owners of that region and involving them in resource management processes (Weir 2009: 120). The operation of state law can only be understood as one strand in this normative complex.

As Sally Merry (1988) points out, work on the mutual influence between legal orders came to focus more on law as a symbolic and ideological system than as a regulatory structure (881). For example, Boaventura de Sousa Santos's (1977) study of law in a Brazilian *favela*, or slum, focuses on a dialectic relation between *favela* law and official law at the level of symbolic resources. In the absence of any official rights to land in the illegal squatter settlement, the Residents' Association both borrows from and inverts the legality of the dominant state system in its treatment of housing matters and disputes between residents, and through the rhetoric and forms of argumentation used. The basic norm of the Association's activities regulating housing, for example, is a complete inversion of state law according to which no resident has any property rights in the settlement. Principles and norms are invoked that expressly distance *favela* law from state law, such as an emphasis on community interest, cooperation and the need for shelter (82, 88–9).

On the other hand, various values or conventions (Santos calls them *topoi*) such as the weight of the written word over the spoken, the use of signatures and stamps or the invocation of impersonal language, are rhetorical techniques that mirror 'official law'. At times, specific principles are borrowed or adapted from state law, such as consent of the spouse or the statute of limitations. According to Santos,

> [i]t is necessary to conceive of [*favela*] law not as a closed system which, despite borrowings, remains independent, but rather as one element within a situation of legal pluralism involving a complex network of relations and feedback (52).

Here is a powerful way to bring the idea of interdependence into a discussion of law. Focusing on participants' perspectives leads Santos (1987) to find not just the intersection of legal systems, but an inherent mixity as 'legal spaces [are] superimposed and interpenetrated, mixed in our minds as much as in our actions'

32 See also Hartog 1985.

(298).[33] Where law as meaning resides in the interpretive practices of individuals in their communities, it is also internally plural or 'finite', in Markell's terms. 'Interlegality' tends to undermine the reification of law by focusing on the open-ended practice of interpretation. For example, if colonial recognition has created 'lawyers' customary law,' then so too is there a 'people's state law' created by their recognition, interpretation and application of state law in their terms: state law in itself is not singular (Benda-Beckman 1984: 32).

In the *Yorta Yorta* case, a rhetorical or linguistic analysis of law might have allowed a more vigorous discussion of the ethnocentricity of the terminology of normative rules, rights and interests that dominated the High Court majority decision and a sensitivity to the constitutive effects of engaging with the common law. Land claims processes force claimants to frame themselves in particular ways in order to be understood, and the Yorta Yorta claimants objectified their ways of life and thought for the court, adopting the language of rights, laws and connection. The constitutive effects of ongoing intersection are visible in the fact that the 'Yorta Yorta Community' emerged as a collective entity, which created scandals regarding the inclusion and exclusion of certain individuals and groups (Morgan 2013). The rhetorical forms, principles or symbols of the common law may also have been inverted by Yorta Yorta people in other contexts, or interpreted to their own ends. The case could also be analysed for the way the specificities of the Yorta Yorta claim affected the articulation and application of native title doctrine.

A shift to law as a linguistic practice and towards the internal perspective and experiences of legal subjects accompanies several critiques of and adjustments to the social-scientific approach. The success of asserting the empirical fact of legal pluralism has tended to turn on some means of identifying law that does not emanate from government institutions as code or decision. As an act of recognition, the structural-functional approach raises similar problems to those discussed in Chapter 2 in that the criteria for identifying law – those legal functions assumed to be universal – are both ethnocentric and essentialist (Roberts 1998: 98; Tamanaha 1993, 2000; Melissaris 2009: 30). Arguing against social-scientific approaches, Brian Tamanaha (2000) points out that functional definitions are under-inclusive: law does many things at once, such as confer powers and status, distribute resources, facilitate relationships, and provide definitions, symbols and aspirations. On the other hand, he maintains that locating law in an essential function such as social order makes it impossible to distinguish between law and all the other rule-based phenomena that contribute to the maintenance of order, like religion, mythology, customs, habits and language (299–302). Consequently, functional definitions include phenomena to which we usually give other names, and exclude what some people would consider as law – natural law or customary law, for instance. Calling the phenomenon rule-system or normative pluralism would be preferable, he thinks, to trying to stick the label 'law' onto everything (306).

33 See also the study of 'integral pluralism' in the factory work place (Fitzpatrick 1984a).

Tamanaha is not alone in his concerns about conceptual clarity, and there is a recurring theme in legal pluralist writings that looser definitions of non-state law are analytically weak. If law is everywhere – even in queues for buses and nightclubs (Melissaris 2004: 75; Reisman 1985) – then it simply disappears into social life and becomes trivial as an analytical category (Moore 1978: 81; Merry 1988: 878; Santos 1995: 429). Tamanaha's (2000) solution to both the essentialist and ethnocentric challenges is to take conventional usage as the criteria: '[l]aw is whatever people identify and treat through their social practices as "law" (or recht, or droit, and so on)' (313).[34]

Tamanaha's conventional approach seems to address the problematic blind spot in Hart's insistence that the rule of recognition for law lies in the practice of state legal officials only. It makes of legal pluralism not just a legal theory but, as Emmanuel Melissaris puts it, a *meta*-legal theory that opens itself up to multiple legal *theories*. But how does it work when brought to bear on Indigenous law and the translations that that entails? Even in the given example, law cannot be 'what (French) people identify as droit'; anyone who has stumbled trying to distinguish between right, law and laws in French[35] will know that even closely related European languages do not provide equivalents (Bix 1999: 10–11). What of law in Hopi, or Gitxsan, or Yolngu? In a subsequent text Tamanaha (2001) asserts simply that translations, while difficult, can be made (169), and that whatever term has been developed to designate state law will do for the purposes of conventionalism (203). Further, the possibility remains that people who speak other languages will have their own socio-linguistic 'thing' that might be studied in terms of its functional equivalent to law.

Placing local terms or categories at the centre of analysis and then engaging in dialogic acts of interpretation in order to talk about them beyond their immediate context has been at the heart of the 'interpretive turn' away from structural-functionalism in anthropology. One of the forerunners of the interpretive approach is Clifford Geertz (1973), who tackles comparative legal studies in his chapter 'Local Knowledge: Fact and Law in Comparative Perspective'. Instead of searching for dictionary equivalents to law in the language spoken in the three societies he chooses to study, Geertz starts with a term that resonates within the respective 'legal sensibility' of each place: *haqq* (reality/truth/validity) in Morocco, *dharma* (duty/obligation/merit) in Bali, and *adat* (social consensus or moral style) in Java (185). In Geertz's study, by showing up how fact and law are differently configured

---

34 This is a change from his earlier criticisms of legal pluralism where Tamanaha maintained that because there was a fundamental ontological difference between state law and other forms of ordering in terms of the institutional power disposed, it made more sense to reserve the term law for the products of the state (1993:192). Note also that although Tamanaha's criticism of functional definitions is that they are circular because they merely subtract the trappings of the state from what appears essential to state law – social control, rules, sanctions and so on – and then look for these criteria elsewhere, he too, is presuming something (convention) that then should define law.

35 For which the translations might be droit/raison, droit/jurisprudence, lois, respectively.

in these contexts (the difficulty often being how to tell them apart) we are led to a reassessment of our own fact-law dichotomy as anything other than natural or inevitable. The interpretive approach thus shares something with Taylor's dialogue on the horizon of value discussed in Chapter 2, in that the basic presuppositions of the constituent parts of the legal universe can be put in question.

For Geertz, the point is not that these terms are key to any universal sense of law; they are merely a way into a 'cycle of terms' in order to unpack their resonances and point to a web of ideas that structure the local legal sensibility. As he puts it, his purpose is 'less to prove something … than to evoke something' (184). Similarly, many legal pluralists are unconcerned by a lack of clear definition and apparent 'analytical weakness' on that count. For example, Moore and Santos are equivocal on whether the diverse phenomena they study are 'law' and are more concerned with processes and 'modes' of legality.[36] As mentioned, Tamanaha (2001) argues that we would be better off doing away with the law label in these cases. If we no longer understand human societies in terms of evolutionary theory that held pre-legal peoples to be less civilized, he says, then we should abandon the assumption of ubiquitous law. Peoples who do not have the English term 'law' as a linguistic convention either have something else that performs law's various functions, or they have a translated version of law (202–5). I think Tamanaha is premature in dismissing the freight of the law label and the 'politics of definition' (Santos 2002: 91). In the context of Indigenous legal and political claims specifically, the assertion of Indigenous law is significant precisely because of the importance attached to legal forms of life, because of the authority that law carries.

What, then, to make of the fact that describing their ways of life in terms of the legal brings claimants like the Yorta Yorta Aboriginal Community within the conventionalist definition? In response to the necessary conclusion that Indigenous peoples could only have had 'law' in the conventional linguistic sense after English was introduced into the continent, we can only say that something happens or changes when 'law' is invoked to describe or rationalize or make claims; that research, conversations, translations, petitions, statements of claim, art exhibitions and so on, are the sites where this happening takes place. In this way, the translation process is in some sense productive of 'law'. But the conventionalist approach is clearly not subtle enough. Utterances containing the word 'law' can be many things – jokes, ironic statements, metaphors, and bald-faced lies.[37] Indeed, it is of major concern to opponents of native title that

36 Moore (1978) tends to write neutrally of the interactions of rules, norms, customs and obligations and sees criteria for identifying the legal as a distraction (56). When Santos (2002) poses himself the question as to why diverse forms of social ordering should be designated as law, he answers 'why not?' (91).

37 While Tamanaha (2009) notes the multiple uses of the term law – laws of nature, grammatical laws and so on – and asserts that the identification of references to law falling within the interest of social and legal theorists is a matter of common sense context and usage (168), he does not address the modes of use to which I am referring.

self-interested statements about traditional law by claimants are simply made up. For Jeremy Webber, Tamanaha's conventionalism is missing a sense of normativity, and thus Hart's internal perspective (Webber 2006: 171, note 5). But another way of putting it is that it is missing a sense of an ability to read the context in which people speak, and thus the difference between propositional statements that are simply logically operative, and performative ones that bring law to life in their making (see Melissaris 2009: 84–100).

Discursive theories of law tend to critique the reification of rules, in which law, an object over there, is imposed on legal subjects, over here. Instead, they make humans the site of law and thus of its inherent plurality. As Roderick Macdonald and David Sandomierski (2006) put it, law is 'imagined by human beings, given expression by human beings, lived by human beings, followed by human beings, modified by human beings, rejected by human beings' (615), a claim to which I will return below. It is no longer external social fact, but part of subjectivity (Kleinhans and Macdonald 1998). Macdonald's project of critical legal pluralism, influenced by Fuller, is to appreciate and foster persons as legal agents rather than legal subjects. However, the subjective element cannot be purely personal or private. As Webber (2006) puts it, it is important for legal pluralism to capture the active, interpersonal dimension in which law is the product of conscious, deliberate human action (169), and so, I would add, the extent to which the meaning of this action is perpetually contingent on the reactions of others.

In contrast to Tamanaha's simple conventionalism, then, I would suggest that the turn to language in legal pluralism has to bring with it the sense of the way words are part of a form of life for a people, a *nomos*, in Cover's terminology. In this vein, legal pluralism has been described as an aesthetic (Manderson 2000: 169–89) or an ethos (Davies 2005: 88). As Marianne Constable argues, thinking about law as language includes consideration not only of acts of speech – both descriptive, propositional statements of principle and constative utterances that perform legal operations, such as promises, declarations and criminal sentences – but also of the background conditions that determine their success. Language relies on a community of speakers who recognize it and who are simultaneously constituted as a '"we" who are speaking with one another' (Constable 2014: 67). Similarly, she continues, '[l]egal speech acts … emerge from and interrupt law as a background practical knowledge of what to do' (68), one based in contextualized experience. Yorta Yorta narratives remind us that the context for practical knowledge is not just human social space but particular places and their ecologies.

A focus on discourse or linguistic speech acts rather than conventional use on its own speaks better to the theme of connectivity and relationship. For Constable, one key relationship is between the speech act and the background practice, or between the explicit and implicit parts of law, and this can bring grounded experience of places into the law picture. But there is also the way in which the possibilities of translation and bilingualism become relevant, as Constable puts it, 'to who "we" variously are or become as we engage with others in public' (70). In his reworking of conventionalism via speech act theory, Melissaris (2009) criticizes Tamanaha's approach for its denial of the possibility of a shared sense of law and hence its assumption that the legal phenomena of different communities are incommensurable with each other (33). Advocating 'interperspectival, critical' legal pluralism – theory that engages both in cross-cultural communication about, and critical reflection on, law – Melissaris stresses the importance of both context-sensitivity and communicability if legal pluralism is to remain committed both to diversity and to theorization (71–4). He also calls for us to think in the fuller sense of law as language or discourse; that is, an understanding of law that entails, prior to the emergence of positive law or even conventional practice, a 'tacit commitment to common normative experiences' that constitutes individuals and collectivities (115).

In sum, certain kinds of legal pluralist theory give us a way to articulate interdependence as dialectical legal orders, spheres or discourses, as an interlegality that is characteristic of law, or as a cross-cultural conversation that contributes to the development of both legal theory and meta-legal theory. Interdependence in these registers is more nuanced and interesting than the *Yorta Yorta* Court's 'intersection' or the fact-law distinction, and certainly is better able to stand up to the self-justificatory accounts of colonial law. However, what brings us closer to the register in which the Yorta Yorta speak about law are those accounts that take explicit statements of law to emerge from the experience of a people of their normative commitments. 'Law as language' takes in not just words, semantics and linguistic usage, but the implicit knowledge of communities of how to act and of what binds them together, and thus the kinds of embodied experiences that seem to underwrite Yorta Yorta claims to native title.

Law, Ideology and Power

If Griffith's socio-legal version of legal pluralism calls out state-centred conceptions of law as the product of ideology and confronts them with legal pluralism as the reality, others have nevertheless been concerned with accounting for state power. For Merry (1988), the fact that state law exercises a coercive apparatus and 'monopolizes the symbolic power associated with state authority' means that it is distinct from other forms of ordering (879). In the terms of this chapter, taking the 'one law' of Kirby J and that of Jackie Holmes Akemarr to be equally meaningful is a significant move in postcolonial jurisprudence, but can seem surreal given the influence that physical and ideological dominance have on the ability of any law to *do* anything. In any analysis of dialectic or relationship, it is much easier to see the impact of colonial state law on Indigenous law than vice versa. And none of these exchanges about law happens in a vacuum with participants innocently bringing their *nomoi* into conversation. The rejection of the ideology of centralism, it would seem, cannot simply ignore the reality of state power. This section will make a few brief comments on the relationship between law, ideology and power.

One starting point is to note that the rise of monistic legal theory was contingent on the emergence in early modern Europe of large states, and the gradual incursion of state norms into those of religious, commercial and customary local communities, following which the former cast the latter as either moral or social norms (Tamanaha 2008: 380–81; Gurvitch 1935). However, it was not necessarily the case that the rise of the state was achieved by brute strength. As Douglas Hay has argued, that the propertied class in a country like England were able to use the criminal law to maintain domination between the seventeenth and nineteenth centuries was not because of their ability to enforce the law – England lacked a standing army or numerically significant police force – but via a combination of ideological elements – the spectacle of majesty, the rule of law protecting individuals against the Crown, and mercy – that supported the class system (Hay 1976).

The monopoly of the state over law was concomitant with the idea of uniformity of laws and the abstract equality of citizens. James Tully (1995) comments that for writers such as Hobbes and John Locke, the sectarian violence of the Thirty Years War provided reasons for a strong central power (67–7, 84). But the belief in a uniform modern constitutionalism also led to measures actively designed to undermine cultural and normative diversity. Policies were pursued so as to inculcate in citizens the 'habits and dispositions which would render a person a "fit member" of modern society': poor laws, the workhouse system, repetitive drills in education and other training, forced teaching of national languages and the introduction of private property in the colonies were some of the means used to 'modernize' customary peoples and instil in them the ideology of the modern state (87–91). So, as Michel Foucault has argued, power in modern societies is characterized more by the dispersed, mundane and productive effects of scientific knowledge and techniques of governance rather than by the top-down exercise of sovereign force (Foucault 1995, 1980: 121).

So far these comments support Griffith's assertion that a state monopoly on law was achieved by the work of ideology. In strands of Marxist tradition, 'ideology' is a 'false consciousness', illusion or cognitive distortion, a tool of the bourgeois class that can – and perhaps should – be overcome in favour of a true picture of the social world, and Griffith's claims mirror this sense.[38] However, as Terry Eagleton (1991) argues, while ideologies can contain falsehoods, in general, in order to be effective, ruling ideologies 'must make at least some minimal sense of people's experience, must conform to some degree with what they know of social reality from their practical interaction with it' (13). Further, 'ideology' has a political or sociological aspect as well as an epistemological one: it can refer to the set of beliefs and ideas used to interpret the world in a way that is 'bound up with the legitimation of certain interests in a power struggle' (15), or more neutrally as advocating or justifying certain social arrangements (Hamilton 1987: 38). Employing these broader senses, Desmond Manderson (2000) argues that while we may be able to off-load the baggage of state ideology, our legal pluralist vision is equally ideological since 'ideology always affects our understanding of the

38 Note that Marx himself never used the term 'false consciousness' nor adhered to a concept of ideology as illusion (Barrett 1991: 5).

world' (170).[39] On the other hand, if the 'illusion' of the monopoly of the state over law were universally believed, then other law would cease to be effectively 'law.' All law, Manderson suggests, is '"a claim" to normative authority, more or less effective' (170).

So what determines the degree of effectiveness? This question troubles attempts to separate law from coercive power. The turn to language, narrative and normative communities that I have adopted might seem to imply that it is simply the strength of our ideological belief – our normative commitments – that makes law outside the state effective. In 'Nomos and Narrative', Cover claims a radical dichotomy 'between the social organization of law as [coercive] power and the organization of law as meaning' that suggests this. Yet later he calls courts 'jurispathic'. How do courts have the capacity to kill law when they do not control the interpretive practices of communities? One answer lies in the symbolic weight of a court's adverse decision and its dampening impact on a community's commitment (although the impact could just as well be a reactive one that strengthens commitment). However, in 'Violence and the Word', Cover (1986) makes it clear that focusing on legal interpretation and the organization of law as meaning is naïve and dangerous if it ignores the physically violent consequences of judicial interpretation (1601). He argues that *nomoi* can only survive colonial and other challenges if bodies are placed on the line: unless we are willing to become martyrs or rebels for our law, then we cannot project the imagined future that is central to law's narratives (1604–5).

In colonial history there is certainly no lack of bodies on the line, and contemporary environmental protests such as those at Elsipogtog in New Brunswick are simply the most recent manifestation of this. But taking violence as the necessary context for Indigenous or any other law is problematic, and there is a rejoinder to Cover based on this point. In Constable's analysis of 'Violence and the Word', she notes that the structural separation between judicial interpretive acts and the enforcement of decisions that Cover describes, while countering a view of law's sovereign power as a matter of judicial will (Cover 1986: 217), nonetheless adheres to the idea of law as the social organization of power in which judges 'trigger' or control the responses of others (Constable 2005: 135). In Cover's own account, the effect of this system of control is destructive of selves and of the possibility of common normative worlds. First, it removes from judges the ability to act, and causes the transformation of enforcers into agents of violence. Second, the pain and fear inflicted on those against whom the law is enforced is never shared; their experience of the law will be radically different to those of institutional actors, for whom either justification or authority is key (Cover 1986: 236–8). Constable (2005) shows that here, contrary to his earlier texts on narrative and its provision of a connection between reality and vision, Cover employs a

39 This is something Melissaris (2009) does not seem to contemplate in his search for an account of law 'undiluted by ideology,' by which he seems to mean the ideology of the state: 47.

sociological account of law as organized violence that is necessary to translate word into deed but that tragically destroys the possibility of sharing a normative world (140). In contrast, Constable argues that '[o]nly where behavior is not controlled or dominated or triggered, whether by social institutional mechanisms of power or by legal entities such as rules, can persons – whether judges or others – initiate and be responsible for action' (143).

If Markell's reading of Hegel in the preceding chapter claimed that attempts by individuals and groups to achieve sovereignty as mastery were futile and based on a mistaken understanding of the human condition of interdependence, Constable's (2005) critique of law as something wielded by an agent to act on the world is that this vision is historically contingent and misses out on an alternative tradition, in which law is more than socially organized violence, and is even associated with a quest for justice that is non-violent (141–2). It is a critique not just of positivism and the republican consensus, but also of the sociological approach that attempts to locate law – to 'recognize' it – in social fact. The anxiety of proponents and critics of legal pluralist theory alike that we can no longer tell anything apart if there are no firm criteria for law, if law and society dissolve into one another, or if legal orders are dialectically entwined, interpenetrating and mutually constitutive, seems to stem from the desire for firm knowledge of the world, for cognitive mastery. Even the critical, discursive approach risks raising the individual as mini-sovereign – she who imagines, interprets and enacts law – at the expense of the experiential law that makes interpretation possible. Stripped of the sovereign subject, law as language is not an instrument of power but a world into which we are born and 'in which we find ourselves limited by something that is not of our own making' (Constable 2005: 146).

A legal pluralist approach to Indigenous rights should not, in my view be staking a claim to empirical validity as Griffiths would have it, or striving for conceptual or analytical strength. Rather, it would be better off asking how to answer a particular question we have[40] (advising a client or understanding how native title has affected Indigenous communities), whether any particular version of law imagines the world in a way that resonates with us (Macdonald 2003: 85) or allows us to engage with the *nomos* of others, and how best to direct the 'application of human energies' (Fuller 1958: 632).

Thinking through whether a legal pluralist ethos would make a difference in the *Yorta Yorta* case is challenging. Acknowledging the normative commitments of all parties – including court officials – as the conditions against which specific legal precepts can stay afloat makes more sense in the case than did the denial of contemporary legal authorship excluded by the doctrine of the monopoly of sovereignty. Had the judges in the majority taken seriously the proposition that they were asking the claimants to prove the contemporary existence of traditional laws and customs, they could not have denied the more extensive claims of legal pluralism that this implies. These laws *could not* be the same laws as at the time of

40 See Boyle 1987: 387.

sovereignty because there is no 'body' of the law, unless it is the body constituted by *Dhungula* and the lessons it teaches us about maintaining healthy country. There would not only be one source of law in Australia, and courts could look to Indigenous law for norms, narratives and practices in making their decisions.[41] If, like Jackie Holmes Akemarr, a claim is being made to 'one law' since the beginning, the court needs to check its interpretive reflexes. What question is the statement answering and is the unity of law over time at a premium? What is 'one' referring to and what is 'law' referring to? Is the one-ness of law being read with some of the earlier theoretical presumptions in mind?

However, there are difficulties in expecting judges to 'apply' legal pluralism. Where engagement with Indigenous law takes place as recognition through the sociological gaze, the pathologies of recognition will follow. The state makes up the rules for recognition, and Indigenous law plays a subordinate role as a cognizable fact. Where Indigenous law is to be taken for its normative value in the decision-making process, an outsider like a non-Indigenous judge may have the usual difficulties of identifying and applying Indigenous law that have plagued all colonial attempts to formally recognize local laws, because they are radically altered by being given a new form, context and language.

What is more, the work of a judge, in that it consists of making a binding decision by choosing 'the' correct law, appears antithetical to legal pluralism itself (Benda-Beckman 1984: 42); the activity of third-party judging itself might also be precluded by practices of dispute resolution or ideas of justice in Indigenous communities. A pluralist ethos would seem to point to some other non-hierarchical, non-conclusive solution. The alternative most often suggested is a negotiated one – whether at the large scale of a treaty or the small scale of community justice programmes, sentencing circles and so on – and usually referred to as the 'political solution,' although we should see this also as very much a legal process. At the very least, institutional change is required to accommodate legal pluralism in a practical way, as Indigenous commentators have argued (Behrendt 2003: 131). However, we should not assume that judges actually do what they purport to do – fix a legal meaning and apply it to the facts. Discursive approaches would allow individual judicial decisions far less control over legal meaning and its finality, even as they authorize the enforcement of their decisions.

The discursive approach to law changes the empirical task that is usually assumed in the recognition of Indigenous law. It implies that meanings for law – and for legal rules, institutions and identities – are being constructed, not just 'out there' in a 'pure' Indigenous realm, but everywhere that there is language and practice, including the court (Macdonald 2003: 98–100). A legal pluralist court – if such a thing exists – sees that it also participates in creating Indigenous law and identity, both by articulating the 'national' law and identity as an invisible standard and by subsequently forcing the minority into a national identity claim. If she must choose one interpretation, one articulation, one law, the judge does so

41 This form of legal pluralism has been suggested for Canada by Borrows, 2005.

in the acknowledgement that this is not the resolution of law, but, as for Cover's jurispathic judiciary, the violence of state power.

Our final reflection on the value of legal pluralism in an analysis of the *Yorta Yorta* decision comes not in taking it as proof of a reality, but as a way of seeing and living in the world. In being able to imagine an alternative to legal centralism, monism and positivism, the orthodoxy of these three aspects of law is itself shown up as a lens rather than an inevitability. A claim for the recognition of Yorta Yorta traditional laws and customs is thus an invitation to engage with the ethos of connectivity.

Conclusion

The separation of fact and law that distinguishes between Indigenous law and state law is built into the structure of litigation, and is assumed in the distinct processes – proof on the one hand, argumentation and authority on the other – through which the two laws are channelled in native title. Several characteristics of the courts' law as provided in the received tradition of legal theory, although explicitly caveated with respect to Indigenous law, nonetheless form the frame by which Indigenous laws are judged. In the result, the territorial exclusivity of state sovereignty relegated Yorta Yorta law to a fact rather than a set of arguments or narratives about law, and the stasis involved in taking law as a body of rules proved inadequate for dealing with law's temporal openness while ignoring other forms of continuity more relevant to Yorta Yorta law, such as the identification of people in the land. The judges consider their law as external to Indigenous law and so fail to see their own judgments as discursive moments participating in the life of Indigenous norms.

An alternative account of co-existence is begged by the heuristic, invoked in several cases, that native title is the result of an intersection between these two normative orders, and 'intersection' has given us a starting point to explore a more robust theory of legal pluralism. This theory confronts the political exigency of the court's understanding of the intersection of Indigenous law and the common law. Kirby J and Jackie Holmes Akemarr may both have their 'one law', but these statements have to be contextualized as normative claims made to hold up against destabilizing challenges, as much as facts about law. Instead of a simple intersection, I have argued for multiple laws of interdependence, from those that speak to the interconnection of lifeforms and arise out of embodied ecological knowledge, to the dialectic between the spoken and unspoken parts of law, and the call and response between different peoples that generate specific reiterations and structures of 'law'.

Legal pluralist analysis would identify some of the sites of this reiteration and some of the pathways of legal structuring. In particular, we could look to written or spoken texts (legislation, judgments, welcome to country ceremonies, paintings, and the land as record of the law), to the knowledge of people about law or about how to mobilize law in social interactions, to the relative status of persons, resources and organizations, and to the discursive resources used to rationalize or justify actions, events, interpretations, claims or decisions, as sites for legal pluralist analysis (Benda-Beckman 1984: 65–8). Such are the implications of a declaration of law's interdependence, and the final three chapters of the book take up the arguments made here that legal pluralism can provide a less Eurocentric and more inclusive ethos for law, and a reason for institutional change.

Chapter 4
Translation: Evidentiary Fact, Language and Law

Introduction

The previous two chapters have elaborated an account of recognition practices in Indigenous rights, first, of Indigenous identity or cultural difference, and second, of specifically legal forms of life. I argued that just as our cultural identity is dependent on interactions with others, so too does law emerge from exchanges of recognition in which law is the dominant language. In contrast to orthodox legal theory, I found that the reliance of officials on unspoken norms of behaviour and broader narratives to make their decisions meaningful in particular ways opens up the decision-making process to the jurisgenerative forces of human communities. The self-conscious articulation of law as principles is a confluence of practice, discourse and imagination, but also the result of exchange between people: we make arguments, express principles and provide justifications that reflect on what we do, and what should be done, in response to questions or challenges by others. This claim for law is a legally pluralist one because it considers law to be a dialogue about meaning with multiple authors. It has neither a unitary existence nor a unitary source.

One consequence following from the argument about discursive legal pluralism in the preceding chapter was that particular sites stimulate the articulation of law and the constellation of terms around it. I suggested that the Yorta Yorta Aboriginal Community's claim was one instance where Indigenous belonging was expressed in terms of traditional laws and customs. A more in-depth analysis of the way in which native title in the courts acts to stimulate Indigenous law would require thinking about the details of the linguistic processes in which peoples' knowledge and experience come to be expressed as law through cognate terms such as rules, rights and property. This chapter will undertake such a study in examining the treatment of evidence, and the role of anthropological experts, in the Australian case of *Neowarra v State of Western Australia*, and argue that not only are the activities of translation in evidence actively constituting the text of the claimants' law, but that the language of translation – the common law – is also transformed in the process.

As we saw in Chapter 2, when recognition of Indigenous rights is characterized in terms of the linguistic process of translation, a particular model of law is at work, as well as a deeper substructure relating language, meaning and the reality that supports it. If translation is the means of recognizing the *sui generis* of native title, then something proper to Indigenous peoples is captured and brought within the common law. The etymology of 'translation' – to carry across – matches a common understanding of linguistic translation as a transfer of something – information or an essential meaning – from one language to another. Language, in this view, is a representation of meaning, and each word names an object in a Platonic link between word and world.[1] If meaning can be picked up and taken across, it is essentially separable both from the original words and from the context in which they are uttered. Translation then, according to E.A. Nida, the influential author of *Toward a Science of Translating* (1964), is the extraction of the structural kernel of the message in the source text and its transfer to the equivalent structural elements in the receptor language, which are then built back up into the most appropriate expressions in the receptor language for the intended audience (Nida 1969: 484–5). A new name stands in for the same thing.

Translation in Indigenous title regimes – to focus on these kinds of rights for the moment – speaks more broadly to the process of representing some aspect of Indigenous peoples' relationship to land in the language of property. In some ways this is simply an example of the more generic hermeneutic process within the common law that ostensibly involves fitting facts into legal categories. Where evidence is seen to correspond directly to something that happened outside of the court, translation in native title functions on the basis that the objective reality of the claimants' laws and customs can be ascertained as facts, represented through language, and then described, with more or less difficulty, in terms of rights and interests. The facts are 'over there' and Indigenous; they are represented in court; they are translated. They are given 'proper' expression in terms comprehensible to the court (*Ward* 2002: [38]–[39]). Translation epitomizes the way in which legal process bridges the separation between fact and law.

The linguistic and cultural differences between the claimants and the court frequently require experts to assist the court in interpreting the facts and thus in rendering the translation. While the testimony of the claimants may be considered primary (*Sampi* 2005: [48]), the preparation of the claim and the hearing itself rely heavily on anthropologists. Anthropology provides an interpretive framework for the testimony of the claimants, indicating the 'meaning and significance of what Aboriginal witnesses say and do, so as to explain or render coherent matters which, on their face may be incomplete or unclear' (*Alyawarr* 2004: [89]).

This chapter provides a brief background to the relationship between anthropological models and Indigenous rights doctrines, and questions the way terminology – so crucial to the characterization of facts and the description of models – has moved back and forth between the disciplines of anthropology and law. Further, it will address the competition between disciplinary methodologies that produce translations of the cultures of rights claimants as facts, contrasting the techniques of participant observation with those of evidentiary standards, witness

1 A view of language famously held by St Augustine, see Wittgenstein 1968 §1; Hobbes 1996 [1651]: Chapter 4 'Of Speech'.

statements and cross-examination. The courts' view corresponds to the 'fidelity' model of translation: judges place faith in the ability of the speech and behaviour of witnesses to represent definitively (or at least, according to the evidentiary standard of the balance of probabilities) their world in court.

However, the importance of context for understanding cultural practices, and thus the context of the processes of ethnographical research itself, has been the focus of recent critical developments in anthropology, and the chapter will go on to develop a critique of language and practice in cultural translation, highlighting the parallels between translation and ethnography. Both have been said to embark on essentially the same enterprise, to represent an original, be it text or culture. Historically they have both mapped out conceptual relations between the domestic and familiar, and the strange and foreign. They have contributed materially to processes of colonization, and to the subordination of non-European others in a conceptual hierarchy that they have helped to create. Contemporary critical thinking in both literary and cultural translation has taken on board the colonial context, the relationships of power embedded in translation practices, as well as the foundational Enlightenment notions that have informed them. The result gives us reason to question the relationship between language and the world on which translation seems to depend, to recognize speaking and writing as material practices that create worlds rather than merely reflect them, and thus to doubt the model of translation assumed in native title. These critical perspectives mirror what I am arguing for as a legal pluralist approach to native title translation: the negotiation of meaning between participants implicated in the production of evidence that undermines the claim of evidence in court to be a neutral description of facts.

Furnished with these insights, I will turn to the Australian Federal Court decision of *Neowarra v State of Western Australia* (2003) to show how the various elements of native title such as the claimant group, laws and customs, and rights and interests are produced in evidence. The frequency with which witnesses refer to specific practices, their assertion of belief, their behaviour in court and various anthropological models are all considered as part of the factual picture. They make up a 'mosaic' of evidence demonstrating the existence of relevant laws and customs that are then translated into native title rights and interests. Translation theory, however, shows us that translation is a discursive process that leads to understanding both the original and the language of translation in a new way. In my account of the decision, I let the critiques of translation help us read between the lines of the analysis of facts that otherwise seem to be neutrally representing the reality of the world of the claimants, and gradually a new vision emerges. The translation of evidence into fact, and fact into law, in legal positivism comes to be seen as productive of particular understandings rather than a one-to-one mapping of inert phenomena or categories. In actively assembling the mosaic in *Neowarra*, the court and the witnesses are not just reporting on 'Aboriginal Law', they are all actively participating in the constitution of it.

In focusing on translation, I have somewhat privileged words and texts in the native title process. I will also, however, address the question of what cannot be put into words and thus defies translation. As Elizabeth Povinelli (2002) asks, what becomes of the ellipsis in the text of the land claim archive that exists because some things are inexpressible, unspeakable and indeterminate (239)? Moreover, what does this wordlessness have to do with law? Is law only what can be spoken? In extending the relationship between practice and narrative, or norms and habit, begun in the previous chapter, I take up an argument by Marianne Constable that positive law emerges when we need to articulate our law because others do not share the same norms and narratives. Law is thus an interplay between forms of behaviour – what we do around here – and a context in which that behaviour is called to account for itself and so comes to be expressed in principled form.

In the relationship between context and expression, acts of translation are also acts of transformation, however, and state law here is no mere audience to a descriptive exercise on behalf of Indigenous claimants. Like a traveller whose sense of normality is thrown into relief as a particularity by an encounter with strange ways, state law is a language reading itself anew through translation. Indigenous law and state law are thus implicated in each other's coming-to-be; they are never 'over there' in splendid isolation. To accept this is to understand that translation in law is relational, constitutive and transformative rather than representative; it is to abandon positivist legal theory's concern with 'what is' and see law as an imaginative craft of 'becoming'.

Translation and Indigenous Rights

There are two levels at which regimes of Indigenous rights might undertake the translation of Indigenous concepts and actions. The first is in articulating legal precepts, whether as part of a statutory definition, or through judicial elaboration. General statements of Indigenous rights often try to encapsulate something that is unique to, and reflective of, the way Indigenous peoples organize their relationships to land, as I showed in Chapter 2. The second level is when judges or finders of fact assess whether any given rights claimants have demonstrated that their practices and attitudes fall within the ambit of the definition. Both levels of translation are thoroughly familiar activities to Western lawyers. At least since the realist movement, law reform has frequently been staked on getting legal doctrine to reflect commercial, social and other realities. In some domains, such as Indigenous rights, the expectation that law will mirror aspects of social practice is additionally inflected by the politics of recognition that we examined earlier. Furthermore, the ability to translate the intricacies of everyday life into the abstract terms of legal principle is the crux of the application of law, depending on being able to interpret evidence based on everything from 'common sense' to the highly specialized knowledge of experts. The particularities of translation in Indigenous rights regimes, of course, reflect that it takes place across cultural differences, challenging the degree to which judges and other legal practitioners can rely on their common sense, resulting as it does from their own cultural location.

The role that experts in culture – mainly anthropologists, but also linguists, ethno-historians and archaeologists – play in Indigenous rights translation is a complicated one. Since the early days of anthropology, its practitioners have influenced colonial policy, including Indigenous rights regimes and jurisprudence. In return, the work of social scientists, and anthropologists in particular, has been shaped by the socially dominant presence of legal discourse and the involvement of social scientists in land and other kinds of claims on behalf of Indigenous peoples. In judicial hearings, the contributions of expert witnesses often pit the methodologies of social science against those of legal fact-finding. Because ethnography, in particular, is built around watching and listening to cultural practitioners, and given that the latter often appear themselves as witnesses in court, from the courts' perspective, the expertise of anthropologists lies in uncertain relation to the knowledge of culture practitioners. It raises the question of representation in both its epistemological and political sense: what is culture and who can speak for it?

Mirrors and Boxes

Anthropological models are particularly evident in the development of Indigenous land rights jurisprudence. Mark Pinkowski and Michael Asch (2004) note the influence of Julian Steward's 'cultural ecology' on the kinds of arguments heard before the US Indian Claims Commission (ICC) from 1946 and, later, in Canadian litigation on Aboriginal rights, regarding 'levels' of social organization and their concomitant institutional complexity. The ICC mandate allowed 'tribes, bands and nations' (three such levels common in anthropological literature) to bring claims. One of Steward's reports for the Department of Justice found that the Shoshone, for instance, belonged to the 'family' level of socio-cultural organization that did not, he thought, have institutions of property, in which case they could not bring a claim (191–3). The trial judge in Canada's *Delgamuukw* (1997) case likewise accepted the government expert's opinion that the claimants were at the 'family level', while the Canadian Supreme Court's finding in *Van Der Peet* (1996) was that, being at a 'band' rather than 'tribal' level of social organization, the claimants' ancestors would not have had the specialization of labour typical in trading economies (197–8).

More subtly, Indigenous rights jurisprudence has been shaped by the very boundaries of the discipline of anthropology that determine what it takes as its subject matter. Like many other ethnographers, A.P. Elkin, the second Australian university chair in anthropology, strove to represent Indigenous peoples as 'bearers of a worthy, noble culture' in order to combat racial prejudice (Attwood 1996: xvi).[2] But Elkin's focus was 'tribes whose way of life was not seriously disturbed', since 'tribal remnants' gave less satisfactory means to understanding the Aborigines (Elkin 1954: vi). So-called 'salvage' ethnography in places like Australia and

2 Somewhat incongruently, Elkin was also a key promoter of assimilation.

North America was buttressed by an academic division: anthropology was a field interested in what Indigenous people did before White people came along; they were 'artefacts of the human past'. History was the story of White people once they got there (Attwood 1996: xii). That the Indigenous past is not considered to be a story of evolution and change (history) continues to be reflected in the role that authentic 'traditions' have in Indigenous rights jurisprudence and the tendency to see the impacts of colonial contact as a rupture with tradition (Ray 2010: 38, 43–8).

In Australia, the commissioner charged with developing proposals for the Aboriginal Land Rights (Northern Territory) Act 1976 (ALR(NT)A)[3] expressly understood his task as trying to translate Aboriginal concepts, to best mirror the way Aboriginal people in that region spoke about their land (Woodward 1999: 16). Following his recommendations, the Act's definition of 'traditional owners' as those with 'primary spiritual responsibility' reflects a widespread anthropological model in Australia that ranks different kinds of rights in country, such as the distinction between primary and secondary rights, core and contingent rights, mediated and unmediated rights, and owners versus custodians.[4] Anthropologists view these models as mirroring the way Indigenous people speak in both their own tongues and in Aboriginal English. For example, Peter Sutton notes that Australian Indigenous people may refer to a primary connection as 'main place' or 'number one country', as opposed to 'number two country' or 'coming in halfway' (referring to a Dreaming track which approaches but does not reach a particular site).[5] However, anthropological models have historically struggled to represent the complexities of Indigenous social organization with respect to land observed in Australia (Myers 1986: 19–20), leading to criticism of the ALR(NT)A that its generic term 'owner' does not adequately capture the complexities of different rights in land (Gumbert 1981: 119–120). Similar debates have emerged in New Zealand about the appropriate corporate groupings to hold fishing rights, especially given their reconstitution after contact (Levine 2002).

As will be discussed below, the representation of culture via ethnography has been understood as cultural translation, through which internal understandings or *emic* terms are translated into external or *etic* ones. Models that explain field data are examples of etic constructs whose relation to reality can be called into question in courts of law, the concern being that something constructed is artificial and can be directed towards particular ends (Thuen 2004: 267). If such ideological constructions might be tempting, it is because the second level of translation in

3 A statutory claims process inaugurated by the Australian Federal government for the Northern Territory after the unsuccessful *Milirrpum* case.

4 For a discussion of the models, see Sutton 2003: Chapter 2 'Kinds of Rights in Country'. See also Peterson, Keen and Sansom 1977; Rumsey 1989: 70.

5 In Western desert languages (straddling Western Australia and the Northern Territory), only some groups of people are named by a term that takes the word for 'country' as its stem: *ngurrara* becomes *ngurraritja*. See Sutton 2003: 11.

Indigenous rights regimes requires the facts to fit the law in order for a claim to be successful. In this second, 'backwards', kind of translation, the aim is not to reproduce for the Court as accurate an account of Indigenous peoples' lives as possible in any terms available in English, but to see whether there is anything resembling the terminological categories specified in the definitions of Indigenous rights among the facts that can be proven, whether there is anything that fits within the legal 'boxes'. This is the case whether or not the definition draws on conventional state law terminology such as possession and rights, or, as is suggested by the *sui generis* characterization of Indigenous rights, has itself already incorporated a first level of translation through the contributions of Indigenous legal concepts.[6]

The Australian High Court in *Ward* (2002) acknowledged the difficulty in translating the spiritual or religious relationship between Indigenous peoples and the land into rights and interests. Such a translation, they said, 'requires the fragmentation of an integrated view of the ordering of affairs into rights and interests which are considered apart from the duties and obligations which go with them' ([14]). The judges here seem resigned to the fact that translation necessarily involves taking things out of context and thus loses the 'integrated view'. They assume, however, that rights and interests are actually there in the first place and able to be separated from their context. The boxes are taken to mirror at least part of Indigenous reality. Other elements that are common to definitions of Indigenous rights are traditions, laws and customs, groupings such as tribes or communities and areas of land and water. Even though the need for translation in arriving at the latter two elements of a claim – claim group and claim area – is not often explicitly acknowledged, owning groups and areas of land are not clearly the naturalized, bounded elements they are in European property discourse. Claim boundaries and group composition are often disputed, and translation in these areas may be likewise subject to difficulty (Smith and Finlayson 1997).

The translation of evidence into legal boxes in Indigenous rights regimes involves the ability of judges to comprehend and describe what Anthony Connolly calls 'culturally different action' and then to evaluate whether that action is properly described by a legally valid concept of Indigenous rights (Connolly 2010: 65–6). Given the widespread importance of 'rights and interests' in Indigenous rights definitions, as well as the influence of H.L.A. Hart's rule-based theory

6 The Treaty of Waitangi in New Zealand is an interesting example in this regard. The 1840 agreement between the Maori and the British was recorded in both English and Maori (as a translation of the English version), and both versions, which differ quite significantly in some aspects, are considered relevant to interpreting the rights of the two parties today, making the definitions of rights a perpetual hybrid rather than a translation. However, not only do Maori terms such as *taonga* (valued possession) now feature in definitions of Maori rights to resources, but the Waitangi Tribunal, a special body convened to hear claims by Maori about breaches of the Treaty and make recommendations to the government as to implementation of the Treaty, can take account of Maori *tikanga* (law/custom) in doing so (Matson 1991: 345–7).

of law, which takes rules as reasons or intentions for behaviours – on judicial understandings of what constitutes something as a valid right (see Chapter 3), the relevant actions for evaluations are those that have the necessary intentional properties.[7] The aim of the claimants' presentation of evidence will thus be to cause the judge to believe that the actions they describe both are genuine, and constitute Indigenous rights. Unless one holds to the total incommensurability of cultures, the premise of the second level of translation is that when the evidence includes accounts of action that are conceptually different to the existing concepts held by the judge, he or she must 'acquire' these culturally different concepts (Connolly 2010: 73–4).

Expertise, Authority and the Representation of Culture

But to whom do the concepts of tradition, laws, rights and interests belong? That is, who has the authority to determine their meaning? From within the court system, the answer is obvious: the judge is the final arbiter of the meaning of legal terms, and (juries not being used in Indigenous rights litigation) the judge provides the authoritative interpretation of claimants' intentional actions presented in evidence. But as the judge makes up her own mind, what are the respective roles of claimant witnesses as experts in living their own cultures, and anthropologists as experts in the interpretation of culture? Several Australian judgments have stated that the evidence of Indigenous witnesses is considered to be first order evidence about traditional laws and customs to which all expert evidence is secondary (*Yarmirr* 1998: 562, *De Rose* 2002: [351], *Jango* 2006: [292]).[8] In contrast to the early days of the USICC, when anthropologists dominated the witness box and 'acted as surrogate Indians' (Ray 2003: 256), recent land claims in North America often also see claimants taking lead roles. According to the common law tradition, experts are there to provide the court 'with knowledge that lies beyond the realm of ordinary judgment and experience' (Ray 2003: 254). Unlike other witnesses, expert witnesses may offer their professional opinions rather than purely reporting what they have observed first hand.

When judges rely heavily on claimant witness statements it sounds like letting the claimants 'speak for themselves'.[9] Anthropologists are said to be merely there to help finesse the translation, to interpret the 'meaning and significance of what Aboriginal witnesses say and do' (*Alyawarr* 2004: [89]), and not to replace what

7 That is, judges are looking for a set of primary actions (e.g. hunting game) together with a set of secondary actions which, by virtue of a critical-reflective content (evaluating primary actions with respect to rules and rights) and a semantic and causal relationship with the primary actions, confer rightness on them (Connolly 2010: 70).

8 This was also the position taken by Blackburn in *Milirrpum* 1971: 169–71.

9 In *Sampi*, for example, in a judgment of 1,152 paragraphs, 593 paragraphs are taken up by quotes of the claimants' oral evidence. There are 176 separate direct quotes or exchanges included.

judges can hear with their own ears. This is particularly so when anthropological models and explanations make use of the same terminology as the legal definitions of Indigenous rights. When Justice Blackburn in the *Milirrpum* (1971) case heard expert evidence expressed in terms of the 'land-owning' or 'land-possessing group', he stressed that this did not prejudice the Court's task of deciding whether this was 'a proper jurisprudential analysis of the relationship' (165). The finding of fact by a judge requires a different kind of expertise.

However, the strategy of letting claimants speak for themselves effectively pitches the fact-finding expertise and methodology of courts against that of anthropologists. The judge in the Australian case of *Jango v Northern Territory* (2006), for instance, thought the court's process benefited from having witnesses take oaths and face cross-examination ([301]). Some anthropologists, on the other hand, have stressed the value of ethnographic methodologies, such as participant observation during an extended period of time, over claimants' statements in court about what they do, and the importance of actions rather than words as a way into the 'hearts and minds' of the claimants (Rigsby 2001: 9), echoing the justification of ethnographic pioneer, Bronislaw Malinowski (1926: 120). Sutton considers that '[i]n classical Aboriginal cultural traditions, it would be abnormal, perhaps even inconceivable, that people would produce explicit, full and objective articulations of how their social order works, comparing ideals with actions, and extracting underlying patterns of typical behaviour' (Sutton 2003: xv–xvi; see also Malinowski 1961: 11–12). He highlights the alien context of the trial in which self-representations of cultural practices are elicited from witnesses over a relatively short period of time by questions from barristers (Sutton 2006: 169).

Furthermore, there is the question of the judge's lack of familiarity with Indigenous cultures and with the problems of cultural representation more generally. In interpreting Indigenous witness statements, judges may be implicitly informed by outmoded stereotypes or cultural models (Niezen 2003: 18–23; Culhane 1992: 72). The trial judge in the Canadian case *Delgamuukw* has been accused of inventing his own anthropology after having summarily dismissed the work of the three anthropologist witnesses and ignoring over a century of disciplinary development away from the kind of evolutionist model that he employed (Cruikshank 1992: 26). More subtly, witness statements can often use terminology – 'rights', 'permission', 'resources' – that may have distinctly different connotations to legal professionals and Indigenous or non-Indigenous lay people, something that may only be apparent to the 'linguist sitting uncomfortably in the second row' (Morphy 2007: 42).

The clash of methodologies is also apparent in the frustration that many expert witnesses experience with the trial process and its formal requirements. Expert reports must conform to the rules of evidence in order to be admissible: they must distinguish between fact, hearsay and opinion, which is not admissible unless it is made wholly on the grounds of the anthropologist's 'specialised knowledge based on training study or experience' (see for example s. 79 Evidence Act 1995

(Australia)).[10] Experts may be pressured by clients' counsel to adopt a particular model or explanation seen as more persuasive for their case, or tempted to reduce the complexity of Indigenous relations to land in order to resemble a checklist of rights and interests. Further, the style of questioning in court forces witnesses to proffer definitive answers on matters that can be neither determinate nor precise (Glaskin 2004: 7). As Steward once remarked in an ICC hearing:

> I have a feeling that Mr. Cobb [the plaintiffs' cross-examining lawyer] regards the scientific process as one of taking hunks of external reality he calls facts. You put them into a machine you call science. You start the machine going and conclusions come out. If the facts are correct, the machine will always produce the same kind of thing.[11]

In contrast, contemporary anthropology and other social sciences mostly take the view that it is often difficult to separate the facts of human action from interpretation; that history, for example, is written out of the concerns of the present and that knowledge is socially constructed in the midst of the negotiation of power between social groups (White 1973: xii; Berger and Luckmann 1966: 126–7). One interpretation might be considered more persuasive than another because it is corroborated or conventionally accepted, in terms of aesthetic values such as coherence, or for ideological reasons (Ward 1990: 152).

Whether the best translators are seen to be Indigenous witnesses, anthropologists, or judges, both the anthropological and the legal methods of investigation invest faith in the ability of witness statements or a text to represent the world of the claimants. The idea that this is a process of translation posits rights, interests, laws and customs as an original text and tends to make invisible the process of translation by comparing methodologies in terms of their accuracy. When the hearing is treated as a question of concept acquisition and comprehension, the political aspects of representation as a struggle for authority – both within communities and between them – are overlooked. For instance, when early on in the *Milirrpum* trial the Yolngu claimants decided to reveal to the judge, in a private meeting, their sacred *rangga* – wooden objects usually kept hidden that their counsel described as title deeds – they expected that, having seen the objects, the judge should necessarily understand their rights to land. But their expectation was based on the fact that, as in *Yolngu* law, the *rangga* themselves were self-evidently authoritative (Williams 1986: 159; Morphy 1983: 301).[12] In a similar example of cross-purposes in the

10 The failure to engage in this intellectual sorting unfamiliar to anthropologists has caused at least one anthropological report to be largely rejected (*Jango* 2004).

11 Cited in Ray 2003: 272.

12 Years later, despite their greater familiarity with mainstream legal processes as 'fact-finding', the Yolngu continue to treat their engagement with the Australian legal system as an opportunity to demonstrate and perform the power of their own law, both within and without the evidentiary frame (Morphy 2007).

context of a US tribal court authorized to apply Indigenous law, Justin Richland notes that Hopi witnesses called as experts on village tradition before the Hopi tribal court treated the hearing as an invitation to give an authoritative opinion as to the outcome of the dispute, while the judge continued to reframe the discourse on tradition in terms of abstract general principles which he, as the legal authority, would then apply (Richland 2008: 73–79). Thus the question of expertise in proving 'culturally different' facts raises the double meaning of representation in its semantic and political senses. Specifically, it is difficult to contain evidence about law or normative tradition as pure information about law lying elsewhere, as such evidence, of its nature, purports to be authoritative.

Understanding Translation: From Mimesis to Transformation

Before embarking on a more detailed examination of the translation of evidence in a study of the *Neowarra* case, I want to deepen our understanding of what translation is. In particular, I am interested in the way that translation has constructed categories of proper and foreign, self and other, and has consequently been a tool in colonial processes.

In both linguistic and anthropological uses of translation there are a number of themes suggested that embody a particular relation between reality and language. The first is the idea of the original, that there exists a concrete, discrete phenomenon, culture or text to be understood and then translated. Second is the idea of matching and equivalence to this original; literary translators often speak of 'fidelity' to the original text, for example, to its style, or to the intention of the author (Steiner 1992: 251; Johnson 1985). Third is the reliance on language as a representation of this original object. Pursuing questions about the epistemological assumptions of translation, as well as the colonial context in which it takes place, will help me critique the use of translation in Indigenous rights and its link to orthodox legal theory as a reification of law.

Jacques Derrida has written about a general 'metaphysics of presence' to which these three themes belong, the roots of which run deep in European philosophy (Derrida 1976: 10–13). Stretching back to a Platonic dualism between pure ideas and their material counterparts in the world, thought is defined as the re-presentation of some essential 'being' that is present, the mimesis of reality. Spoken language has the most direct relation to thought; it is the original signifier of meaning. Writing is then a secondary order representation, 'a sign of a sign'. For all elements in the chain: being → thought → speech → writing, the latter phenomenon is considered to be exterior to the former, the former is presence to the latter's absence. Theory makes thought present to consciousness, for instance, by re-presenting it through language. At the core of this system of representation, argues Derrida, is a yearning for original pure presence, a meaning that transcends all signs. One of its effects is the effacement of the materiality of language. Within this system, translation is seen as a transfer over to a new language of what is signified in the old, even though translators of all but the most trivial texts will have experienced that this is not what happens.

The deconstruction of the assemblage of language, writing, meaning and objects – the core of post-structuralist theory – has formed the basis for a critique of translation that has been taken on board to some extent by both anthropologists and literary translators. Questioning the effects of representation also has serious consequences for understanding the involvement of both these professions – and their representations of non-Europeans – in the colonial project. Both cultural and literary translation in the colonial context were made possible by a mindset intent on 'othering' non-European peoples, as well as by the physical control of territories that made such activities relatively 'safe'. Translation in turn became necessary and instrumental as a technique of colonial governance. The following sections will trace the role of translation in the reification of culture and the relationship between Europe and its colonies; the impact of the linguistic critiques on anthropology; and the consequences of these critiques for native title translation.

Translation and the Constitution of the Other

> The Translator considers thought content a prisoner which he transplants into his own language with the prerogative of a conqueror. (Jerome, Patron saint of translation)[13]

Translation has a specific history in the West relating the domestic and the foreign, the self and the other. The word 'translation' comes from the Latin derivative *translatio* of the Greek *metapherein*, both meaning 'to carry across'. Aristotle defined metaphor as the transference of an alien term into a familiar context, but he also included it in the category of 'strange or foreign words' (*tois xenikois*) as opposed to 'current or proper words' (*kurion onamaton*) (Aristotle 1961: Chs. XXI and XXII). Metaphor, or translation, thus has, as Eric Cheyfitz points out, a built-in 'territorial imperative', a division between the domestic and the foreign, the familiar and the strange, the proper and the figurative (Cheyfitz 1991: 36). The first terms – domestic, familiar, proper – become aligned together, at home; the second are always displaced.

Cheyfitz (1991) argues that translation has long been bound up in the history of European imperialism. In medieval thought, he explains, the theory of *translatio imperii et studii* legitimized the transfer of political and cultural empire from one people to another, which, at the time, justified the inheritance of both the imperial and cultural legacy of ancient Rome and Greece by medieval European peoples. In Cicero's *De Inventione* the wandering savages are at once transformed into settled peoples, when they are convinced by, and taught, eloquence. This trope was acted out upon the arrival of the English in the New World, where the forced

13 Cited in Friedrich 1992: 12–13.

learning of English – as promoted in the Virginia Company's 1609 *Instructions* edict to educate the children of Algonquian leaders in English language and manners – became a key strategy in the domination of local cultures that continued into later centuries with residential schools (Cheyfitz 1991: 6–7; Miller 1996: 106–7).

More pervasively, European activities of translation were, in Cheyfitz's analysis, a kind of foreign policy that determined the relations between the English colonists and the local peoples. The Algonquian would be translated into English and not the other way around. The problem of translation is both acknowledged and repressed in the education edict: the universal use of English masks the turmoil of intercultural interaction necessarily taking place out of sight of the written record. For example, when the right of the English to be present in Virginia is explained, in *A True Declaration of the Estate of the Colony in Virginia*, to be because an Algonquian king sold the land in exchange for copper, the Algonquians appear implicitly to be working in the same political, legal and economic register as the English, one where this kind of exchange can make sense (Cheyfitz 1991: 7–8). The colonizers thus translated the territories of the New World into 'property' to be exploited by Europe through these wilful textual descriptions, and followed later with the force of physical dispossession.

The story of translation in the Americas was not so uniformly one-sided, of course. In various situations, it was necessary for Europeans to present their objectives in local linguistic and symbolic idiom. For the Jesuit missionaries, speaking Aboriginal languages and translating the word of God into the vernacular was seen as key to persuading 'minds and hearts' (Blackburn 2000: 101). Further, a range of partnerships from trade to military alliance to land cession treaties were sealed using adapted Indigenous rituals (the exchange of gifts, smoking pipes, protocols like the Haudenosaunee Condolence ceremony (Pomedli 1995) and the presentation of Wampum belts (Borrows 1997)) and employing Indigenous idiom (the covenant chain, the one bowl).

In post-Renaissance Europe, translations of literary works from outside of Europe – such as Sir William Jones's 1789 translation of the Sanskrit play *Sakuntala*[14] – seemingly gave European readers access to the culture and knowledge of other peoples. Translators of Sanskrit and Persian texts were said to have helped 'open' what became known as the Orient, digging 'a channel between the hemispheres of human genius'.[15] Tejaswini Niranjana argues that Jones's Sanskrit translations and others like it powerfully constructed a version of 'the Hindu' which then became the basis, in an iterative fashion, of European discourse on the topic, and eventually, a received truth about India (as backwards, weak, unreliable, inefficient and cruel) (Niranjana 1992: 12–14).

---

14 See Figueira 1991. Religious texts were at first the main targets of translators: the Koran into Latin in 1143, into French in 1647, the Parsi Avestas in 1771 and the writings of Confucius in 1861 (Girardot 2002).

15 Raymond Schwab (1934) cited in Said 1979: 77.

Edward Said (1979) has also shown how stereotypes of 'the Orient' in general helped define for Europe an image of itself in opposites (1–2). Niranjana (1992) stresses the core role of translation in fixing this propaganda as knowledge. Being generally unreliable, the English claimed, Indians were deficient translators of their own texts. But because good translation was seen as transparent, a European translator was doing no more than presenting what the Hindus really were on about, and so could effectively speak for them – it was, after all, their own script (13). The idea of the original meant that behind the script lay 'a' Hindu character, psyche and way of life. The colonial subject, and the difference between the European self and the colonial other, is established through translation. But this was not merely a discourse circulating in European intellectual circles: Niranjana argues that because of the freighted value of European languages, texts and education, colonized peoples have also come to see *themselves* through this lens, a point that Franz Fanon (1967) has also made in relation to African peoples (ch. 5). Niranjana (1992) contends that an anglicized Indian 'would have preferred, because of the symbolic power conveyed by English, to gain access to his own past through the translations and histories circulating through colonial discourse' than through texts in a local script (31). Translations then arguably did more than represent or misrepresent: they became acts of recognition that effectively constituted differentiated cultures and subjectivities.

Although a great number of foreign texts that were translated during the process of colonial expansion had the effect of demonstrating the need for and rightness of European occupation and domination of the rest of the world, the availability, for the first time, to a European public of dramatic masterpieces from outside of the Greek/European tradition[16] also had the effect of mounting a conviction that 'all ethnic groups' are capable of producing great art. The idea of culture – a complex of learned behaviours and symbolic orders – as an attribute of all human societies was, towards the end of the nineteenth century, part of the universalist perspective that shifted the study of colonized peoples from the domain of the natural sciences to the generalized 'study of man', anthropology. Armed with the Kantian philosophy that human knowing was mediated by universal structures of the human mind, anthropology could look beyond the surface differences of the way people lived in order to perceive what was common to all. Early anthropology, however, had a tendency to see social phenomena as developing through stages (a model revived by Steward in America), and posited the literate, segmented and industrialized cultures of the anthropologists as more developed than those they were studying.[17]

The seminal work of Claude Levi-Strauss on kinship, law, and myth was in part an effort to de-throne European thought from this privileged position. In his

16 Which had been preserved and transmitted to Europe by Islamic scholars.

17 Evolutionism is associated in anthropology with Maine, Spencer, Tyler and Morgan, although the idea of human progress through stages has a much older pedigree: Bettinger 1991: 9–11.

fascination for form over content, he attempted to show an underlying structure of thinking which was unchanging and common to humankind. Each language and culture around the globe was simply an actualization of a universal thought structure. Levi-Strauss's structural anthropology placed a premium on meaning and signification, and depended on a conviction that all human behaviour was presumptively meaningful (1967: 80). Levi-Strauss was particularly inspired by the structural linguistics of Ferdinand Saussure but understood Saussure's claim to be that language is but one kind of signifying system. All (meaningful) aspects of culture can thus be read in the same way as a language: by identifying the way that conscious linguistic or symbolic phenomena (signifiers) link to the concepts that are signified, and then the way these signs (the pairs made up of signifier and signified) differ from others according to a systematic and possibly unconscious infrastructure. Cultures can be described as a signifying system consisting of a determinate set of relationships between phonemes or units of meaning. The stories contained in myth, for instance, are infinitely translatable, because they revolve around core thematic binaries that are common to all myths: completeness/incompleteness, selfishness/altruism, autochthonous/non-autochthonous, natural/unnatural (1963: 202–12).

Levi-Strauss's understanding of a kind of bed-rock of truth underlying anthropological data is evident in his elaboration of social structure. He claims that social structure is the model built up around the empirical reality of social relations; sometimes the members of the subject group will have their own conscious models, but these can be inaccurate and prevent good analysis: '[f]or conscious models, which are usually known as "norms", are by definition very poor ones, since they are not intended to explain the phenomena but to perpetuate them' (1968: 281–2). While Levi-Strauss acknowledged that each culture has its theoreticians whose contributions deserve the attention of anthropologists, he was also critical of the approach of Marcel Mauss and Émile Durkheim that took the conscious representations of the 'natives' as the starting point for categorizing native thought: these representations 'may be just as remote from the unconscious reality as any other' (1968: 282). Instead, the task of the ethnographer is to 'read and then reinscribe the implicit meanings that lie beneath/within/beyond situated speech' (Asad 1973: 160).

Notwithstanding Levi-Strauss's reservations, trying to get at how other people think – 'the native's point of view' in Malinowski's famous phrase (Malinowski 1961: 25) – generated one of the principal methodologies in anthropology, that of ethnographic participant observation. Diverse and unpredictable as cultures are, anthropologists needed to become acculturated to their subjects' worlds in order to understand them. They would live with them, learn their language, eat what they eat; in short, they would become 'native'. Pioneered by Malinowski in British social anthropology, and Franz Boas in American cultural anthropology, participant observation was seen as the way to counter ethnocentricism. Rather than being manifestations of the same basic human structures, elements of each culture related to peoples' radically different ways of seeing the world and could be meaningful only in those terms.[18] In order for these ways to become intelligible to the anthropologist, he or she would have to put aside their own received ideas of what constituted, for instance, kinship, religion or property.[19]

On the other hand, the outsider perspective of the ethnographer was vital to a scientific assessment of a group's culture, because, being a structure beyond the ken of any one member of that group, it had to be put together by the ethnographer. Malinowski wrote of the Trobriand Islanders that:

> [No individual has] knowledge of the total outline of any of their social structure … For the integral picture does not exist in his mind; he is in it, and cannot see the whole from the outside … The integration of all the details observed, the achievement of a sociological synthesis of all the various, relevant symptoms, is the task of the Ethnographer … .the Ethnographer has to construct the picture of the big institution, very much as the physicist constructs his theory from the experimental data, which always have been within reach of everybody, but needed a consistent interpretation (Malinowski 1961: 83–4).

Participant observation was an attempt to bring the scientific authority of anthropological training – theory, abstraction, analysis of data and a global perspective – to the interpretation of culture, thus providing something that neither the locals, nor the 'amateur' travel writers, missionaries, or colonial administrators, even with their years of personal experience, could do. At the same time it brought the authenticity of the 'I was there' type to what had previously been the desk-bound retrospection of professional anthropologists (Clifford 1988: 26–34). While the privileging of experience comes straight out of the modernist empirical tradition – where knowledge is gained through the senses – in ethnography, as in other human sciences, the understanding engendered by 'being there' is of a special kind. Encapsulated in the German word *verstehen*,[20] it is empathy born out of concrete perception, a rapport with people and the sensitive sharing of their world, which guarantees ethnographic authority (Clifford 1988: 37).

Just as William Jones had promoted the importance of translating the Sanskrit texts that enabled 'indirect rule' of India (that is, according to local Hindu law) (Said 1979: 78), the special expertise of anthropologists in understanding how Indigenous peoples 'thought' and how their societies were organized was sold to

---

18 The so-called 'Sapir-Whorf hypothesis' – that language determines (or at least influences) the way we think of the world and that the distinctions made by language are arbitrary and so relative – is an example of this approach. See 'The Status of Linguistics as a Science' in Sapir 1966.

19 This made anthropology a natural ally for those putting Western metaphysics in question in other domains such as philosophy. See 'Structure, Sign and Play in the Discourse of the Human Sciences' in Derrida 1978: 282.

20 The term originates with Max Weber, but also Wilhelm Dilthey (1914), 'The Construction of the Historical World in the Human Sciences' in Rickman (ed.) 1976.

government as being indispensable in the management of Indigenous populations. Malinowski, for instance, vaunted social anthropology as providing scientific recipes for the controlled transition of African states to indirect rule, creating 'in Native authority a devoted and dependable ally, controlled, but strong, wealthy and satisfied' (Feuchtwang 1973: 92). The Australian government began to train its administrators in Aboriginal Affairs in ethnology in 1914 (Feuchtwang 1973: 82). Even for those anthropologists in the twentieth century who prided themselves on producing ethnography free of the earlier ethnocentrism and a sense of European superiority, the colonial context was an implicit part of their practice. Since most anthropological research was funded and supported by colonial administration, ethnography tended to elide descriptions of the impact of colonization on local populations that might have been taken as criticism, and so presented its subjects as reified cultures existing in the continual present (Feuchtwang 1973: 90, 96).

The reification of culture was also achieved by the idea of anthropology as cultural translation. The social structures empirically observed by ethnographers became represented in the analytic labels – the *etic* terms – of their discipline. At least in the practice of cultural anthropology prominent in America, language and the representation of culture became central to what anthropologists do. On the other hand, the accuracy of the translation was understood to be compromised by the limits of the language in which the anthropologist wrote. Sometimes the *emic* terms used by the locals were left untranslated. Boas, for example, preferred to use the Kwakiutl word *numaym* (glossed as clan in his early work), explaining it as a bundle of privileges for which there is no English equivalent. The use of the word *Altjeringa* in Central Australian ethnography instead of 'Dreaming' or other English words is another example. Whichever linguistic strategy was used, Niranjana suggests, ethnography is a kind of mimesis of reality 'that effaces the materiality of language, which then becomes a mere transmitter of an essential meaning' (Niranjana 1992: 55). What is needed to expose the colonial epistemological project is a critique of language as representation.

The Critique of Representation

The idea of mimesis, and translation as the transfer of meaning into new contexts, depends on words being the counterpart of ideas or meanings. Around the turn of the nineteenth century, Saussure had loosened the link between word and world by showing that the sign, the association between word and concept, was meaningful not absolutely but only in its difference to other signs. With some quick inter-linguistic comparisons – *bread, brot, pain* or *law, recht, droit* – both the associations and their relative differences are shown to be arbitrary and dependent on conventions proper to each language. Fifty years after, the influential linguistic philosophy of Ludwig Wittgenstein also took convention to be core to meaning, but his emphasis on language as use avoided the structural fixity of Saussure's systems: rather, the associations between words and meanings change iteratively through interactive and dynamic linguistic practices (Wittgenstein 1968: 11).

Wittgenstein explained the acquisition of language as a process of analogy: we learn to perceive the meaning of words – even the most literal meanings – by their repeated association with many different objects, events and contexts, rather than by direct correspondence between word and object.

Just as language is learned this way, so is it constituted. Language grows and changes through usage, through evolving associations, and so at its most basic level is itself analogic or metaphoric. For Wittgenstein (1968), it is *use* rather than direct representation that provides meaning, so that language is a 'form of life' rather than an abstract system of signs (§ 19). In his famous example, English speakers may not be able to define the concept of 'game' but we can all use it accurately and in ways that others will understand. The core relationship in meaningfulness is not a one-to-one mapping of words and concepts, but an organic association of 'family resemblances' understood – and practised – through use. Thus Wittgenstein undermined the metaphysics of presence where language is always in search of an original.

In very different ways, but with a similar resulting focus on practice, use and time, Derrida has also attacked the representational relationship at the heart of translation. Derrida follows Saussure in contending that meaning is constituted through differentiation in linguistic signs – a cat is a cat because it is not a dog and so on. However, he takes the importance of differing further so as to stress that, even if dog is excluded from the concept of cat, it is nonetheless necessary to it. Meaning arises out of the absence of another sign, rather than the presence or identity of the concept in the sign in question. In order for 'cat' to make sense, it must do so in reference to 'not dog', 'not horse', or to 'furry quadruped', in other words to other signs and aspects of language such as negation ('not') rather than in reference to the real animal. In contrast to Saussure's synchronic or static structure, Derrida claims that signification relies not on a pre-existing set of differences, but an ongoing diachronic production of those differences through use, where meaning is continually deferred to the next use.[21]

In this critique of language, not only is the meaning of a sign always deferred to other signs and other uses, but, as Derrida has shown elsewhere, the means of establishing truth always rests on a metaphoric ground (particularly the kind of spatial imagery I have just used with 'rests' and 'ground').[22] One way of characterizing this claim is that nothing exists outside of representation (or, if it does, we can only know it through concepts formed in language). Derrida's ontology is debated, but the least we can say is that language cannot ground its truths outside of itself. Conceptual knowledge is 'aporetic' in nature; it rests on 'constitutive blind-spots' in language in that we do not notice the metaphoric qualities of statements that we take as factual (Norris 2002: 144). On the other hand, although language is not a transparent conduit *to* the world, it is a material thing itself. It is something that we do, practise, speak, listen, read and write

21 See for example 'Différance' in Derrida 1982.

22 'White Mythology: Metaphor in the Text of Philosophy' in Derrida 1982.

actively in conjunction with other people in space and time (Austin 1962); it is made up of breath, movement, ink and paper (Kristeva 1989: 18–42); it is an event, performative and creative. Meaning is not *in* the text but is made through the activity of reading in its surrounding material context.

This view of language dismantles the view of translation as the reproduction of meaning, as Walter Benjamin argued in his influential 1923 essay 'The Task of the Translator' (Benjamin 1969). But if translators are not reproducing the original, what are they doing? There may no longer be any pure original meaning behind language to be faithful *to*, but there is what is being read, and the attempt to translate it, writes James Boyd White (1990), 'brings us again and again to face that which is particular or unique to the language and its context, to the speaker himself, and therefore cannot be translated' (xvii). It is this experience of untranslatability – the experience of the otherness of the other – that gives translation an ethical component. That the experience of this impossibility is perhaps the true recognition of difference makes translation, as White has claimed, a model for justice (1990, xvii).

But facing this difference is inherently destabilizing for the self. While contemporary literary translations seemed to be praised for their seamlessness, and the 'invisibility of the translator' (Venuti 1995), Benjamin advocated translation that always bears the mark of the foreign language, and that allows the target language 'to be powerfully affected by the foreign tongue' (Rudolf Pannwitz, quoted in Benjamin 1969: 81). We can hear, for example, that the odd syntax of Robert Browning's 1877 translation of *Agamemnon* from the ancient Greek – 'they hymn their hymn, within the house close sitting' – jars the ear and produces a 'centaur-idiom', neither Greek nor English (Steiner 1992: 332). This new cadence in our own tongue has conceivably influenced the development of English lyrical writing since then.

In an example closer to the topic at hand, the sense in which, in Australian Aboriginal English, people speaking about 'caring for country' etc. – as if it were a proper noun – is uncomfortable to the English ear, with its understanding of country as an object or a political entity, is one which obliges differing concepts of place, as well as the work done by language, to come to the foreground. And as Cheyfitz (1991) has claimed, the force accompanying the 'wrongness' of metaphor actually allows it to open the space between signified and signifier, permitting a community of dialogue between writers and readers, an equivocal play of voices (38). This point takes translation away from the metaphysics of presence, from re-presentation of an original, and into an ethical mode where the language of translation allows itself to be transformed by the encounter with the untranslatable.

The challenge faced by anthropology in this critique of language and translation has had three layers. First, the claim of ethnography to represent an originary culture is questioned. Ethnographers are engaged in a process of actively creating a culture, such that the main activity in ethnography is not observation but interpretation – 'constructions of other peoples' constructions of what they are up to' (Geertz 1973: 9). Clifford Geertz, influential in this approach, treats cultures as assemblies of texts – a sometimes illegible manuscript – to be read, rather than an object to be described (1973: 9).[23] So although participant observation is indeed a methodology based on experience, what is experienced is the ethnographic event – the material circumstances of interpretation and textual production – rather than an unmediated culture or people.

The second challenge is that of authorship; a text must have an author. The ethnography as text is written by the ethnographer, and its authority comes conversely from the demonstrated intimacy with local life, and the disappearance of the writer from the scene as he or she takes on the status of the omnipresent narrator (Clifford 1988: 40). Through the coherence of the account presented, the culture as text, however, ends up being ascribed to a single authorial group – the Nuer, the Trobriand Islanders, the Walpiri – with stable cultural attributes and intentions. What these textual representations mask, as Talal Asad reminds us, is that it is people rather than a society who speak (Asad 1973: 155). The ethnographic text is neither a pure product of the ethnographer nor of 'the society' but a mess of individual acts of communication. The ethnographer is often heavily dependent on key 'informants' who spend time answering his or her questions and who have a certain ability to take – and an interest in taking – a distanced and critical stance on what it is that they do and think. The ethnographer is interested in 'that', and locals will also engage in thinking about what his or her questions could mean, what kinds of communication are possible, and what sense 'that' could have to an outsider. The result is often a product of constructive negotiation between two or more active, interpreting speakers (Clifford 1988: 41).

Some ethnographies have chosen to highlight this dialogic approach to writing ethnography. Deborah Bird Rose (1992) makes her status as 'student' of the culture – the ignorant stranger being taught how to behave – the core of her ethnography in *Dingo Makes Us Human*. Victor Turner's *The Forest of Symbols* presents a three-way collaboration between his main informant and their interpreter, giving 'visible place to Indigenous interpretations of custom' (Clifford 1988: 52). At the very least this style introduces other voices into the cultural text, but more profoundly, it brings to life the discursive process, mediated by multiple intentions, understandings, perspectives, through which translations are negotiated between the ethnographer and the practitioners of the culture. Consistently with this, a collaborative approach to research in Indigenous communities has now become the model advocated by various research bodies, signalling the political aspects of inclusion and exclusion, subject-hood and object-hood, in research (AIATSIS, Canadian Institutes).

The third challenge is the overdetermined context of ethnographic research, and the inequality of languages and peoples in the dialogic production of 'culture'. In terms of semantic production, the context can make the 'that' of ethnographic exchange into an extremely charged referent. For example, in a close reading of the colonial archive surrounding Spencer and Gillen's 'pioneering' work on Arrernte ritual sex in Central Australia in the 1890s, Elizabeth Povinelli wonders about the

23 See also Ricoeur 1971: 537–44.

linguistic and demonstrative manoeuvres that would have taken place in order to arrive at a statement like 'licentious sexual intercourse prevents decorations from falling off during ceremonies' (Povinelli 2002: 89). In the throes of frontier devastation, the Arrernte had been offered food and protection in exchange for information about their rituals. In various exchanges about 'ritual sex' – pointing, diagrams, substitutions like 'that' – the attempt to find out 'what was really going on' would have been obfuscated as much by what the Arrernte were quickly learning about settler morality/judgment and its impact on their lives as by the impossibility of words to refer to the same objects across cultures (or to participate in the same language games). Beyond the personal relationships between ethnographer and informants/collaborators, it is the authority of capitalist and industrial institutions, always in the background if not the foreground, that oversee the present practice, and future use, of cultural translations (Asad 1973: 163).

Strategies of Translation

Clearly there is not just one way to translate. From the stylistic raids of the Renaissance, to the racial caricatures of the Orientalists, or contemporary trends in literary translation which advocate either the invisibility of the translator or fidelity to something in the original text, different translation strategies embody different senses of responsibility to others. The inherent violence of translation referred to by Cheyfitz is an implicit theme in many of the critiques of Indigenous rights canvassed in Chapter 2, usually expressed in terms of the erasure of the specificity of Indigenous peoples when they, or their culture, are represented in the terms of settler law. And yet there are those who suggest that some approaches to translation, notably those that proceed through negotiation and dialogue, can avoid this erasure of difference.

In writing of translation in Australian native title, Paul Patton (2000) identifies two different techniques of translation (28). In the first, which Patton claims is used by Justice Blackburn in *Milirrpum*, the translator assumes the need to first determine the 'real' nature of Aboriginal land tenure via anthropological translation, and then to compare this to common law property to see whether a translation into a proprietary right can be made. Because the descriptions of Yolngu life in relation to land seem to speak more of 'cogent feeling of obligation to the land' than 'ownership of it', Blackburn J finds that this relation is not proprietary in nature (*Milirrpum* 1971: 270). To the Yolngu and many others, this 'translation' seemed arbitrary: 'if *djalkiri* is obligation, why don't you people respect obligation?' (Murray 2003: 78).

In the second strategy of translation, taken up in *Mabo,* there is a *prima facie* position that Aboriginal peoples had proprietary rights over the land in which they lived. The assumption is that occupation[24] of a territory was in some way

24 Overlooking the not insignificant issue of what constitutes 'occupation': see *Marshall* and *Bernard* 2005: [41]–[66].

meaningful and thus capable of being understood as proprietary in nature. The warning against 'mere analogies' of English jurisprudence made in the influential 1921 House of Lords decision in *Amodu Tijani* could lead us to resist treating alike those things which are different and to deny legal protection, as did Blackburn J, or it could give us a reason to abandon cultural equivalence as a basis for recognition. The second strategy begins with what George Steiner describes as the 'radical generosity' that *all* translators must initially bring to their task: an act of trust, based on assumptions about the coherence of the world, that there is something there to translate (Steiner 1992: 312). The 'reality' of Aboriginal land tenure, and the difficulties of translation, would only then figure as a second step in providing the content of the property right recognized.

The two strategies respectively involve choosing to transform the Indigenous interest to fit in with pre-existing categories, which Blackburn J declined to do, or modifying existing law to accommodate the new kind of interest, which is what the *Mabo* judges chose. Patton (2000) claims that this choice is the perennial lot of a translator working between languages: 'either the foreign term must be treated as equivalent to an already existing term of the home language, or the home language must be modified in order to accommodate the foreign term, either by simply importing it into the home language or perhaps by coining a term that is new to both languages' (35). Although 'native title' would appear to be such a neologism, we have seen that the moment of equivalence critical to Blackburn J's translation is merely postponed to the second stage – native title still has to be expressed as rights and interests (a mere analogy with English jurisprudence) to be protected.

The violence of equivalency, of making something stand in for something else, seems, as Cheyfitz claims, inherent to the very concept of translation. Similarly, Steiner (1992) describes a schema in which the initial attitude of trust is followed by a move of appropriation, violent in nature, during which the original text is comprehended (literally, seized or 'taken with'), the code is *broken*, 'the original meaning is brought home captive by the translator' (314). However, he goes on, the sense of despoliation is an illusion, because a good translation will enhance the original rather than destroy it. A translation always stands in relation to its original, the two are read in light of each other and, through this dialectic movement, both home and target language are transformed. Even the fact that it was deemed worthy of translation can enlarge the stature of the original. After the initial violence of capture, there is a compensatory movement of 'bringing back'. In this return of equilibrium Steiner sees translation as a moral stance: 'fidelity' in translation is neither literalism nor 'any technical device for rendering "spirit",' but is rather that which seeks to restore the balance of forces disturbed by the original appropriation (318).

Steiner's theory of translation has been criticized by those with an eye on colonial histories, because the asymmetry between languages renders any balanced exchange impossible and makes any claim to have benefited the language of the colonized a dubious one (Niranjana 1992: 59).[25] This seems to be the basis of criticism, expressed by Stewart Motha (1998), that the possibility for dialogue (the condition for ceasing practices which essentialize or efface Indigenous difference) 'is closed off when concepts like "native title" or a property right are introduced as the mediating device for the relationship between the two groups' (27). It is the sense that the terms and parameters of translation – 'the commodity form of ... property law', 'the logic of Western thought and language' (Kerruish and Purdy 1998: 163) – are imposed by settler law that makes it unjust. Just translations are those which are consensual and negotiated through dialogue, rather than imposed and monologic.[26]

Steiner is not unaware of the effect of power on the equilibrium of translation,[27] although it is not a major feature of his exposition. However, these criticisms do not detract from a core part of his theory, one which is emblematic of my argument for law in this chapter. It is that '[n]o language, no traditional symbolic set or cultural ensemble imports without risk of being transformed' (1992: 315). Steiner's idea of 'bringing back' could be called a third strategy of translation, but for the degree of choice that this would imply. Even in situations of domination where no official purchase is given to dialogue between the oppressed and the oppressor, it is the *nature* of language to be dialogic, as we have seen in Wittgenstein and Derrida. If property is used as a term of translation, it is not a full-stop, but a work in progress. While it may be an imposition, the translation of Indigenous claims into property is part of a process of meaning-making that is dialogic *in spite of itself*.

Patton (2000) seems in some ways to have taken this on board. In commenting on Blackburn J's attempt to keep property 'proper' by excluding the possibility of analogy between Yolngu *djalkiri* and common law property rights, he points out that 'the subsumption of some particular relationship under a given category is at once both the process by which we form "proper" concepts and the process by which we form metaphors. As a result, the boundaries of the proper are never finally settled and the very nature of the process of legal translation ensures that retranslation can always produce a different outcome' (34). This is a powerful insight and one that has not been brought to bear on Patton's conclusion that native title has not created a 'third term' but merely a lesser form of English property, a 'mere analogy of English jurisprudence' (37). Taken further, we would have to understand the point about metaphor to be that property itself is not a stable category and is affected by native title translations.

In sum, the fact that Indigenous rights may be conceived as a project of translation indicates that there is a proper domain, the familiar ideas of property for instance, and a foreign one, the *sui generis* of Indigenous place relations.

---

25 See also the feminist critique of his gendered images of translation: Chamberlain 1988: 462–5.

26 See for instance Uhlmann 2001.

27 See for example the comment on the failure to preserve local language in the face of invasion: Steiner 1992: 315.

But translation is the very process by which we make these categories; they are made and remade every time we use metaphors, which is every time we use language. Legal decisions – as to what is in and out of a particular category – are an archetypal example of this reiterative process (Davies 2002: 336). But decisions about meaning can never be unilateral and permanent; meaning is always deferred to other terms, to other users, in an ambiguous play.

The deconstructive approach to representation undermines the common assumption that language can give direct access to reality. In that the Indigenous *sui generis* must make itself known in court through language (or, as we will see in the next chapter, through other symbolic means such as paintings), what can be recognized through translation is only an already constructed text. That such a text, saturated by the larger colonial setting and its specific manifestation in the native title hearing, is not an objective reality 'out there' cannot be accounted for in modern law's evidentiary and proprietorial divide between law and the world. Within this setting, a multitude of desires and perspectives are interacting to produce the 'traditional rights' which native title will protect. The lesson that Steiner, Benjamin and Derrida invite is that the dialogic nature of meaning-making in language means that translation is both constitutive of the original and transformative of the recipient.

Neowarra v State of Western Australia

Neowarra is one of a series of Australian decisions following the *Yorta Yorta* case discussed in Chapter 3 that has seen the rise to importance of the notion of 'normative society' in determining aspects of a claim. As in *Daniel* (2003), *Alyawarr* (2004), the Wellesley Islands claim (*Lardil Peoples v State of Queensland* 2004), and the Bardi and Jawi claim (*Sampi* 2005), *Neowarra* defines the appropriate native title holders as those people united by a normative body of laws and customs. Normativity is key to the finding in *Yorta Yorta* that the 'traditional' requirement of s. 223 of the Native Title Act means substantial continuity since 'sovereignty' in the acknowledgment of laws. In *Risk* (2006), *Bennell* (2006) and *Griffiths* (2006), the continuity issue centred on whether the claims demonstrated the interruption or adaptation of traditional laws. In *Neowarra*,[28] the normative character of current practices and beliefs was challenged by certain of the respondents, and we get to see the judge work through how to draw out 'normativity' from the evidence. The richness of the expert evidence and witness testimony included in the judgment text makes *Neowarra* a particularly apt case study for translation in native title.

The terms of backwards translation are provided by s. 62 of the Native Title Act, and an original – the evidence – must be found for which these terms are

28 Similar challenges were made in *Jango* (2006) and the Goldfields claim: *Harrington-Smith on Behalf of the Wongatha Peoples v Western Australia* 2007.

the equivalent. There must be a *native title claim group*;[29] a *claim area* of land or water, to be identified by a map and by physical description or other information; a description of specific *rights and interests* claimed; details of the *factual basis* of the claim, including the *association* between the native title group and the land and waters, the existence of *traditional laws and customs* giving rise to native title, the *continued possession* of such rights *in accordance with* traditional laws and customs, and any *activities* that the claim group may carry out on the land.[30]

The Magic of Description

The most remarkable thing about *Neowarra* for our purposes is the seamlessness of the Indigenous world that appears in the text, and the *absence* of the messiness of translation. The palpable solidity of clan systems and marriage rules, spirit ancestors and the organization of clan estates is there, not just in the authoritative voice of the judge and the experts, but springs up out of the mouths of Aboriginal witnesses. For example, *dambun* = estate. In the words of Justice Sundberg:

> The claimants' society is divided into clans through a patrifilial connection with a particular tract of country – an estate or dambun. [D]ambun means 'own place', 'own block', 'camp', home', 'our country' ... [M]embership carries with it rights in relation to the estate, expressed with different degrees of emphasis and exclusivity [such as] the right to exclude people from a person's country. [D]ambun are classified according to the moiety system, each being either Jun. gun or Wodoy (*Neowarra* 2003: [204]).

Wanjina = a class of ancestral creator beings:

> Not only did Wanjina lay down rules of conduct; he was in the nature of a creator being. Paddy Neowarra, for example, said that people, animals, trees, rivers were all 'under Wanjina'. Some witnesses who painted Wanjinas on to the landscape, as in a cave or on a rock wall, did so by way of assertion of their entitlement to clan country. Thus, when asked whether he had to see anyone's permission to paint the Wanjina in Guyugongo country, Dick Tataya replied 'No, I'm the boss for it' (*Neowarra* 2003: [166]).

Wurnan = trade system:

---

29 Note that the claim is to be registered by an individual or individuals who are authorized by all persons holding native title rights i.e. 'the claim group' in s. 61.

30 Note that in the definition of native title in s. 223, association is termed 'connection', the area is 'land and waters', but otherwise the key elements of the definition are there in the application requirements. These elements are likewise reflected in the required components of a native title declaration, that is, what the judge is required to 'find' in respect of the native title claim.

> Professor Blundell continues: 'The Wurnan … is "like a map". In space, each segment of the Wurnan is appropriately called (in English) a "channel", and trade items flow from clan core to clan core along and between the two Wurnan segments' (*Neowarra* 2003: [262]).

Wunggurr = primordial water serpent related to spirit conception:

> An explanation of the Wunggurr concept or belief was given by Scotty Martin … : 'Wherever you found or dream the kids next to the Wunggurr country or Wanjina country, whenever that boys or girls born, after that country you got to give the little kids the name. Because, see, the little one – little baby come from there out of that Wunggurr water or Wanjina country'. … A Wunggurr place can be found outside a person's clan or even language country … The significance of this is that a person can have rights in his or her own clan estate and in another estate in which that person's Wunggurr place is located (*Neowarra* 2003: [178]).

In the smoothness of these translations, *dambun* becomes estate, *wurnan* becomes a trade system. This is not to say that the complexity of these terms is undermined. The *wurnan*, for instance, is also described as an ordering model for all humans and all of nature divided between the Jun.gun and Wodoy moieties, and its pattern of exchange extends beyond material goods to songs, rituals and marriage. Its map-like nature even specifies the organization of decision-making councils and the care of widows and orphans. The effect of these descriptions, however, is that, whatever sense it might have to native speakers, *wurnan* becomes a trade system, a cognitive model, a map and a law about sharing. It is, despite the complexity of the description, reduced to and reformulated by that description.

The 'Recognition Level': Figment or Translation?

On the other hand, it is in the space of contention that the work of translation is more apparent, and we see not only the shift between the register of the religious or the spiritual and the legal register of rights and interests that bothered the Australian High Court in *Ward*, but also how the things that people do and say is made into the text of their relation to country by being read in particular ways by the court.

In *Neowarra* the disagreement between the applicants' anthropologists (Alan Rumsey, Anthony Redmond and Valda Blundell) and the respondents' anthropologist (Basil Sansom) concerned the group 'level' at which the native title holders should be recognized. The claimants sought recognition of an 'umbrella' group, called the 'Wanjina-Wunggurr community' or the 'Wanjina tribe', made up of three different language groups in the claim region, Ngarinyin, Worrorra and Wunambul, and within them the various clans associated with the estates or *dambun*. The umbrella group was identified by the claimants' anthropologists as those sharing a set of beliefs in the two ancestors Wanjina and Wunggurr, or generally sharing a 'cultural domain'. They argued that only this level would enable native title recognition, first, of the 'multiple and cross-cutting ties' that people might have to different areas of land other than via patrilineal inheritance (such as through marriage or 'spirit conception') and, second, of the fact of a shared culture. This cultural domain was argued to be the entity that is reproduced over time and gives a 'blueprint' for more specific relations like clan estates ([89]).

The state, through Professor Sansom, argued for recognition at one of two levels: either at the smaller group level at which the people speak about belonging to or owning the sets of physical sites that make up the *dambun* on the basis that this was the significant group from the perspective of Aboriginal law, or, alternatively, at the level of 'language tribe'.[31] For instance, a Ngarinyin person's language identity is hereditary, and creates a basic link to Ngarinyin country because the country itself is stamped in the Dreaming with the Ngarinyin language identity. As Sansom said in evidence, 'Language thus stands for and embraces a jurisdiction – its dicta are the very dicta in which the provisions of the law find their expression' ([195]). The general interest of the Ngarinyin language group in Ngarinyin country was that of 'the proper administration of the law by members of the constituent clans of the Ngarinyin people' ([85]).

One aspect of the dispute was whether the larger group level existed 'in reality;' the other was whether this group was the appropriate entity to hold native title. Sansom argued that not only did the larger group not exist as a culturally significant entity for Aboriginal people – for example, there was no Indigenous language term for it – and as such was an anthropological figment, but also that to recognize native title rights at this level would 'do violence to traditional and customary practice' in which clans had primary responsibility for *dambun* ([89]). It would treat as equivalent all the various links that people have to land and undermine the customary requirement 'that certain core rights be privileged over others' ([84]). Professor Blundell, on the other hand, defended the notion of the cultural domain as an anthropological *construct*; that is, a representation of an inside view of culture for the purposes of analysis and comparison, as distinct from a *figment*, for which there is no corresponding phenomenon in the society ([110]). Blundell explicitly described her analytical location of smaller clan countries within the cultural domain rather than just the language countries as a 'translation of the way [she thinks] people conceptualise their connections with land' ([90]). They did not have 'a' word, but they had many ways of referring to this larger group, such as 'the three tribes' or 'the Wanjina tribe' ([99]).

Disputes over the validity of group ascriptions in terms of the Native Title Act have been quite common in litigated claims (Lavery 2004). In several cases in the Northern Territory and Western Australia particularly, the claimants have been a group constituted on the basis of shared language, law or a community identity.[32]

31 This was stated to be Sansom's preferred model: *Neowarra* 2003: [388].

32 *Wandarang People v Northern Territory* 2000 (twelve estate groups and four languages); *Ward* (Miriuwung and Gajerrong language groups); *Alyawarr* (seven estate groups and four languages); *Sampi* (Bardi and Jawi language groups).

As in *Neowarra*, state governments have consistently tried to argue for recognition at the smaller level such as clans, estate groups, or the traditional owners defined in terms of 'primary spiritual responsibility' or 'patrilineal descent' that are the cultural entities recognized under the Northern Territory Aboriginal Land Rights Act.[33] This undoubtedly stems from a perception that a recognition of these groups would minimize the number of rights holders and thus the gains of the native title determination, or, as one writer has claimed, is 'a deliberate attempt to reduce the claimable land and increase the level of proof required to [sic] a parcel by parcel connection' (Strelein 2005: 7).

In *Neowarra*, the difficulty of trying to take 'the natives' perspective' on groups is circumvented because Sundberg J approaches translation from within the limits of s. 223 (1) of the Act that defines native title as the 'communal, group or individual rights and interests of Aboriginal peoples'. He reasoned that neither the *dambun* nor the language group level would reflect all the kinship links people had with various *dambun* or language areas. This approach imported a kind of democratic ideal of inclusiveness into native title.[34] Nor would anything but the recognition of the Wanjina-Wunggurr community allow for the possibility, shown in evidence, of succession to *dambun* when the last clan member had died ([387]–[388]). The dispute became a question of semantics in the match between the evidence and the Act. Sundberg J held that achieving such a match requires not a mapping of the people who assert particular rights to areas as 'holders of native title', but an assessment of the group that sustains a normative system according to which the multitude of rights are held. Here, the question 'whose laws and customs?' is answered only by the Wanjina-Wunggurr community ([393]).

The umbrella group is still required to 'exist', but this is read through the lens of native title doctrine: the entity would exist if 'the claimants regard themselves as part of a community' through evidence of 'an emphasis on shared customs or traditions' ([386]). Statements such as '[w]e are all *Wanjina* people belonging to this country' and '[w]e are all the one people that connect to the *Wanjina*, no matter what tribe we are' were typical of this evidence ([167]–[168]). Sundberg J thus implicitly agreed with Blundell that if the cultural domain was a construct, it was also a translation of the way the claimants thought. Insofar as it was a dispute between professional anthropologists, Sundberg J preferred to take the word of those (Rumsey, Redmond, Blundell) with extensive experience in the field over that of Sansom whose research he felt had a 'desktop quality'. Further, because the Act defines the native title holding community in terms of the observance of laws and customs, it is, in part, the meta-narratives or *nomos* – about the *Wanjina*

33 Note that this Act preceded the Federal Native Title Act by 20 years and generated specialist language, claim culture and expertise that have inevitably shifted across to the Native Title Regime. State and territory land rights Acts operate concurrently and non-exclusively with the Native Title Act; they may identify different sets of rights holders or territories that depend on their differing criteria.

34 See Correy 2006: 344 on the inclusive ideals of the registration test in NSW.

spirits, for instance – which give an overall structure of meaning to the Wanjina-Wunggurr community's specific rules of social organization and land usage and distinguish them from those of their neighbours.

Sansom's proffered 'original' of estate or language groups was not rejected because it did not exist, but because it was not the appropriate original to be translated backwards into a native title group. Through the filter of the Native Title Act, the claimants' community becomes defined in the case by their shared observance of traditional laws and customs. Sundberg J's conviction that the Wanjina-Wunggurr community is the only group description consistent with the evidence subsumes all the alternative translations within it. It becomes the authorized version, but seemingly authored by the singular 'community'. One quote from Redmond indicates the context-dependent and provisional nature of this translation: 'the Wanjina-Wunggurr community has been created as a shorthand for an entity defining itself in this situation in relation to a western legal process' ([395]). This community has, in effect, been 'found' in translation (Geertz 1983: chapter 2). It may be an anthropological construct, but is no less real for that fact.

The Body of Law as Mosaic

How does the Court come to identify 'the Wanjina-Wunggurr normative community' or a 'right to exclusive possession' in this case? Following the elaboration of a critical approach to anthropological translation above, a context-sensitive inquiry would lead us to ask how the claim began to be formulated, what conversations were had between individual claimants, between them and their Native Title Representative Body, the lawyers, the anthropologists. We would want to know more about the making of the reports of the anthropologists, historians, linguists and archaeologists, about the hearing and the oral evidence. Were there 'numinous' moments of emotional awareness or 'Verstehen' that never made it into the transcript (see Shaw 2001)? What, physically, was acted out at the hearing? In conventional legal discourse, these are 'supplementary questions' that relate neither to fact nor to law, although I will take some of them up in the next chapter as being crucial to both.

For now, I will analyse the text of the judgment. What is its author doing in claiming to present the translation of another world? Let us consider the feat of translation performed by the parties in arriving at the normative system of Wanjina-Wunggurr. The applicants' anthropological report described the cultural domain as a distinctive ensemble of traditional elements: belief in *Wanjina* and *Wunggurr*, *dambun* estates associated with one or more named *Wanjina* creator beings, and an exogamous patrilineal moiety or 'skin' system that governs who can marry whom. In the list-like account of evidence of laws acknowledged and customs observed the judge adds to these elements: other stories that people knew about, the ability to speak the languages from the claim area and knowledge of the language identity of different places, various rules such as the marriage prohibitions relating to the skin system and avoidance relationships, rituals such as male initiation, the practice of 'smoking' visitors,[35] and the public performance of songs, widow mourning rites, the *wurnan* trade system, and looking after country.

First, we have the structuring of what the claimants say, and what is represented in what they say, into the categories of belief, ritual, stories and so on. Aside from being structured through the judge's textual organization, the categories evolved dialogically, such as in the exchange between counsel for the applicants and Scotty Martin Walagmuro about *Wunggurr* conception. Counsel asks, 'So, what, that baby is there somewhere in the water, is it? How does that work?' Confronting what might be the familiar scepticism of *gardiya*,[36] Walagmuro switches from a language of 'what happens' (seen in the extract on *Wanjina* above) to one of belief:

> Well, what I believe the – what a story was telling me before, any kids that come out of the water or this must be *Wanjina* give you that – those kids. That's what I believe (*Neowarra* 2003: [178]).

Second, we have the equation of laws and customs with the beliefs, rules, stories, practices, knowledge, social structures and rituals enumerated which is implied through the layout of the judgment in headings ('Laws Acknowledged and Customs Observed') and subheadings ('Wanjina', 'Wunggurr', 'Wanalirri', 'Moieties', 'Clans and Dambun' etc.) rather than through explicit discussion.

Again it is contestation that brings the process of translation to the fore: faced with the contention by one of the respondents that the role of *Wanjina* is uncertain among the claimants or that there is no uniformity of practice, Sundberg J replies that rather than a 'melange of confusion', the evidence is a mosaic of individual witnesses describing their own level of knowledge about these laws and customs but that 'assessed as a piece, [t]he mosaic discloses that *Wanjina* created the land and waters and what lives on or in them, and laid down laws and customs around which the Aboriginal people have constructed their lives' (*Neowarra* 2003: [177]).

The mosaic, like the ethnographic text, is being constructed on the basis of a supposedly external perspective that can turn an array of individual utterances into a whole. The fact of the existence of law and custom can be concretized by a statistical count of how many witnesses told, for example, the Wanalirri ancestor story (30), how many did not know the story (3) and how many did not mention it (23) (*Neowarra* 2003: [191]). We have here the ethnographic model of Levi-Strauss and Malinowski where the whole can only be seen from outside, and by reading what is implicit in the accreted evidence the judge can get at the true facts of the claimants' native title. The active involvement of the anthropologist and the judge in the articulation of a recognizable whole – a body – of Wanjina-Wunggurr laws and customs undermines, first, the separation of fact from law on which legal

---

35 The practice of passing a smoking branch close to a person so that the smoke will cleanse them.

36 White people in Indigenous languages of the Kimberley region of Australia.

positivism is based, and second, the metaphysics of presence and representation in which the articulation in court ostensibly merely names something that exists outside.

In the following exchange we get the sense that counsel for the applicants is trying to get at something behind the words of the witness:

> *Mr Blowes*: So who can speak for this Nyalinja, this Fish Hole area?
>
> *Tiger Moore Rowarr*: Well … far as I know I can run it from here, only Durack River through to Speewar.
>
> *Mr Blowes*: You can run it; what do you mean, you can run it?
>
> *Tiger Moore Rowarr*: Well, I can hold it all, say it, or say something for it.
>
> …
>
> *Mr Blowes*: … So you hold this, you said like you hold this part; what do you mean by that?
>
> *Tiger Moore Rowarr*: Well, I have to hold this part, if I can, like just sort of rule it. I'm ruling it; rule this part of this country.
>
> *Mr Blowes*: Yes. And when you say you rule it, what do you mean?
>
> *Tiger Moore Rowarr*: Well, just like I owns it.
>
> *Mr Blowes*: All right. And when you say just like I owns it, what do you mean?
>
> *Tiger Moore Rowarr*: Well, owns it mean I'm the boss of it.
>
> …
>
> Rule it mean you got to own it, you got to rule it and you're the boss of the country.
>
> *Mr Blowes*: And … when you're a boss of the country, what can you do on the country?
>
> *Tiger Moore Rowarr*: Well, I'll just check on the country, if they don't destroy it. Wherever my sacred sites and wherever, whatever, painting or whatever on the cave, just like the one we just saw back there, and if nobody's going to control it or rule it, if it's going to be destroyed what will happen with Aboriginal people (*Neowarra* 2003: [276]).

Sundberg J concluded that although the phrase 'right to speak for country' was often used without any indication of what it amounted to in practical terms, 'on reading the whole of the evidence it is clear "speaking for country" means ownership of it'. In the end, the terms 'own', 'run', 'speak for', 'hold' and 'rule' used by witnesses were credible similes for 'exclusive possession'. In addition, exclusive possession was an appropriate translation because the claimants occupied and used areas and sites in the claim area, and there were no rights to the claim area asserted by neighbouring Aboriginal groups (*Neowarra* 2003: [378]–[379]). But the march of similes in this exchange starts to break up the link back to the real thing being represented (the witness's 'right to country') because the words are excessively substituted for other words. The substitutions effectively put the process of translation into the spotlight. The witness is searching for words that will make sense to this lawyer.[37]

Acknowledging the impact of the native title process on translations can cause problems for claimants. To be successful, the claim must be described in a way that fits within the legal framework but is *not oriented to it*, as Povinelli observes of recognition-based legislation in general (Povinelli 2002: 253). A claim will not be traditional and therefore not genuine if some part of it can be seen to be a result of the claims process itself; the translation must be a 'credible simile' rather than an opportunistic one. For instance, a group that has gained its identity through the process of organizing a land claim is not therefore a community united by *traditional* laws and customs, unless the accretion of groups can somehow be traced to 'traditional' processes such as marriage, adoption or succession to country whose people have died.[38] In *Neowarra* the finding of unity through observance of traditional law obviated the state's argument on this basis. But the distancing of the 'original' of Indigenous law in space and time is obvious here, as is the orthodox model of translation: the court forum and processes are not part of Indigenous law, which exists out there and long ago and is only represented in court.[39]

Rejecting a group identity claim because it is seen as a recent fabrication ignores the way that native title is a 'total social fact', in Marcel Mauss's terms, as James Weiner argues (Weiner 2003: 98). Peoples' interests in country and their interpersonal relationships cannot exist outside of context, and native title – including anthropologists' and lawyers' attempts to configure and recognize traditional law – is now one of those contexts. The South Australian Hindmarsh Island Bridge affair will provide here a useful way of reworking the conventional idea of translation as carrying over some core of fact from Indigenous law to

37 Or perhaps this exchange was foreseen and trying emphatically to make a point for the benefit of the judge.

38 See *Sampi*, and *De Rose* 2003.

39 Although site visits in preparation of the claim were not discounted as evidence of 'looking after country', and Sundberg J noted that court visits to the sites still required certain preparatory rituals such as 'smoking': '[i]t is not easy to quarantine these visits from the laws and customs that govern Aboriginal behaviour' (*Neowarra* 2003: [299]).

its recognition under state legislation.[40] Although this was a matter under the Aboriginal and Torres Strait Islander Heritage Protection Act (Cth) 1984 and not a native title claim, the crucial elements are similar: the proof of Aboriginal cultural significance via an investigation that involved anthropologists and Indigenous witnesses, and the requirement that the culture be traditional and not of recent invention.

In 1993 a group of Ngarrindjerri women in South Australia sought to invoke the Heritage Act to prevent the construction of a bridge, which would have destroyed a site associated with the 'secret women's business' or sacred laws, under provisions for the protection of sites of Aboriginal cultural significance. A dispute erupted, with a second group of women saying the secret women's laws did not exist, and the proponent women saying that this second group just had not been told. An anthropological report was hastily written (also secret) and a Royal Commission enquiry called, which managed, through powers at its disposal, to keep the object of its enquiry relatively opaque.

The claim was finally declared to be based on a fabrication and the bridge went ahead, but, in the meantime, the Ngarrindjeri secret women's business gained a national profile. Through the complicity of the anthropologists, the Royal Commission and the media, the secret women's business achieved the same social effect that all regimes of secrecy have: to publicly differentiate between groups in society which are inside and outside the secret (Weiner 2001: 155). At the meta-level of the *nomos* of 'secrecy' the Commission and other agencies and individuals themselves helped act out aspects of Ngarrindjeri culture, which then cannot be said to exist 'out there' and apart from the claims process. To say this another way, the rituals, symbols and discourse of settler law get pressed into the service of 'internal' matters of Indigenous law, just as versions of Indigenous law get pressed to serve the function of claiming the separation of law from fact, the difference between the common law as the one Australian law and Indigenous law as the fact of social existence. This, to me, is the cogent 'intersection of two normative orders' in native title. It also shows Ngarrindjeri culture finding itself in the methods of translation in which they, the anthropologists and the Commission were all involved.

Rules, Norms and Principles: Found in Translation

In light of the discussion of H.L.A. Hart and the requirement of normativity in *Yorta Yorta* in Chapter 3, I am interested in pursuing a further example of the mosaic: that part involved in ascertaining the *normative* aspects of the claimants' law. The rules that stand out in the test for normativity, and that are used to support the evidence of general observance of a body of laws and customs, are those that resemble the type of commands or prohibitions familiar from European positive law: for instance, the 'marriage rule that a Jun.gun person could marry a Wodoy

40 For an overview, see Edmond 2004.

person, but not another Jun.gun person' (*Neowarra* 2003: [199]) and the rule that one must not utter the name of a recently deceased person (*Neowarra* 2003: [257]). As we shall see, these specific examples of translation link practice and discourse in a way that illuminates an understanding of law more generally: they suggest that it is always produced in translation, in the tension between the spoken and the unspoken, but moreover that practice and discourse are necessarily moved in the process.

Although they resemble positive law, however, the rules are not proved by reference to an Indigenous pedigree or valid source, such as 'Well, Wodoy and Jun.gun, they gave the rules that – when they was in the Dreaming. "Your children marry my children"' (*Neowarra* 2003: [200]). Rather, their existence is established in terms of a factual pattern. For the marriage rule, this was found in witnesses' accounts of their own and others' marriages. A statistical breakdown of right-way and wrong-way marriages was provided. Sundberg J comments that Heather Umbagai, in her discussion of young people marrying the wrong way, 'clearly viewed the development with great disapprobation' (*Neowarra* 2003: [219]). The deceased's name rule was also 'observed' via peoples' behaviour in the hearing. The occasional slip by court personnel in mentioning the name of a deceased person 'was greeted by a murmur of disapproval from … other witnesses at the back of the Court' (*Neowarra* 2003: [257]). The rules, even though not followed all the time, constituted obligations or standards of behaviour because their breach occasioned consternation in, or disapproval by, other members of the group.

According to both jurists and anthropologists in *Neowarra*, a rule exists because people can be observed to follow it and because they demonstrate a particular attitude with respect to behaviour in conformity to it. It seems a carbon copy of Hart's theory of (primary) rules as a combination of convergent behaviour and the internal attitude of the participants, their rational choice to behave in conformity with a rule. The rule in its propositional form is rarely given by Aboriginal witnesses, even though they do use the language of law and rules, for example 'that marriage rule'.

How then do we *arrive at* the expression of the rule – how do we translate it – from these non-verbal and otherly-expressed things? The judge simply states that there is no doubt that people declined to say names 'because of the existence of a rule that said they must not say the name' (*Neowarra* 2003: [257]). Support for the rule that 'a stranger must always ask permission' to enter a person's country (*dambun*) was elicited by counsel in repeated exchanges where witnesses were asked what they would do in hypothetical situations: what would happen if a stranger wanted to come and look at this place? (they got to ask me); can you push out the Liyarr mob? (no, they're our relations); what if the Bararungarri people want to come here? (they're welcome); someone from Turkey Creek? (they got to come through me so I can show them around); what would happen if a stranger built a place on your country? (there will be big trouble, we will kick them out) (*Neowarra* 2003: [302]–[304]). Sundberg J writes that 'the only general rule that can be stated is that a "stranger" must always seek permission' (*Neowarra* 2003:

[302]). The rule emerges through a Socratic process of consolidation, articulation and abstraction.

Sundberg J attributes behaviour to rule following because this makes sense in terms of temporal causation and rational choice: the rule comes first and we choose to follow it. We saw in the last chapter that the conscious behaviour of rational actors was core to Hart's distinction between habit and rules; indeed the idea of rule following and normativity depends upon the temporal priority of rules to behaviour. Our critical take on translation, however, would have us complicate the causal chain. Hart also claimed that the internal perspective manifests itself in rules given as reasons for actions or for the criticism of others. Just as an anthropologist can elaborate a social structure that explains peoples' behaviour, rules can articulate why we felt we had to behave in a particular way, and, as Levi-Strauss would have it, perpetuate behavioural phenomena. The articulated rule may not be fabricated or baseless, but it is a reflection on something beyond itself; it is the translation that makes the rule.

The distinction between rules and habit blurs into something perhaps better described as a relation between discourse and a modal 'must',[41] a feeling of obligation, or between discourse and *habitus*, Pierre Bourdieu's term for the practical knowledge of how to act – a bodily competence – in given situations (Bourdieu 1977: 78–82). The old ladies who muttered disapprovingly when counsel said the wrong name during the hearing might have been thinking of a rule, or they might have reacted instinctively because it felt wrong. Whether it is Hart's officials articulating the rule of recognition based on the unspoken conventions of legal practice, or Ngarinyin invoking the Dreaming to explain local marriages, both are referential practices not indexing the content of law as 'rules' but pointing elsewhere to the inexpressible modal must.

We have some insight here into how translation was and is central to the growth of positive law as the dominant form of law. As Marianne Constable (1994) explains in speculating on the origins of law in Norman England (82–90), in any situation of conquest, there is a dislocation between the shared knowledge of 'what we do around here' – the *habitus* – of the victor and the vanquished. The conquerors wish to impose their law on those ignorant of it; they must enunciate that law in ways capable of being followed, hence the necessity for positive principles or rules. The conquered peoples wish to claim recognition of their law; they must articulate it likewise. It is when this articulation becomes considered as a translation that the original 'text' comes into existence: the original customary law is thus a back-formation of its explanation to others.

This pattern is, I think, more ubiquitous. On smaller scales, and in more everyday situations, claims are made, principles spelt out and stories told when a challenge is made to what we do or believe we should do. Law is neither the unconscious 'before' (Hart's 'habit') nor the constructed 'after', but the interdependence of

41 The expression comes from Elizabeth Povinelli's (2002) discussion of the representation of the Dreaming in Western legal processes (254–62).

the two. The same relationship applies to other kinds of 'befores', a different language, another form of expression. Following on from the speech act theory used by Constable and discussed in the previous chapter, positive legal forms emerge in the need to communicate explicitly to strangers, but the resources for building these structures are the lived, accumulated, and perhaps unconscious, social conditions of the actors. The generation of this law is inherently hybrid, it is the product of encounter and difference, as Jeremy Webber (1995) has argued in documenting the emergence of a 'normative community' between the Aboriginal peoples and colonists in Canada. There is no separate sphere of Indigenous law as fact and common law as law. People create patterned practices, make arguments which gain legitimacy, develop expectations as to the behaviour of others, and tell stories that make sense of all these things, in interaction with others.

In Australia, some have observed in these discursive interactions a kind of reverse mimesis, where legal categories that are supposed to be translations of Indigenous life in turn become hegemonic discourses that structure or consolidate Indigenous social relations (Povinelli 2002: 3; Merlan 1998: 150). Simon Correy (2006), for instance, argues that prior to the *Mabo* decision, there was a shared history of dispossession and forced migration among Aboriginal people in New South Wales revealed in rhetorical appeals to solidarity and a loose identification of groups centred on residence and extended family. The advent of native title problematized social reality for Aboriginal people in NSW, who can no longer take their intersubjective relations for granted given the appearance of a process that demarcates social reality and provides certain social relations – 'traditional owners' or 'biological descent groups' – with specific structural and ideological advantages over others (344–5). In evidentiary hearings, witnesses are urged to articulate and make judgments about their own and others' internal orientation to 'law' and thus to calibrate their perception of their being in the modal language of obligation – should, must – and the causal language of rules.

Indigenous rights regimes have opened social life to reflective self-conscious and critical apprehension; they have caused Indigenous people to develop new theories of themselves (Niezen 2009). More than being mere imitation, the impact of translated terms and new organizational structures can be seen as a kind of social technology that is used to transform social life in inventive ways (Martin 2003: 6). Whatever the importance of a concept of the Wanjina-Wunggurr community to the *Neowarra* claimants before the trial, with the recognition of native title, the 'three tribes' have become a corporate entity that operates in native title's institutional context.

The practitioners of the common law are perhaps not as susceptible to Indigenous representations of courts, evidence, principles and decisions. The effects of translation go both ways, however, as I have argued. The adoption of Aboriginal English expressions such as 'country' and language terms such as *dambun* produce a 'centaur' legal idiom that puts the 'proper' discourse of common law property in a new light. When the state argues for the limitation of recognition to the specific sites that have been visited and cared for in recent times, Sundberg J invokes the importance of Wanjina in connecting sites to larger areas of country through the beliefs of the applicants which is in contrast to the 'pinpricks on a map' that might result from recognition based on common law ideas of use (*Neowarra* 2003: [289]). Suddenly Western property seems overtly Cartesian.

The need to respond to different aspects of the claim and the evidence offered for and against it causes lawyers and judges to articulate the common law in particular ways, to develop theories of the common law in reaction to potentially destabilizing challenges. The process of analysing the normativity of Wanjina community laws and customs provokes an exegesis of what norms and rules are *for the rest of us*. It changes our understanding of normative community. In the choice between two translations of social organization (the two anthropological models), Sundberg J instantiates the democratic ideal of inclusivity in native title when he chooses the umbrella group. In seeking the existence of law in the calibration between behaviour and belief, the judge accepts evidence that not all, especially the young, observe the rules. He invokes the truism that breaches of rules merely serve to prove their existence, and claims that all teenagers are likely to rebel against the ways of their elders, thereby creating a moment of universality across cultures (*Neowarra* 2003: [344]–[345]). As Geertz (1983) has written, the experience of unfamiliar cultures sets off diverging commotions in our minds and brings to the fore our own imaginative concerns (50–54). It would take a closer reading than I have space for here to identify the imaginative concerns of Sundberg J's law completely, but in these brief examples the translations betray his concern for conformity/non-conformity, inclusion/exclusion, sameness/difference and speech/action. In short, in translating other cultures we find our ((re)created) selves.

Conclusion

Both the interpretive model of anthropology and the translation model for the recognition of Indigenous law as fact by the court conjure an objective Indigenous culture as a unified text. What is hidden in these models is the situated and discursive production of 'culture', 'rules', or 'normative systems' (as these named phenomena). Whether through the myriad interactions between ethnographers and informants, or the formal presentation of evidence in court, the coherent text of Indigenous law and culture is produced through communicative acts by (and between) specific persons in particular contexts until what emerges is a generalized 'cultural domain' authored by a generalized 'community'.

What comes to be articulated more widely as Indigenous law and culture, and the arguments made which reflect a normative universe, is the product of discursive relations over time between Indigenous peoples and a range of representatives of settler society, from missionaries and anthropologists to government agencies and lawyers. Recognition through translation then implies more than affixing a common law 'post-it note' to a fact of Indigenous law: it is a productive moment for both sides. As with literature, it is the reading that makes a text into a unity. As with literary translation, it is the necessary rapport between original and translation, the reading in relation to the other, that brings to each language a new awareness of *itself*. This interaction affects law at the level of the imagination, changes our capacity to understand what law can be and thus makes it become something else.

In *Neowarra*, a translation is produced in which a group of people can be recognized as having exclusive possession over an area of land. The complex negotiations that produced this seamless text are mostly hidden from view, but occasionally we witness the courtroom as an ethnographic event in which court personnel are interacting with the claimants, interpreting practices and constructing cultural mosaics. We see witnesses choose their responses in terms of what the 'court's law people' indicate they are able to understand and accept. We have briefly considered the relation between the spoken and the unspoken, and the ability of the judicial text as a material object to structure what witnesses say and do into laws and customs through its organization. The next chapter will take up an analysis of some supplementary forms of evidence that cannot be reduced to textual representations, focusing on the impact of holding hearings 'on country' and the use of painting as proof. In those things that escape translation, those things that remain utterly other, I will argue that the pluralism of native title is realized. Facing the inadequacy of translation, the translator lives the fact of the 'irreducible outness' (William James, quoted in Davies 2005: 94) of another law.

Chapter 5

Proof: The *Ngurrara Canvas*

Introduction: 'Walking All Over Their Painting'

On the front cover of the *Oxford Companion to Aboriginal Art and Culture* an Indigenous man in a red loincloth appears dancing on a brightly coloured canvas (Kleinert and Neale 2000). He is dwarfed by the size of the painting, and is doubly lost amid the 'riotous colour', the lines, circles and swirls of his platform, the *Ngurrara Canvas II*. The man is Nyilpin Spider Snell, an artist from the Kimberley/ Great Sandy Desert region in the north of Western Australia, performing the *kurtal* or snake dreaming dance in Canberra to 'remind those sitting on the High Court of the depth of [his peoples'] claim' (Winter 2002: 6) In this chapter I will use the meaningfulness of this painting as evidence of Indigenous title to support my argument that legal pluralism involves a dynamic learning process about law in which there are multiple teachers and multiple students.

Indigenous peoples have long been making legal claims in their own forms – title deeds in song (Koch 2013), treaty ceremonies (Pomedli 1995), wampum belts (Wicken 2002: 89–93), petitions adapted from traditional art forms (de Costa 2006a) – and some contemporary courts around the world have accepted that 'alternative' forms of proof related to Indigenous oral cultures are admissible in evidence (*Pueblo De Zia* 1962: 505, *Van Der Peet* 1996: [68], *Svartskog* 2001, Parsonson 2001). But while oral narratives, paintings, dances, and site visits are taken at first to be simply new kinds of proof, they turn out to be a locus for opening up larger questions about the nature of truth and what it is that is being proven.

The *Ngurrara Canvas* is a collaboration involving around 50 artists, produced when the Walmajarri, Wangkajunga, Mangala and Juwaliny peoples were asked to prepare a map of their traditional area to support a native title claim. They decided that each person would paint a section that represents their own areas of responsibility on the land and in lore. The result, although not employing cartographic conventions, is described as a map: it shows the freshwater holes (*jila*) and other sites in the desert in spiritual and physical relation to each other, and also represents the relationships between the painters themselves (Chance 2001: 28–40). In giving evidence about the connection of the claimants to the land during a plenary session[1] before the National Native Title Tribunal in 1997, each

1 Claimants have to pass an initial registration test with the Tribunal, demonstrating that there is sufficient factual basis for the claim: Native Title Act 1993 (Cth) s. 190 B(5).

witness stood on their respective portion of the canvas and recounted the stories associated with it.

But what exactly does a painting prove? One painter described the importance of the *Ngurrara Canvas* as follows:

> I believe that [native title] is about blackfella law. The painting is only for proof. When I go to court to tell my story, I must listen very carefully before I open my mouth. Maybe the *kartiya*[2] will say, 'We don't believe you' ... That's why we made this painting, for evidence. We have painted our story for native title people, as proof. We want them to understand, so that they know about our painting, our country, our ngurrara. They are all the same thing (Ngarralja Tommy May in Chance 2001: 38).

In one respect, the painting is seen as a way to communicate knowledge to non-Aboriginal people and to the courts. Proof of knowledge about country and traditional law is the measure of entitlement under the Native Title Act. But the knowledge of which Ngarralja Tommy May speaks is not something the painting 'points to'. This would be the conventional understanding that evidence is something that testifies to the external real world of facts. The painting is the country, we are told: 'They are all the same thing'. This statement suggests that evidence about traditional knowledge is itself evidence of a different way of knowing. The painting is powerful because in proving a different kind of title from that familiar to the common law, it engages in the very question of what entitlement is. The painting is not just a fact about law; it is law.

Second, the painting is seen to address the need for credibility in making a claim, the need to appear truthful. The relation of truth to evidence in Western law is complicated. While the function of evidence is to elicit the facts, where facts are taken to correspond directly to an external reality, the court usually has before it only some form of statement that the facts claimed are true. Evidence is then what allows the court to increase or decrease the weight of probability in assessing that a claim is true. This might include evidence about the character of a witness in order to infer the likelihood that they are making truthful statements. Assessments of credibility are also likely to be influenced by more subtle cultural indicators such as dress and manner (Timony 2000). So what is it about a painting that could show the credibility of a witness? Do paintings have their own truth?

Third, the painting is described as representing a map of the claimants' country.[3] Maps of the more conventional variety have been central to Indigenous title claims, as they have been central to the development of modern land law, and to the project of colonization in general. Boaventura de Sousa Santos (1987)

2 White people.

3 Aboriginal paintings from other regions have also been described as geographic maps: for example Pintupi Western Desert acrylic dot paintings (Myers 2002) and Yolngu bark painting in Arnhem Land (Morphy 1998).

has written that both maps and law make claims to authoritatively represent reality. The use of such a painting in evidence may undermine the exclusivity of both Western cartography and Western law because it suggests that in order to recognize a different kind of title, state law might also have to consider a different way of conceiving of entitlement and representing the land. It thus underscores the multiple dimensions of any development in the law and the interdependency of law on other ways of knowing. The painting may well act as a kind of map in the claimants' case, but it does more than just indicate the geographic parameters of the claim or describe a parcel of land. It makes a claim about the basis for entitlement and the manner in which it can be proved that resists reduction to a set of rights and interests over a bounded territory.

Thus in this chapter I will disassemble the painting's function along three axes, all of which see it targeting a particular orthodoxy in the common law and pushing towards a realization of the transformative and plural character of evidentiary practices in native title. I first take up the claim that the *Ngurrara Canvas* is law. Although subordinated to the category of 'fact', the painting must be taken on its own terms in order for it to be meaningful as proof, which means accepting a very different person–place relation as the basis for entitlement and the point that, for the claimants, the painting embodies the law. The most obvious challenge posed here is to the idea of the state as the sole source of law, but other assumed attributes of law – that it consists of public, verifiable and positive statements of principle, for example – are also resisted.

Next, I will argue that the painting makes a claim to credibility that confronts conventional legal understandings of truth because it operates aesthetically, rhetorically and therefore a-rationally. Finally, I will consider that to read the painting as a map entails a challenge to the European valuation of land, the way it is thought and depicted. Where maps have historically colluded with property law in order to communicate a particular mode of entitlement, the canvas insists on disrupting the universality of this vision. In all three instances, there is a strong normative aspect to the canvas, an argument about how to see the world, which is missed in a conventional reading of it as something purely factual, purely aesthetic or purely cartographic. I will show that it is this much larger challenge that must be met if Australian law is to reject *terra nullius*, as the recognition of native title in *Mabo* (1992) purported to do.

The *Ngurrara Canvas* operates in a number of frames.[4] It contains designs that originate in body and ground painting associated with traditional ceremonies and law, but it is transposed onto the Western format of a flat canvas and in acrylic paint of a much wider palette than was earlier available. It is not a map of the claim area in the conventional sense anticipated by National Native Title Tribunal personnel, and yet it is comprehensible as such in the context of a growing public

4 My intellectual debt here is to Howard Morphy's (1991) image of the frame in relation to Yolngu art and Richard Mohr's (2002) analysis of change and continuity in law with frames as a semiotic device.

awareness of the way Indigenous art can represent traditional relationships to 'country'. It articulates a claim in a language alien to the rational legal discourse of the court, and yet it can still have rhetorical power: '[i]t was, one tribunal member said, the most eloquent and overwhelming evidence that had ever been produced [in the tribunal]. The Aborigines could proceed to court' (Brooks 2003).

Ngurrara as Law

Indigenous Law as 'Fact' in Native Title

Among other things, the Walmajarri, Wangkajunga, Mangala and Juwaliny groups had to prove they had a connection to the area claimed under traditional laws acknowledged and traditional customs observed by them (Native Title Act 1993: s. 223 W). In *Mabo*, Justice Brennan had written that the content of 'native title must be ascertained as a matter of fact by reference to those laws and customs' ([64]). The existence of Indigenous law is a necessary, although insufficient, condition for the recognition of native title (*Fejo* 1998: [46]). As we saw in Chapter 3, the High Court stressed in the *Yorta Yorta* (2002) case that claimants would have to demonstrate that they continue to practise traditional laws as laws and not, for example, as a mere community narrative of what used to happen (Gleeson CJ, Gummow and Hayne JJ: [30]–[42], Callinan J: [185]). Evidence for native title thus consists of claimants' knowledge about traditional laws as well as proof that these laws are still followed. And yet, the status of the state as the sole source of law in Australia is consistently affirmed in native title jurisprudence (*Yarmirr* 2001: [115]; *Yorta Yorta* 2002, Gleeson CJ and Gummow and Hayne JJ: [43]). The puzzle in which legal pluralism is at once required and denied is solved, in the court's logic, by relegating Indigenous law to the domain of fact.

As with Aboriginal rights in Canada, the reference to Indigenous laws and customs is indicative of the court's *sui generis* characterization of native title: it is not bound to European conceptions of property, but has its own character (*Mabo* 1992, Brennan J: [49]–[50], Deane and Gaudron JJ: [63], [84]; *Delgamuukw* 1997: [114]). The ability of this character to be determined by Aboriginal laws and customs is limited, though, because native title is strictly a proprietary right, and is always subject to the overriding authority of the common law. Thus, in *Ward* (2002), recognizing native title is said to involve the translation of a broad Indigenous spiritual relationship to land into proprietary rights and interests (15). As the previous chapter has demonstrated, 'the facts of Indigenous law' are ascertained by collating and abstracting rules, beliefs and social phenomena out of what people say and do. Evidence about asking permission to enter a certain territory, for example, is indexed to a rational principle – a rule that a certain person has the right to exclude others – and the qualities of longevity, widespread acceptance and obligation revealed by the witnesses give the practice the 'necessary' normative or rule-like character according to European observers.[5] Indigenous law as fact precludes any threat to the state's monopoly over sovereignty. Likewise, it leaves unchallenged the idea of law as a discrete body of rules, or the idea of entitlement as arising from rules regulating the use of land.

Different Evidence and Evidence of Difference

In contrast, the procedures for proving native title, as they have evolved under the Native Title Act and in Federal Court practice, seem to augur transformation: a 'profound shift' (in the words of Court Registrar Louise Anderson) in the common law. Native title is said to challenge 'the Court, the parties, and the broader Australian community to reconsider fundamental questions such as Australia's history, concepts of ownership, time, spirituality, and even the content of truth itself' (Anderson 2003: 124). Through s. 82 of the Native Title Act and changes to the Federal Court Rules, court procedures have been adapted to take account of cultural concerns of Indigenous claimants that differ somewhat from the preoccupations and standard practices of the common law. For instance, Rule 34.122 (formerly Order 78(ii)) of the Federal Court Rules suggests that evidence about customary law may be given 'by way of singing, dancing, story telling or in any other way than in the normal course of giving evidence'. It is often through the difficulties encountered in the process of obtaining and seeking to understand evidence that primary judges encounter differences in 'fundamental questions' that a fuller treatment of native title as the recognition of difference would have them take into account.

The following four qualities of knowledge have attracted commentary in the context of native title.

> *Propositional logic*: while the examination of witnesses often uses propositional logic to produce contradictions in witness statements and thereby conclude that only X or Y can be true, anthropologists have reported a lack of concern among some Aboriginal speakers with apparent contradictions (*Lardil Peoples v State of Queensland* 2004: [71]).[6] The point of contrast is the degree to which statements must be taken as context dependent; removed from that context, two 'truths' may contain contradictory propositions. Other differences between Aboriginal and standard English, speech styles, and modes of questioning are commented on by Neate (2003) and Eades (1988).
>
> *Written as opposed to oral knowledge*: although s. 82 of the Native Title Act permits the court to waive rules of evidence, such as hearsay, so that the oral nature of Indigenous tradition can be accommodated, there is an

5 See *Lardil, Kaiadilt, Yangkaal & Gangalidda Peoples v State of Queensland* 2000: [76].
6 See *The Lardil Peoples v State of Queensland* 2004: [71].

inherent bias towards the credibility of the written word (Kerruish and Perrin 1999; Reilly 2000).

Open as opposed to closed information values: the trial process is premised on the optimum availability of facts, and Western political cultures place a high value on information as a public good. Commonly, the accessibility of knowledge in Australian Aboriginal cultures is highly selective and dependent on age, sex and spiritual affiliation. Details about peoples' connections to places, which are the focus of proof in native title, are the very facts most likely to be highly secret. Court practices have been adapted to some degree in trying to respect (particularly the gender aspects of) restricted knowledge or 'secret business' (McIntyre and Bagshaw 2002).

Abstract or universal knowledge as opposed to highly particularized knowledge grounded in places and rituals: Aboriginal 'country' is literally the basis of knowledge and authority for Indigenous claimants. There is a metonymic association between following the law, walking the country, and doing ceremony such as singing, dancing or painting the country. Evidence in native title is often given in 'on country' hearings in recognition of the inability of some claimants to speak about country without it being beneath their feet (Trees 2002).

These points of contrast (crudely drawn) in thinking and being problematize the project of translation that evidence purports to be achieving. The common law has carefully restricted native title to proprietary rights. However, once traditional laws and customs become a reference point, the practice of claiming native title soon causes those attempting to identify proprietary rights to engage with the tangled cosmos of ideas of which property is a part. Ways of knowing are directly implicated in what something (a painting, an account of hunting and fishing, a Dreaming story) is evidence of and why.

We can examine more closely how the *Ngurrara Canvas* works as fact in the Walmajarri and Wangkajunga peoples' claim. From a close viewpoint the painting is made up of abstract components – concentric circles, dots, arcs and lines – which the claimants identify with physical, geographic locations, as well as the occasional figure – a tree or a *kurtal* dancer. That the painters talk about 'getting the boundaries right' between sections of the painting, that the other side 'is not my place' (Ngarralja Tommy May, in Chance 2001: 35, 38) makes it sound as if the claimants have differentiated rights of 'access' and 'ownership' across those physical locations, which are fairly readily translatable as proprietary rights. And yet, '[t]here is no grid-like effect to demarcate separation of territories but a blending of adjacent areas, the flow of the painting imitating the flow of peoples' movement through the country and of family connections over space' (Pat Lowe, in Chance 2001: 30).

Throughout Australia, designs were and are used in a number of situations: on rock walls, on bodies during ceremonies, etched or painted onto stone or wooden *tjurunga*,[7] on the ground for ceremonial or simply illustrative purposes. To the south of Ngurrara country, the Walpiri of the Western Desert use sand designs to accompany stories and gossip, so that children learn these markings as an integral part of speech (Munn 1973: 63). Their word *guruwari*[8] expresses the conflation between places, the Dreaming Beings in the creation stories and visual representation: it means both the design and the marks left by ancestors on the ground (Munn 1973: 119). The iconography of *guruwari* also embodies the realm of law, providing a lexicon for the creation of obligations and kinship by the ancestor Beings.

For the Yolngu in the north, Howard Morphy (1998) describes a conflation between bark designs, Dreaming stories and topographical features: bark paintings recount the journeys of the ancestors, shaping the land as they went. Both designs and landforms are 'continuing manifestations' of the activities of the ancestors (218). Consequently, narratives, paintings and related ceremonies about ancestor Beings can be thought to provide a sort of alphabet that allows people to get to know their country, and conversely, to construct and reconstruct the story by reading the country (Schreiner 2007: 195–9).

Ngurrara painter Pijaju Peter Skipper talks about the painting as being both *wangarr* (shadow or image) and *mangi* (essence, spirit or presence) of the land, both a representation of the absent land and an embodiment of it. The land in turn contains 'the stories and the bodies of the old people' (Chance 2001: 33). Each section of the painting simultaneously renders the stories associated with each place. It is these stories to which the entitlement implied by boundaries can be traced. Once the identification of individuals with particular totem ancestors is added, however, the web between individual people and specific places, designs, songs and stories binds them in a relationship of 'ownership' quite unlike the possession of an object held by a subject person, familiar in Western property.

Within Indigenous law, various ceremonies of design creation are often part of a ritual obligation, and transferring those designs to canvas has been seen as a continuity in that obligation, especially where it has been impossible to visit and physically maintain sites (*Neowarra* 2003: [340]–[341], Myers 2002: 16–20). The development of painting for a Western art market has meant that many communities are used to employing art to communicate with a non-Indigenous public and in relation to the goals of recognition, land rights and economic independence, as will be discussed below (Myers 2002: 5–6, Morphy 1998: 16–20). Using painting in an unconventional manner as proof, in order to gain control over traditional country, can be recuperated within the duty frequently voiced as the obligation to 'care for country' as this latter notion shifts to accommodate new circumstances, and so the execution of the painting itself is also a manifestation of people continuing to follow the law.

7 Sacred object, in Arrernte language around Alice Springs (Pannel 1994).

8 A type of men's ceremony and corresponding designs.

In the logic of native title, the 'tradition' of designs, boundaries and Dreaming stories is the frame of reference that gives a painting value as evidence. Designs originating in sand, rock, bark and body painting embody relationships between ancestors and law, living people and places in the land, which make them crucially relevant to what is being translated in native title as property rights. In evidence, the painting illustrates the rights (such as those indicated by boundaries) and the origin of those rights in a system of law (such as Dreaming stories), and facilitates the oral evidence of the witnesses. The very production of the painting lends proof, following *Yorta Yorta*, that these people not only hold the requisite knowledge about their country, but continue to practise it as law. The painting succeeds in proving this in large part because, according to the painters' ways of seeing things, the designs are so intricately bound up in the land that 'they are the same thing', that walking on the painting 'brings [the] country up closer' (Chance 2001: 40).

But the significance of the painting relating to proof of title has to be decoded. It is, aside from reflecting general characteristics of Aboriginal acrylic painting already familiar in contemporary Australia, opaque to uninitiated non-Indigenous peoples. As for any other translation, the grammar and idiom of this code have to be respected and followed in order to render it legible. Its norms have to be taken seriously. How else does a dot establish a title, than if the law binding that dot to a whole conceptual universe is followed as a principle of interpretation – as a law? In native title doctrine, Indigenous law is not 'law' in any normatively significant way for the court. But because of the need to translate, to take seriously what Indigenous law 'is', the 'fact' category, like the 'property' category, is a leaky one. For one moment, non-Indigenous triers of fact have to suspend their disbelief and put to one side their knowledge of how the world works and interpret it through other principles. The canvas is law because it participates in an interpretation of a normative relationship and does not simply represent a physical fact. To understand that the painting is *wangarr* and *mangi*, to understand what it is that the painting 'says' about a witness's rights and connection to country, observers have to submit to the painting's normative vision of how the world ought to be: that we all have an obligation to follow the law in the land.

Ngurrara as Truth

There is one further hurdle of disbelief that the claimants face, however: this is not about the difference of the evidence in itself, but its authenticity. Like Ngarralja Tommy May, other painters are confident of the ability of the *Ngurrara Canvas* to convince *kartiya* of the truth of their peoples' claim.[9] For the court or the tribunal, the truth of the claim will come down to the authenticity of what is presented as traditional laws and customs connecting the claimants to the land. How is it possible for the canvas to do this work?

9 See also ABC Radio National 1997.

The Normal Course of Evidence in the Common Law

In the conventional view of law, evidence is the process by which the facts of the case are brought before the judge or jury so that they may establish what happened. Once facts are characterized, the relevant legal principle will then be applied in order to produce the decision of the case. The assumptions of what William Twining (1985) calls the 'rationalist tradition' of evidence scholarship, implicit in most contemporary work on evidence, are that events and facts have an existence independent of human observation, that true statements correspond with facts, and that present knowledge about past events is theoretically possible, if typically incomplete (12–14). Although in practice we can never perfectly establish the truth of a statement of fact, we can filter the process through the rules of admissibility, so that only evidence that tends to increase or decrease the probability that a statement of fact is true is allowed to be introduced. This includes details suggestive of whether the witness is being truthful or otherwise; that is, their credibility.

The 'normal course of evidence' is taken as a reasoned process of revealing the world through the senses of the witness or the court itself, via eyewitness or expert testimony, documentation or exhibited objects. These either constitute the 'fact' in question itself (the witness saw the accused stab the victim) or by inference attest to the occurrence of the fact in question (the witness saw the accused running away from the victim with a bloodied knife in hand). A brief survey of contemporary texts on evidence indicates that there are few challenges to this paradigm (Cross and Tapper 1985: 16–37; Ligertwood 1993; 4, Howard 2000: 2). Peter Murphy (1995), for instance, admits that 'facts' in court are a matter of what the court can be persuaded to believe rather than what is true, but proceeds as if this process of persuasion is non-contentious or uninteresting (1–16).

And yet, as evidence is a matter of persuasion, it is never a purely 'rational' exercise. Whether facts are true or relevant to the question on trial, or can be inferred from other facts, depends on the experience or intuition of the trier of fact. Persuasion takes place by rhetorical and emotional means as well as by 'logic', as practitioners are well aware. But the challenge that these points pose for the rationalist tradition is more than just an admission of some extra factors added to a core of facts, or a suspicion that the work of most litigators lies in manipulating the trier of fact into arriving at the judgment that will suit their client. None of this challenges the proposition that the truth is 'out there'. The relevance of outlook and experience, however, goes also to the heart of the concepts of logic, rationality and knowledge itself, as feminist and critical race scholars have argued: our background, values and experience affect not only what we know, but how we know.[10]

Critical legal scholars have likewise argued that the process of judgment in court is neither rational nor determinate, and that both facts and law are highly constructed, dependent on language, reasoning and discourse for their

10 See Alcoff and Potter 1993; Delgado 1995; Harmon 1999; Nicholson 2000.

representation.[11] Consequently, 'the legal representation of fact is normative from the start' and is telling of a particular way of imagining the world (Geertz 1983: 174). The fallacy of the correspondence theory of facts (where statements are considered to correspond directly to aspects of or events in the real world that exist apart from human discourse) is hinted at by the vernacular of practitioners who often speak of the narrative 'coherence' of evidence as a test for the plausibility of that evidence (Twining 1985: 183; Jackson 1988). How we assess the truthfulness of a story depends on how well it 'hangs together', and this relies in turn on cultural experience with styles of narrative. Playing on standard stories also has the effect of pre-empting judgment. For example, if a woman can be cast successfully as a damsel in distress, or a wicked stepmother, we can guess whether the decision will be in her favour or not.[12]

Other scholars point to the integral role our senses play in the way we respond to law; that it is sometimes the aesthetics of legal drama and discourse that makes certain decisions possible. For example, Desmond Manderson (2000) argues that it was the visual impact of the scarred body of the plaintiff in *Natanson v Kline* (1960), her heart beating visibly through ribs damaged by radiation in a mastectomy procedure, that led to a new legal principle of informed consent, when those before her had failed in similar claims (41). The aesthetics of a body, or a painting, or a legal judgment, imply a moral standard. Likewise, they demand a moral judgment.

Perceiving evidence as rhetorical, narrative, aesthetic and normative puts paid to the premises of the rationalist tradition. Instead, the hearing of evidence produces a sort of translation of what is taken to be the 'real world' – other places and other times – into the terms of law; it renders a world in which law's principles make sense. In the process it establishes both the separation of law from society and its mastery over society. The translation and the constitution of the law/world hierarchy is a play which is dramatized in various ways – the architecture and dress of the court, the presentation of witnesses, exhibits, experts and documents.

Conventionally, however, for all the symbolic significance of wigs and gowns in evoking the majesty of the law, and the historical origins of the forms of court order, these aspects of law are mostly considered to be little more than window dressing, peripheral to the substance of either law or fact (Haldar 1994: 188). But the window's frame, like the frame on a painting, plays a role that is not merely extraneous. It constitutes the object, says what is inside and out, is at once a part of the scene while seeming external to it. It tells us, in both legal and aesthetic terms, what is available for judgment (Derrida 1987a: 57).

The frame here is more than just the interpretive context of a 'frame of reference'; it has the sense of selection, delimitation and constitution. The frame as an analytic device is bound up in the philosophical question of 'the limit'. In distinguishing between a thing and what it is not – a painting from

11 See Hutchinson and Monahan 1984.

12 See Sarmas 1994.

the wall, an object of beauty as opposed to its ornamentation, fact from law, law from everything else – there is a question of what happens at the border (the limit) between the thing and the not-thing. A frame (*parergon*) does the job of maintaining this limit; it 'delimits' the subject (work, *ergon*) captured within it. But the status of the *parergon* as neither inside or outside, and yet maintaining the inside from the outside, makes it a paradox. In order to imagine how the *parergon* operates, Jacques Derrida, in *The Truth in Painting* (1987), denotes the frame structurally with the figure of a laced boot (from Van Gogh's painting, *Boots with Laces*): it laces the edges together by passing through them in a repeated and reversible movement, from outside to inside, from under to over. A frame thus 'cuts out but also sews back together. By an invisible lace which pierces the canvas … passes into it then out of it in order to sew it back onto its milieu, its internal and external worlds' (304).

Consequently, when the courtroom, the gavel, the leather bound law report say 'what passes by me is the law' they are neither superfluous, nor quarantining the law off from the world, but are rather performing this lacing role. It is by virtue of the law's frame that the outside becomes represented in the *ergon*, that scraps of the world, 'footprints, fingerprints, chance memories captured by a witness', come to correspond to 'the "whole truth and nothing but the truth" of an event' once brought within the walls of the court (Haldar 1994: 192). In native title cases, some of these frames help constitute the world for the court: a microphone in a bush hearing turns a person into a witness, a piece of canvas makes *ngurrara* into a map, a loincloth signifies Aboriginality. Frames are the means by which things become what they are. The two senses of frame – *ergon* and frame of reference – are related, for something does not become a 'thing' to be interpreted until it has been framed 'off' from everything else. Each framing then also implies a frame of reference, a weaving between the thing and its context.

The Painting as Supplementary Evidence

The positivist paradigm for evidence would take paintings, dances, songs and pitching the court in a desert riverbed to visit country, as merely novel ways to introduce facts about Indigenous rights and interests in land into evidence. But how are these 'facts' communicated? Without further explanation, a man dancing on a canvas does not immediately say much to a court. An explanation can indicate the significance of the dance, the song, and the iconography to the facts at issue: how the claimants are connected to the land and what their rights are over it. But then, as far as the court is concerned, what does the painting add to the explanation? The presentation of cultural evidence communicates in ways supplementary to the facts proper: by appeal to the senses through colour and rhythm, a sense of space and a smell of dust; and by referents in intercultural knowledge between Indigenous and colonial cultures. Does it *look* like an authentic demonstration of Aboriginal law and culture? Does this man seem to know how to move about the canvas in an Aboriginal way? Does it tell the story that the court needs to hear?

For the court, evidence will be judged credible if it gels with expectations of authentic culture (the 'feel' and the 'look') and if the witnesses display 'genuine' knowledge in their testimony. For this, any observer will rely on a repertoire of cultural precedents, among them a likely awareness of paintings as a particularly high-profile site for debates about authenticity and Indigenous culture in recent decades. The use of acrylic colours to paint Dreaming designs on boards for sale emerged in Papunya (in the Central Desert) in the 1970s. With support from the government under the new policy of self-determination, and interest from painters for whom commercial values complimented their own views of the paintings as culturally 'dear', a modest market developed in 'Aboriginal acrylic paintings'. While Indigenous artefacts had earlier held only ethnographic interest for Western audiences (Short 1991: 218; Morphy 1991: 22), they now represent a category of 'fine art' in galleries the world over (Myers 2002: 64).

The appeal of these paintings to a Western public has been multifaceted. In Australia, a new 'national consciousness' led people to formulate Aboriginal culture as distinctive of a uniquely Australian identity that was significantly linked to its land. Internationally, responses to Aboriginal art were themed around an interest in 'the Other' and a nostalgia for place and spirituality, a 'conceptual return to our lost ("primitive") selves' (Myers 2002: 283–6). While acrylic paintings represented an idea of Aboriginal authenticity, however, debates raged around the negative effects of commercialization and industry on the 'traditional' nature, and therefore the value, of such art. On the other hand, it seems that despite the use of new materials and the influence of advisors in tailoring work for a market with particular visual expectations (Myers 2002: 284, 289), the paintings continue to hold the layered significance of designs that were previously painted on bodies, objects and in the sand, to enact stories from the Dreaming and the geographical places belonging to the painter.

This is what interests the court – that something traditional 'is there' in the painting. But like most work in galleries, acrylic paintings are intercultural objects, produced out of a complex of government policy, the consumer market, art criticism and land claims as well as distinctly Indigenous purposes. Non-Indigenous ideas of 'pure tradition' are in themselves hybrid events, products of the colonial encounter and textually mediated efforts to explain the inexplicable. The *Ngurrara Canvas* has a specifically contemporary purpose, but is also continuous with an inherited mandate to look after country; it is not a 'title deed' and represents something quite different to 'property', and yet, if reiterated over time, it can come to be understood in those terms because property and title deed will *themselves* undergo a semiotic shift (Mohr 2002: 13).

So the world of facts in native title does not exist 'out there'; it is created for the court by the supplementary evidence in the physical and aesthetic being of the painting or other evidence. In the *Neowarra* example from the previous chapter, a principle of exclusive possession comes into being when, through the event of oral questioning, someone articulates what they do when asking permission. The manifestation of Ngurrara/country in the canvas brings the claimants' law into the terms of the law of the court at the same time as it marks a distinction between the two. More than pointing out that the painting convinces us of the truth of its object because it matches stereotypes of cultural authenticity, I am arguing that the 'excluded supplement' of the common law proper, whether a-rationality and aesthetics in the question of proof, or Indigenous law in the question of sovereignty, always makes a return and so effects a transformation on what is proper to the law. The general point here is that the recognition of native title is not the application of a label (property) to an external phenomenon (Indigenous law) by an unassailable common law. What is there in evidence is mixed up in the exigencies of proof: all law becomes articulated and made present in certain ways in response to a challenge by an interlocutor or a need to explain and justify and so is intrinsically hybrid.

In stating that the 'facts' of Indigenous culture and law do not exist in any objective way for the court, I do not mean that giving evidence is meaningless, or that evidence is a chimera. Giving evidence is a practice itself, meaningful, for example, in terms of obligations to care for country or to represent Dreaming relations in pictorial form. It is also a practice for *kartiya*, one that constitutes spaces and relationships in particular ways and one that is required to transform law into a concrete experience (Tait 1999). But just as personal experience and intuition are brought to bear in judging the truth of evidence, so new evidence teaches us new ways to read and judge the truth of evidence, forming restructured understandings that are carried over into our approach to the next case and so on.

The pedagogic potential of proof seems to be particularly dramatic when the court hears evidence given 'on country'. If, in the usual environment of the courtroom, symbols and practices work to consolidate the power and authority of Western law, then being a visitor on, for example, Walmajarri homeland potentially destabilizes that frame of reference by immersing the court in another world. If evidence is the law's way of framing the world to make it available for judgment, then the intercultural frames of a native title hearing push towards the possibility of other views on the world and other sorts of judgments. Like the canvas, the hearing on country does not just depict boundaries and rights in land, but *why* land matters: it demonstrates what land is and why particular relationships are sought to be protected, and effects a transformation in understandings of property. A closer reading of the *Ngurrara Canvas* as a map of country will provide one example.

Ngurrara as Map

Through the approximations I ascribed to Indigenous visual culture above – iconography, representation of topography, lexicon – the common reference to paintings as maps is understandable; they both encode the land. Within the native title frame, paintings can thus be accepted in the role of marking out an area of claim, in the way that a cartographic map would. And yet, unlike a topographical map, it would be useless to an uninitiated person trying to find their way, for the map and the canvas are premised on incongruent ways of reading the land. The question I wish to address here is what this habit of reading has to do with entitlement to property.

Cartography and the Common Law

In addition to the principles of proof discussed above, property has its own requirements. In the Torrens system of land titles now operating in Australia, proof of title depends on establishing that the person claiming title is the person who is registered as the proprietor of an interest on the register of the state or territory-wide Land Titles Office (or equivalent).[13] This system is the apotheosis of a long process of the 'dephysicalization' (Vanderveld 1980: 329) of real property in the common law, where title to land was gradually, and now almost completely, removed from material events on the land.[14]

In spite of this development, the common law presupposes a resource of memory. In medieval and preliterate times, where the performance of rituals such as turning turf or exchanging objects marked the conveyance of land to a new owner, the objects worked as a guarantee of title 'only because they were fixed as reference points within a medieval art of recollection, which recorded cultural events by associating them metaphorically or metonymically with things and their images' (Pottage 1994: 361). So the functional locus of title was in the local knowledge about boundaries and transfers; the ritual of transfer merely underlined the accumulated practice of neighbours and past owners as to who held what rights and where.

The advent of cartography eventually facilitated the removal of property from local knowledge onto a more abstract domain, first of the paper title, and more recently, of the register. In a more rapidly changing social, political and economic context, individual memories could no longer give certainty. Increased communication led to a perception of local spaces as parts of a whole, matched by the increased availability of maps, which placed land onto a homogenizing linear grid. Industrialization led to a growth in urban areas and rapid changes in topography that confused and outstripped local memory, at the same time creating the need for, and perception of, land as a commodity. Proof of title in the common law context is thus dominated by a logic of interchangeability and abstraction. Every time we use the title system, we bring that logic into being as a (naturalized) way of perceiving land.

Native title evidence is introduced into this frame of reference. Memory and practice as a resource in proving title is at once deeply familiar and pointedly forgotten in modern property. It is easy to accept that a painting stands in for memory in the same way as a title deed (or the register) does for common law

13 As long as no exceptions to the indefeasibility of title apply: for example, Real Property Act 1900 (NSW), s. 42.

14 Some rare exceptions include the doctrine of adverse possession, and the provision of easements by prescription.

property, while overlooking the performative, constitutive role that earlier rituals actually played and that the technology of title continues to play, and so missing the subtleties of what native title is performing and bringing into being.

In Australia, the same disciplines of cartography and property that in England facilitated industrialization worked in concert to offer up a vision of a land available for acquisition. The commodification of space was the text and the pre-text of colonization. Since its inception in the European imagination,[15] *Terra Australis* was represented cartographically as a blank space within the initially vague outlines of its coast (Ryan 1996: 115–17). The impression of collusion between this and the legal doctrine of *terra nullius*, a legal blank space, is hard to avoid. Once physical colonization of Australia began, representations of its landscape in the sketches and journals of early explorers followed a similar trope. The monotonous, undifferentiated mass of land in the interior resisted being read, for example, for signs of water, in the way that 'normal' landscape could be read.[16] Landscape also became monotonous because of the imperative to move through space in exploration: the apparent absence of geographical 'milestones' frustrated an explorer's desire to sense progress and direction (Carter 1988: 27).

New maps inscribed colonial qualities over Indigenous (unreadable) ones: the blankness was marked by features of European creation: fences, houses, roads. Locations were, and are, specified through coordinates of latitude and longitude that take Greenwich, London – the heart of the British Empire – as their point of reference (Reilly 2003: 3). Indigenous place names were laid over with names bestowed by explorers who created a landscape in the act of naming. Names reference the imperial act of possession or the experience of exploration itself: Victoria, Queensland, Cape Tribulation, Lake Disappointment.

In an attempt to manage the vastness and unfamiliarity of the land, both written accounts and early landscape painting made use of the comforting European ideals of the 'picturesque', an aesthetic in which the land appears as a scene arranged for the viewer – vivid green foliage, ornamental avenues of trees and the like – and, moreover, as naturally awaiting the arrival of sheep and cattle (Appleton 1975: 25–39; Ryan 1996: 74–6). Rightfully enjoying the view facilitates a sense of rightfully enjoying ownership. Kooris,[17] when present, were corralled by the 'picturesque' as part of the scenery – they belonged to the known rather than existing as knowers (or owners) themselves and so did not disturb the fantasy of *terra nullius*.

Although native title is a form of land ownership that in some sense operates outside the grid of registration, it is in another sense incorporated into the same

15 Pythagoras devised a concept of a southern landmass counterbalancing the northern one in the fifth century BC, and a *Terra Australis* appeared on the medieval *mappae mundi* (Eisler 1995: 8–11).

16 A similar experience was had by European settlers of the Canadian prairies, who were at a loss to know how to paint in the 'absence' of scenery (see Rees 1982).

17 As early landscape painting was mainly from areas in the South East, the people depicted were Kooris.

non-Indigenous view of land through the processes of representation used in native title claims. Maps, as Alexander Reilly explains, are everywhere in native title, and '[t]he ability to represent relationships to land and waters cartographically is central to the process' (Reilly 2003: 3). Maps are used to specify the external boundaries of the claim area and the extent of other land tenures,[18] and to indicate the various aspects of the claimants' connection to the country through symbols that represent Dreaming tracks, and other sites of significance to them, alongside the symbols of European settlement, such as roads, fences and homesteads. These maps embody both the possibility of co-existence, and the limitations of the recognition of Indigenous relationships to country, because in being reduced to a singular, unambiguous cartographic discourse, Indigenous spaces are subjected to a deeper process of colonization.

The significance of maps as representations to questions of proof is that they belong to an aesthetic that semiotically communicates entitlement. The act of representing space positions people with respect to the world. Perspectivalism 'helps constitute an apparent divide between the "sovereign eye" of the observer and the space of the "external world"' (Blomley 1998: 575) that makes domination and surveillance possible and natural (Cosgrove 1984: 25). In cartography, even the implicit sense of observation is erased. The flatness of projection is a view from nowhere and the naturalness of this particular vision is perfected. The cartographic aesthetic thus achieves the necessary conditions for ownership: a subject 'eye/I' that can only relate to the objectified land through possession, and a grid of infinitely exchangeable portions. It also excludes other perspectives by creating the illusion that these qualities inhere in the land rather than exist as properties of vision (Bender 1999: 32).

The *Ngurrara Canvas*, on the other hand, has a spatial organization in which there are no portions, only places known and named. If dot paintings can sometimes resemble aerial photographs, they are far more significant for positioning people in, in relation to, and because of, the landscape. Such land could never be a possession; it is more like family. The relationship is one of care and stewardship. The map of country that it paints is full; full of people, history, law, stories, connections, allusions and symbolism.

The *Ngurrara Canvas* is coined as a map because that is the term to which the claimants responded. The analogy also permits the uninitiated to understand the painting as a representation of the relative position of places in the land. But the painting embodies an alternative aesthetic that contests all three aspects of the dominant legality of entitlement: objectification, commodification and exclusion. As a map, the painting is not simply assimilated to the Cartesian worldview, but participates in shifting the terms in which maps are understood. It introduces a multiplicity to the monopoly over vision, a perspective in which people are in, not absent from, the map, and a relationship with land that forms an alternative mode of entitlement. It is an argument for justice in aesthetic terms.

---

18 Required by Native Title Act 1993: s. 62.

To the court, the *Ngurrara Canvas* both represents and demonstrates, through performance, the existence of property rights via matters of entitlement under traditional law. But what the painting represents and performs is something larger than what is forensically captured as the frame of traditional law: Western titles are also performative, and in this intercultural arena, the evidentiary process hosts a shifting conversation about what land (and with it identity and entitlement) can possibly mean, and performs the fact of that plurality. Although not superseding the technical requirement in s. 62 (2) (b) of the Native Title Act that a cadastral map of the claim area be provided – and so never 'officially' a map – *Ngurrara* as map nonetheless puts into relief the fact that land titles are a complex of habits of vision, practices with respect to the world and the methods of representation that link the two. In particular, it is the tension between the painting's aesthetic qualities and the image of the standard map that heightens the sense of fullness and of the abundance of non-assimilated meanings of country and refuses the physical, aesthetic and normative implications of *terra nullius*. It deconstructs the very optical basis for how we see and therefore *what* we see when we look at the land.

Physical Country

If *Ngurrara* is a map, this map also *is* the country. Giving evidence on the painting is the next best thing to standing on the land (Chance 2001: 40). Where physical country is understood to be fully integrated both into an Indigenous notion of law and one of identity, it makes sense that, as Kathryn Trees has explained in relation to the hearings for the Miriuwung-Gajerrong claim, witnesses do not merely feel more comfortable giving evidence on their home country than in the foreign territory of a courtroom (although that is one way of expressing it); their ability and authority to speak about certain places may literally depend on their being physically present (Trees 2002).[19]

The practice of permitting hearings 'on country' seems to go further than merely increasing 'access to the facts' because it contemplates the normative impact upon the witnesses of being on country. Chief Justice Black (2002) of the Federal Court writes that:

> The new practice is a recognition that, for many claimants, their relationship to country is not able to be explained in the abstract, and that it is necessary to be on country to gain a true appreciation and understanding of that relationship and the claimants' evidence about it. It is also an acknowledgment that, under traditional law, some evidence can only be given on country, and that there will be many cases in which it would be quite wrong to expect claimants to talk about their relationship to country by reference to maps prepared by non-indigenous people (18).

19 See also comments by Justice Sackville about the striking 'contrast between the demeanour of witnesses when testifying in the courtroom and when giving evidence more informally on-country' (*Jango v Northern Territory* 2006: [296]).

Under the Native Title Act (s. 82), taking account of the cultural concerns of claimants and witnesses is part of the balancing process of procedural fairness. But is there more at stake? If giving evidence on country is a source of authority for Aboriginal people, is there a conversely unsettling process going on here for the court? How does it affect the processes of law 'for judges to sit in the desert under trees or in tents for 4 – 6 weeks at a time to hear evidence, with limited facilities and very few formalities' (Black 2002: 18)?

The physical site of the court and its surroundings are conventionally seen as extraneous to the operation of law. As we saw, however, this supposed window dressing communicates a great deal about the law, and even makes judgment itself possible. Even in a desert setting the idiom of order familiar in courtroom architecture (Haldar 1994) is apparent in the habits perpetuated: during the Miriuwung-Gajerrong hearing, a picnic table was transformed into a judges' bench with a red cloth; maps and stacks of legal papers reinforced the value of the written word; the judge and the lawyers sat on raised chairs and heard from witnesses while they, too were sitting in chairs rather than on the ground; microphones designated who the court would listen to; the whole arrangement enhanced the position of the judge – the performance was for him, who sat in objective distance from it all (Reilly 1998: 203–5). Sometimes such degrees of formality are even requested, as when the Karajarri community invited the court to robe to reflect the significance of the proceedings for the claimants (Anderson 2003: 135).

There are clues as to how an experience of physical country might affect judgment. Reilly (1998) writes that the court looked uncomfortable in its new setting on the riverbed of Miriuwung-Gajerrong country (205). In *De Rose v State of South Australia* (2002), Justice O'Loughlin mentions six of the thirteen sites visited during the hearing. Unusually for a native title judgment, he gives some brief descriptions of physical aspects of the sites. For instance, the site at Intalka was described as 'a rocky gorge of spectacular beauty, spoilt by the presence of three large rusted water tanks' ([384]). Some of the significance of the places to the claimants was described: where the ancestor Beings had travelled through, places of danger and death and the association of ancestor Beings with physical features of the land was a recurring part of the hearing ([387]).

We can only speculate as to the effect on the trial judge in *De Rose* of travelling round to these various sites with elderly Yankunytjatjara and Pitjantjatjara people, at times obviously impressed by the landscape and the stories associated with it.[20] Perhaps there are some clues to his surprising findings that the claimants had lost their spiritual connection to the place (*De Rose* 2002: [910]–[915), however, from the fact that the claim area comprised a cattle station. Alongside emu eggs transposed into boulders and *tjukurpa*[21] tracks there were fences, water bores and cattle. This is contested land, and the presence of European artefacts in the

20 For example, *De Rose* 2002: [410].
21 Dreaming, or Ancestral Being.

landscape seems to represent a *fait accompli* in the competition between two groups of people.

Just as the legal doctrine of *terra nullius* was accompanied by cartographic and artistic representations that all spoke to a particular way of seeing the land and the Kooris, Murris, Wiradjuris and others who lived there, a reversal of the doctrine relies on an ability to see the land as peopled by legal agents, as belonging to someone, as known to someone. It is possible to consider that hearings 'on country' merely enable a more comprehensive presentation of the facts required to prove native title. This is a perspective that poses few challenges to the positivist conception of law and evidence. However, I would argue that a hearing on country enables the change of view required to fully reverse *terra nullius* in all its constituent parts by physically locating the court in what was previously a blank space, and populating it with ancestors, stories, law and people themselves. In contrast to the orthodox conception, this argument proposes a law that is part of a larger complex of seeing, representing and being in the world.

Conclusion

When the Australian High Court in *Yorta Yorta* spoke of native title as an 'intersection between two normative systems' ([39]) it was as a device to explain the recognition by the common law of rights arising in traditional Indigenous law: the intersection happened once, at the time sovereignty was claimed. Because there can only be one law and one sovereign, recognition relates to property rights alone. But the reference in the definition of native title to the internal perspective of claimant groups – what does Walmajarri law say – means that in the process of proof, what Walmajarri law says about property rights soon unravels into larger and more fundamental questions. Partly because of the requirements of proving customary entitlement as a fact in court, and partly because the Federal Court has been directed to take Aboriginal and Torres Strait Islander cultural concerns into account, some kind of 'profound shift' is visible in the necessity to take seriously the daily realities of the claimants' lives and the way they think: there are unfamiliar rules about who can speak about what and where they can speak; some people aren't supposed to look at other people; this rock is an emu egg; strangers have to be 'watered' before they enter this place; this painting is the country.

The need for elements of Indigenous law to be taken as principles of interpretation in proof in state law processes means that the intersection of the 'two normative systems' is not a dead letter, but a live quotidian interaction. The dynamics of this interaction can be understood in part by considering how forms of evidence particular to native title, and especially paintings such as the *Ngurrara Canvas*, communicate their significance by operating within multiple cultural frameworks. A painting that draws on traditional designs from the Kimberleys (a region in the north of Western Australia) works on levels pertinent to the painters in terms of embodying Dreaming stories and their connections to places and ancestral Beings. It is one way of fulfilling a traditional obligation to 'care for country' and it in fact performs that relationship to country. For the court, this manner of proof is inevitably read against common law notions of proof, title and the modes of imagination and representation, such as cartography, that support them. Reiteration over time of Indigenous modes of expressing connection to country through Dreaming stories and designs can begin to be read as these Western phenomena – maps, title deeds – within both contexts. In response, the phenomena themselves begin to undergo shifts.

But the intersection is more than simply the traditional law and custom frame caught within the common law frame. Such a painting is not a 'purely' Indigenous object, produced for internal purposes. There is a recent and high-profile history of Aboriginal painting for a Western market that involves desires for cultural pride and economic independence on behalf of the painters, as well as changing Western aesthetic criteria, ideas of landscape and, for non-Indigenous Australians in particular, a search for a distinctive national identity. The *Ngurrara Canvas* was painted for an additional specific purpose, the native title claim, but its power as a communicative tool relies on this history of Aboriginal mainstream art and the ability of a non-Indigenous audience to perceive the painting as meaningful. Through its address to the senses, the *Ngurrara Canvas* may also compel others – without further rational explanation – to recognize in the common law what is a compulsion under law for the claimants.

Lastly, the use of the painting as a physical platform for delivering evidence on country introduces a final frame that draws all the others together. To stand on a painting that represents parts of the country in order to talk about those places and its laws embodies the connection in Walmajarri, Wangkajunga, Mangala and Juwaliny ontology between land, people, stories and designs and so brings home a knowledge about land that is radically different to that of the court. But its spatiality allows it to invoke the concept of maps, while challenging the way of seeing, and understanding land, that Western cartography represents. Standing on a painting that is a map of country drawn from another way of seeing thus confronts the physical and the representational aspects of *terra nullius*: we are here on this country and this is the way it looks to us.

This intersection through the processes of giving evidence is not, despite my emphasis on dialogue, a fluid semiotic free-for-all. Meaning (or knowledge) and power are bound together, and in native title, it is the *kartiya* who have the power to disseminate some interpretations, to quash others, and to back those interpretations with the force of the state. After all, the *Ngurrara Canvas* does not fulfil the requirements of s. 62 for a map of the claim area. Others have despaired that what is proper to Indigenous peoples, whether in art or in native title, is inevitably erased by the colonial leviathan that at best holds an inventive monologue with itself. Such a view would mean that even when, like the Ngurrara claimants, agency is asserted through cultural means, the terms on which claims are received are not of their making: if not property, title, or proof, then dance, painting and the designated identity of 'Aboriginal or Torres Strait Islander' trap them in a diorama from which there is no escape. While it may return land to their control or engender pride in aspects of their culture, the native title process is stressful, often requires the breach of secrecy laws, and always demands that claimants represent themselves through foreign languages, ideas and technologies.

In contrast, I do not claim that in using the *Ngurrara Canvas* as evidence some kind of 'true' recognition of the painting's meaning has taken place, but rather that the processes of interpretation and meaning making are more complex, plural and shifting than the conventional model of proof would allow. In a 'clash' of laws, judges may wield the force of law, but the source of law as legal meaning remains a deeply social, and inescapably plural, process.[22] For law more generally the implications are that some of law's neat divisions have to be rethought, in particular, the singular location of law in the state, the separation of fact and law, the rationality of proof, and the idea of property as distinct from a broad ontology of place.

As Fred Myers argues, by the very fact that it provokes exposure to a paradox, Aboriginal art has influenced the parameters of art criticism and discourse. The same prospect exists in native title: the involvement of Indigenous claimants in native title processes is not only supplying answers to the questions posed by law, but changing the nature – the how and the what – of the questions themselves. In this case, the *Ngurrara Canvas* has entered into the discursive terrain of facts, maps and painting, but its aesthetic has begun a transformative dialogue with those terrains. Not only will the claimants have learnt a great deal about their own law in painting it for the court, but the court and its attendants, and those picking up the *Oxford Companion to Aboriginal Art and Culture*, will experience the normative shift that the painting's aesthetic provokes because law, truth and justice are also about ways of seeing. Thus the unofficial law of native title is dependent everywhere on larger semiotic habits that must always be reiterated and performed, and so are never fixed. This quality opens state law to the transformative power of its encounter with Indigenous law.

22 See Cover 1983.

Chapter 6
Negotiated Agreements

Introduction

Given the critique of legal orthodoxy sustained in the preceding four chapters, and the argument for an understanding of law as contingent and intersubjective, the obvious next step is to move the engagement between Indigenous and non-Indigenous peoples, and the engagement between their discourses and practices of law, out of the legal institutions structured by positivism and into a forum that would facilitate open communication, mutual respect and negotiation. Indeed, in a number of jurisdictions there has been a stated preference by a range of different stakeholders for negotiated solutions to Indigenous title claims, both as a quicker and less costly alternative to litigation, and as a more appropriate strategy to encourage reconciliation between settler governments and Indigenous peoples (Tehan 2004; Scholtz 2006).[1] More prevalent still is the turn to negotiated agreements with Indigenous stakeholders in matters of environmental regulation and resource development, such as through mining Impact and Benefit Agreements. However, the idea that we can 'step out' of law is simplistic, and this chapter will argue that a critical, discursive legal pluralism can add significant nuance to the legal dimensions of negotiated agreements.

Contemporary Indigenous land negotiation policies began in the 1970s with Canada's 1973 Comprehensive Land Claims Policy and Australia's Aboriginal Land Rights (Northern Territory) Act 1976 (Cth).[2] In New Zealand, a formal policy of 'direct negotiations' in 1989 replaced ad hoc negotiations over grievances relating to breaches of the terms of the Treaty of Waitangi 1840, and continues to operate as an alternative to pursuing claims through the Waitangi Tribunal (established in 1975). Australia's Native Title Act 1993 (Cth) provided the first nationwide negotiation policy, requiring that applications for the recognition of

1 See also statement of Aboriginal and Torres Strait Islander leaders at Eva Valley, Coombs 1994: 231–4; Australian state government statements cited in Aboriginal and Torres Strait Islander Justice Commissioner 2003; judicial statements in *Delgamuukw* 1997; *North Ganalanja Aboriginal Corp v Queensland* 1996 (Brennan CJ, Dawson, Toohey, Gaudron and Gummow JJ).

2 Although this legislation established a Commission to make recommendations to the government on the validity of claims, once ownership was transferred to Aboriginal hands, the consequent absolute control over access held by the traditional owners gave an effective veto over development, and necessitated their involvement in any development on that land.

native title be first dealt with through mediation by the National Native Title Tribunal (NNTT) in an attempt to reach a 'consent determination' concerning the existence of native title (s. 86B). In a comparative analysis, Christa Scholtz (2006) notes that the decision to implement such policies involves not only a choice to recognize land rights, but also an assumption by the executive branch of responsibility for the outcomes rather than delegating the resolution of claims to a judicial or quasi-judicial body (15). Courts and governments alike have identified the 'unique character' (Native Title Act: Preamble) of Indigenous rights as a reason to seek the conciliation, or reconciliation, of parties via various forms of consensual agreement. For stakeholders more generally, much of the support for alternative dispute resolution (ADR) processes comes precisely from the value of these methods as alternatives to litigation: agreements are seen as an 'antidote to the sterility of the law' (Ritter 2004); they are the practical or political, as opposed to the legal, solution.

Even where a formal policy has not been adopted as an approach for the resolution of Indigenous rights claims per se, negotiated agreements with Indigenous peoples are proliferating in more diffuse ways around resource management. For instance, in the US, where a formal land negotiation policy has not existed since 1871, claims to water rights on arid and semi-arid reservation lands[3] are often settled by negotiated agreement spawning what one author has called a 'second treaty era' (McCool 2002: 8). Canada and Australia both require negotiation in certain circumstances over resource development projects affecting Indigenous rights stemming from the Crown's duty to consult in Canada (Newman 2009), and the right to negotiate that accrues to Indigenous parties who have fulfilled the criteria to become registered as claimants with the NNTT in Australia.[4] Finally, environmental and resource management regimes often include a formal role for Indigenous peoples in different stages of decision-making, while at the international level, the right of Indigenous peoples to 'free, prior and informed consent' that would involve them in development project decision-making is gaining some traction (Szablowski 2010: 112–13).

In this chapter I focus on negotiation and agreement-making as legally plural events. As a purportedly flexible alternative to 'the court's law', agreements are one of the most obvious places to look for the 'unofficial law' of Indigenous rights, and so a promising arena in which to develop a legal pluralist understanding. I do so by testing four different conceptualizations of the negotiation process. I argue for the recovery of certain plural aspects which help not only in the analysis of the complex factors in Indigenous rights negotiations, but also to articulate the ethical challenge posed more generally by this book: what is our responsibility if law works in conditions of interdependence?

3 See *Winters v. United States* 1908.

4 Leading to what are known as 'future act agreements'. Registered claimants also gain the capacity to enter into more general 'Indigenous land use agreements'.

In the first common conception, agreement-making is held out as the political rather than the legal solution to native title, in which it is hoped that all parties will benefit from exercising their own decision-making capacities instead of having a decision imposed on them by a court. As I will elaborate, there is a perceived opposition between the formality of law and the informality of negotiation that appears to permit parties to resolve their disputes 'without the law'. Analyses of informal justice processes, however, note several normative continuities between the zones of the formal and the informal that make negotiated outcomes complicit with, and constitutive of, state legal power. Critics readily admit that negotiated agreements do not live up to their promise of providing a space for parties to exercise their freedom because they are overdetermined by colonial power relations. However, these critics have underestimated both the ways in which informal processes are sites of state legality via the inscription of normativity in negotiating subjects, and the susceptibility of state law to other kinds of legality because its agents are also responsive subjects. Rather than a conceptual choice between a law-free space, or one exclusively dominated by state power, the idea of inscription focuses on the iterative and intersubjective nature of normativity that makes it inherently responsive and ultimately unstable.

The second conception figures negotiation as happening outside of but in the 'shadow' of the law. Analyses of negotiations speak of native title rules and procedures as endowing parties with certain bargaining advantages or 'chips' that come into play with a multitude of other economic, political, cultural and personal factors. In these images – the bargaining chip and the shadow – law has a concrete or determinate existence, bounded in space. In terms of the impact of the law on the negotiation process or the outcome of the agreement, however, there is no such object. There are only representations of law, interpreted individually by parties, deployed rhetorically, fused with other arguments and principles. The fact that even the 'content' of positive state law depends on legal reasoning, which in turn depends on rhetorical *topoi* and logical forms drawn from the general cultural milieu, makes law perpetually open to and integrated with the common sense of individuals and groups.

The third conception focuses on functional effects in the claim that agreements constitute a *de facto* recognition of Indigenous peoples' sovereignties or a *de facto* treaty making process, a claim that has been particularly important in Australia given the unequivocal official stance on the issue of Indigenous sovereignty and the absence of any formal treaties. This conception also mirrors the legal pluralist argument that pluralism is a fact because it focuses on the practical significance of agreement-making, its social functions and effects. However, in the face of a resistance to *naming* negotiated agreements as treaties, the idea of *de facto* recognition cannot explain the symbolic significance of language. Why does it matter to call something law (treaty, sovereignty) or not? While the *de facto* approach to agreements recognizes the dispersal of law in social practices that challenges legal centralism's location of law in official edicts, it could articulate more clearly the discursive relation between official law and these practices.

Rather than try to determine whether an agreement is or is not a treaty, we should concentrate on how agreements and arguments about them are transforming our understandings of what 'treaties' are.

The fourth conception of agreement-making is an intersection of different cultural and legal domains as visualized through a Venn diagram of overlapping circles. Again, this mirrors a version of legal pluralism: the one that sees pluralism as the co-existence of different legal orders in the same social space. The model is similar to the popular conception of native title in Australia as the 'recognition space' between Indigenous law and the common law. The problem here is the assumption of pre-existing corporate entities – Indigenous law or state law – that come together to make a third, an agreement. We have seen throughout this book the many different ways in which law depends on interpretive practices, and so never attains a stable, uniform whole. As the product of discourse, it is only known via individual perspectives and is only articulated interactively.

Analysing these different approaches to the same phenomena will allow me to test the limitations of orthodox legal theory that I have investigated in different contexts throughout this book and to consolidate some of its arguments for legal pluralism. In general, although all four conceptions have heuristic purposes and are suitable for some kinds of analysis, they mostly miss the radical potential in the constitution of legal meaning *through* the negotiation process, and thus the space for transformation, that exists because our concepts of law are irretrievably affected by the process. Any approach to law that does not accept the dependency of legal meaning on these discursive interactions runs the risk of reifying legal phenomena and then allocating resources based on a test of cultural or legal authenticity that assumes these things really exist. It is the untenability of that particular aspect of legal orthodoxy on which I will focus in Chapter 7.

The susceptibility of law, and people, to change through participation in the re-iterative processes of legal meaning-making has serious consequences for a theory of intercultural justice. If law is indeterminate and has multiple locations in human symbolic practices, then native title is not the intersection between pre-existing differences but, in anthropologist James Weiner's (2006) phrase, a 'differentiating activity' (17). This turns the intersection question on its head, as it were: instead of asking how it is that two different things intersect in the same space, we start with one situation, one moment, or one person and ask how differences get produced. The kind of 'call and response' pattern that leads to naming law in negotiation, as in other aspects of native title, makes law and the articulated differences on which it relies interdependent and relational from the start.

Political Justice: Negotiation as an Antidote to Law

The preference for consensual processes reflects a perception that, in Richard Bartlett's (2000) words, 'any dispute is best settled by agreement … [Negotiation towards an agreement] can readily accommodate uncertainties in the legal strength of the positions of parties and it enables the development of an ad hoc settlement tailored to the particular circumstances' (404). According to this view, the problem with litigation is that it is formal, adversarial, and focused on determinative findings of fact and law. In the courts' terms, Indigenous rights exists as a syllogistic either/or, and what can be given a hearing are very specific and technical issues of 'relevant' fact and law, rather than accounts relevant to the parties' own sense of justice, which makes the process alienating. A legal decision is seen as a unilateral exercise of the state's power. Negotiated agreements, according to their supporters, can be informal, culturally sensitive and empowering for parties. They offer the chance to tell the stories that the participants wish to tell, the flexibility to craft innovative solutions that reflect all parties' interests and that are not limited in scope or subject matter, and the promotion of solidarity or positive ongoing relationships between parties. With consent as the grounding rationale, agreement is additionally said to be an exercise in communal autonomy and self-determination.

The institutionalization of alternative methods for resolving Indigenous rights claims follows the wave of support for ADR in many jurisdictions which, taking off in the 1980s, saw the introduction of specialist non-adversarial tribunals, of mediation and arbitration as an option for litigants, especially in family and commercial matters, and of community dispute resolution centres (Astor and Chinkin 1992: 1–11; Barrett and Barrett 2004). As an 'alternative' to formal justice, ADR is structured by its opposition to the state. In its version as private and community dispute resolution processes, it is conceived of as a challenge to the power of the state or an affirmation of its limits: there are some things that the state does not do best (Fitzpatrick 1992a: 200). In particular, shoring up a zone of freedom from state intervention gives back to citizens what is proper to them – their own disputing – and empowers them by teaching the skills to resolve disputes autonomously, and to participate in and build authentic community (Christie 1977).[5]

However, recent analyses of alternative conflict resolution, influenced by Michel Foucault's thesis on the discursive nature of power, have called into question its simple opposition of formal/informal or control/autonomy (1979, 1980). In contrast to the sovereign model in which a central authority wields power over us like a sword, disciplinary power works by normalizing our practices through persistent and diffuse corrective training, 'omnipresent surveillance' (1980: 214), and the inscription of ways of being and knowing by parents, schools, health and social workers, law enforcement, human sciences and the media. Foucaultian analyses of informal as against formal dispute resolution note normative continuities over the two domains, such as the rational individual, and the value of order over dispute. Where mediators are involved, critics argue that the extent to which certain selves are formed by disciplinary mediation techniques, whose exercise of freedom then secures the legitimate zone of control claimed by state law, makes the domain

5 See also Pavlich 1996b: 710–11.

of formal and informal mutually constituting.[6] That is, we are never 'free' of the legality of the state.

Of course, negotiations over Indigenous lands could not, in any case, have aspired to constitute a 'zone of freedom' from the state whenever the state itself is a party. As for providing a purely 'political solution', the various institutionalized forms of negotiation are often tightly framed by the formal legal system. For example, in the Australian native title context, consent or voluntariness is compromised in a number of ways: determinations of native title must pass through mediation before litigation is an option (Lane 2000b: 48) and their content must satisfy the court as being 'appropriate' (Native Title Act 1993 (Cth): s. 87). More generally, while the absence of evidentiary rules and other formal aspects of litigation might make the process more adaptable to the needs of the parties, and address the cultural prejudice built into those rules, this is mitigated in a number of ways. In particular, governments generally require prima facie proof of rights (via an anthropological 'connection report', for instance) as a precondition for entering negotiations that deploys ministerial official's understanding of state law criteria for title and evidentiary thresholds.[7]

Moreover, what is continuous across the domains of litigation and mediation is the pervasiveness of the colonial relation and the imbalance of power that disadvantages Indigenous parties in numerous ways. Informal dispute resolution has been severely criticized as disadvantaging minorities or being inappropriate where there is a history of violence or oppression between parties.[8] Indigenous participants have experienced negotiations over their rights as 'culturally intimidating' (Patrick Sullivan, in Jackson 1996: 38) and while the personal element *can* create empathy and understanding,[9] it can also exacerbate hostilities (Atkinson 2002; Dodson 1996b: 9). Dispossession and the historical disadvantage of Indigenous peoples can be the cause of entrenched power imbalance in agreements (Dodson 1996b: 9; Dodson, in Jackson 1996: 42), such that the legitimacy of non-Indigenous law and rights to land is at all times taken for granted, while Indigenous law and rights are something that must be proved (Borrows 2002: 101; Bauman and Williams 2004).

Although negotiations over Indigenous lands can take many forms, the influence of the Harvard Negotiation Project strategy – where parties are instructed to approach their dispute as a problem to solve, and to concentrate on

6 See Matthews 1988; Fitzpatrick 1992a; Pavlich 1996a; Andersen 1999; van Krieken 2001; Brigg 2003.

7 See Australian Institute for Aboriginal and Torres Strait Islander Studies 2013 and Aboriginal Affairs and Northern Development Canada 2003.

8 See Delgado, Dunn, Brown, Lee and Hubbert 1985: 1387; Grillo 1991; Cobb 1997.

9 'Once the traditional owners start to talk about country, and what country means to them and what it is they want, you know, which is usually cultural heritage protection, access for ceremonies, the capacity to take kids out there and get them off the streets and put them in touch with their culture … you can just see the light bulbs go on with pastoralists and other interest groups' (Mediator Interview #3, 3 November 2003).

creative solutions to how their interests may be met mutually, rather than on their entrenched 'positions' – is widespread.[10] For instance, the British Columbia Treaty Process was established with the intention that negotiations between First Nations groups and the government would adopt this style of negotiation (de Costa 2006b: 19), while the Australian Native Title Tribunal has outlined a similar strategy for its mediation service.[11] The ideal is that the objective of 'certainty' in development and planning touted by many stakeholders, but particularly by governments and industry proponents, would then come not just through producing a detailed document specifying parties' rights and obligations, but through engendering the greater sense of responsibility in all parties for the solutions reached through a participatory process.[12] On the other hand, interest-based negotiation is criticized as essentially asking vulnerable parties to forgo their rights in forgoing their positions, or even as providing a smokescreen for government parties' 'take-it-or-leave-it' approach: interest-based negotiation is presented as being honest about one's intentions, and the symbolic effect of attaching 'the valued normative criterion of honesty … is to disguise the instrumental, positional basis of the non-Aboriginal government's negotiation policy' (Woolford 2004: 120).

In many critiques of power imbalance in negotiations, power is something exercised by settlers or their governments against Indigenous peoples. Foucault's understanding of pervasive disciplinary governance, however, sees power also operating in more subtle ways. Alternative dispute resolution rests on certain premises, such as the ideals of peace and harmony,[13] that are far from universal: for instance, fighting may be seen as enjoyable or entertaining, violence and conflict a way of forming and maintaining groups rather than threatening community cohesion (Brigg 2003: 290). Even when peacemaking and community harmony are consciously invoked as drawing on Indigenous traditions, as Laura Nader and Jay Ou (1998: 27), and Emma LaRocque (1997: 3) have argued, this tends to be an idealization that downplays traditional punitive or retributive responses, or Indigenous histories respecting the dignity of the individual. Interest-based negotiation has also been questioned on the basis of cultural appropriateness (Brigg 2003: 295; Myers 1986: 160–63; Macdonald 1988); in particular, Mark Doxtator argues that Aboriginal people in North America would tend to emphasize understanding and working at achieving and maintaining a balance in place of a

10 See <http://www.pon.harvard.edu> Fisher and Ury 1991; Moore, 2003.

11 See for instance Neate 2003; Neate, Jones and Clarke 2003. Note the Tribunal acknowledges that issues such as 'reconciliation', the empowerment of parties and the strengthening of relationships are important, and so promotes techniques of 'storytelling' that are said to bring the human element out of the issues, encourage inter-personal recognition or enable compromise. See for example Winslade and Monk 2000.

12 National Indigenous Working Group on Native Title 1997; Agius, Howitt, Jarvis and Williams 2003: 2–4; Aboriginal and Torres Strait Islander Social Justice Commissioner 1997: Chapter 1; Neate 1999.

13 See Nader 1991.

'one shot' agreement (cited in Imai 2003: 591).[14] Attitudes to disputing are, in turn, closely linked to notions of the self: as a bounded, autonomous individual, or as embedded in interpersonal ties and other links to the non-human world.

Rather than see the negotiation space as a normative vacuum, vacated by law so that pre-existing legal subjects may exercise their freedom, Foucaultian critiques of informality suggest ways in which alternative dispute resolution may be seen as helping to constitute participants as legal subjects, and so extending the regulatory reach of state law. Studies of mediator techniques show mediators not only steering participants towards a preferred outcome, but also using techniques that subtly discipline them into behaving appropriately; into becoming rational, responsible, non-disputing individual selves (Pavlich 1996b: 717–28; Greatbatch and Dingwall 1989): 'there is pressure on disputants to perform their stories and selves in ways understandable to the mediators and intelligible within the goals of the mediation session and accompanying assumptions about peace and conflict' (Brigg 2003: 295). For instance, ground rules establish a controlled non-violent interaction during mediation as well as the distinction between the mediator's role – responsible for process rather than advocacy or advice – and the participants' role – responsible for the content of the dispute and its resolution. The focus on individual responsibility separates disputants from broader politics and networks, and discourages them from interpreting their dispute as part of broader social issues relating to race, culture, gender and power (Astor and Chinkin 1992: 15; Abel 1981; Brigg 2003: 293).

The mediator may use an array of techniques – ignoring, encouraging, cajoling, shaming, rebuking, joking, relaxing, summarizing – both to reframe discussion and to discipline participants. As mediator Morgan Brigg (2003) notes, all of these constitute 'subtle injunctions, inducements and rewards' – that parties should be 'rational rather than emotional, constructive rather than destructive, conciliatory rather than combative' (295). Story-telling techniques, aimed to help one party appreciate the perspective of the other, also work as a kind of self-examination or catharsis that Brigg relates to the western trope of the confession, which always positions the confessing subject in relation to an authority. Just as technology (Foucault 1980), myth (Fitzpatrick 1992b), narrative (Cover 1983), film (Kamir 2005) and children's stories (Manderson 2003), are said to be necessary to law because they create a world in which its precepts make sense, it seems that mediation helps make the kind of subjects that are needed for modern law to function. Significantly, though, this happens not through coercion but through submission; it is not legal prescription but legal inscription, in which the law is written into our behaviours and identities, and subjects come to discipline *themselves* (Manderson 2003: 90). The pervasiveness of law as inscription is important in a legal pluralist

14 This view is supported by the contrasting metaphors for historic treaties: the Iroquois called them a covenant chain linking the parties that had to be periodically polished to keep it shiny rather than a contract representing a unique moment of a 'meeting of the minds'.

account because it notes the normative tendency of all discourse and the multiple ways that state power can be deployed.

The analysis of law as inscription takes us beyond the recognition of the plural forms of state legality, however. Although the characteristics of ADR – informal, private, interpersonal – and the techniques of mediation *do* actively work to produce selves and communities that are consonant with state legality and which reiterate the structural oppressions on which it is based, the very fact that these forms must be constantly enacted and reiterated through personal interaction in order to exist makes them unstable and essentially open. Here, then, is a way to relativize the role of the state in power relations and to conceive of power itself as plural or finite in the sense referred to in Chapter 2.

When state power is understood as a stick wielded over others, it appears that resistance to the exercise of power in the context of mediation is either disciplined or rejected. As Brigg recounts from his own experiences of intercultural mediation, if there is an intervention from a party during a mediation session that challenges the liberal premises of mediation, it may be met either by a redirection back to the 'real focus' of mediation, or by a conclusion that the party is beyond assistance and thus 'outside' of the domain of mediation. The rejection of mediation events that are 'not working' as aberrant helps to rationalize and constitute other mediation events, and the operation of power in them, as normal, and affirms the autonomy of mediation. Even here, the continual experience and labelling of events as normal and not-normal makes the autonomy of mediation practice temporary and contingent.

Focusing on the micro-processes that take place during these personal interactions, however, Brigg observes something more at stake: the agent of state power – here the mediator – is him or herself a subject. The disciplinary potential of mediation relies on the effective capacities of the mediator, and the ability to engender empathy, trust and encouragement in participants that ensure their compliant responses. On the other hand, this also opens the mediator up to being affected by others. When conflict threatens mediation with failure, the mediator will experience an ethical dilemma (however momentary) in choosing whether to prioritize the party or the political and ontological commitments of mediation, or in choosing whether to discipline or reject the disruption. As Brigg (2007) remarks, some troubling events cannot be contained or processed by liberal governance, leading mediators to 'improvise their mediation practice in ways that transgress the boundaries that are established through training and accepted practice' (39).

As the public statements of some Australian NNTT mediators indicate, they are aware of the cultural assumptions in mediation and do their best to make mediation a true alternative to litigation by being sensitive, in their management of the mediation process, to the different meanings Indigenous peoples might ascribe to conflict, to the implicatedness of whole networks of kin and community in the native title claim, or to the important place of anger and other emotions. It may be that mediation which focuses on stories, emotions or reconciling damaged relationships is actually consistent with the way some Indigenous peoples understand conflict and the self, although caution should be exercised in making assumptions on that basis (LaRocque 1997). Some of the imbalance towards western values may be able to be redressed by asking Indigenous elders to participate as mediators, as Madeleine Sauvé (1996) and Larissa Behrendt (1995: 73–96) have argued. More radically, there is the possibility for settlers to be trained in Indigenous mediation methods, such as through the Mawül Rom project in Northern Australia's Arnhem Land (Newman 2004).[15] While the investigation of alternatives to state law is, in context, important in designing negotiation strategies or mediation for dealing with disputes over Indigenous rights that are respectful of Indigenous participants, the multiple forms of state legality deny such a simplified opposition between state law and the rest. Further, Brigg's personal insights into mediation practice point to a larger possibility for the susceptibility of all law to others given that it is acted out through humans in their effective responses to others. The result may not change, but the person will. The effects of any exercise of power are beyond absolute control, unstable and potentially transformative.

Bargaining in the Shadow of the Law

While state law may, as in the case of Australia's Native Title Act or judicially ordered consultation in Canada, prescribe agreement-making and its forms, it also influences the process and outcome of negotiation in more diffuse ways. Commonly, formal rules that go to the substance of Indigenous rights, and even those that pertain to procedure, are understood as distributing bargaining advantages between parties which they then bring to the negotiating table (Bartlett 1996; Corbett and O'Faircheallaigh 2006/7; Cairns 2011: 171; McHugh 2011: 47). The effect of courts' decisions on agreements reached outside the courtroom was coined as 'bargaining in the shadow of the law' in an influential article by Robert Mnookin and Lewis Kornhauser (1979), who argued in the context of family law that the recognition by courts of entitlements or a pattern of favouring certain claims – giving custody to mothers, for instance – confers on parties a 'bargaining endowment' that adds to their general power to influence the other party.[16] Their study of divorcing couples showed that judicially applied principles of property distribution or custody affected the outcomes of negotiated settlements for the very obvious reason that failure to agree might provoke the dissatisfied party to litigate, at which point the court's decision would determine the matter. The threat of an imposed decision gives an incentive to reach agreement; the prospective content of that decision gives parties a measure of how far they should be prepared to bend.

15 The project has offered a Master of Indigenous Knowledges (Mawul Rom) at Charles Darwin University since 2011.

16 See also Smith, Blagg and Derricourt 1988.

More interestingly, however, Mnookin and Kornhauser showed that the court-sanctioned rule did not map in a linear fashion such that negotiated outcomes matched adjudicated ones. Rather, parties' behaviour was influenced by a whole range of factors tied to the litigation of disputes – the transaction costs (financial and personal) of litigation, the potential remedy and the degree of uncertainty of outcome, for instance – as well as the parties' personal preferences as to outcome and their willingness to take risks. In strategic negotiating behaviour, no party will settle for an outcome that leaves them worse off than if they had gone to court – including the transaction costs of undertaking litigation – but that calculation is an individual and subjective one.[17]

The bargaining model is prevalent in analyses of Indigenous rights agreements (Nader and Ou 1998: 25; Szablowski 2010: 117; Humphrey 1998; Sexton 1996; Bartlett 1996). The pragmatic observer knows that the abstract recognition of rights in court decisions or legislation is only of concrete value to the extent that it can be translated into what Indigenous peoples can *do* with their rights. The *substantive* rule may be that Indigenous title or rights are protected by state law where it exists, but in practice the substance of the rights depends on the fine print of the *procedural* rules and, because Indigenous rights must always be worked out on the ground between a range of different actors, the rules become mere bargaining tools among a multitude of other economic, cultural and political factors relating to the specific people involved (Blowes and Trigger 1999; Wootton 1996; Szablowski 2010: 116–23).

For example, in the agreement between gold miner Zapopan and the Jawoyn Nation prior to the Native Title Act, it seemed that the potential 'transaction costs' gave the company an incentive to negotiate even when a successful native title claim was by no means guaranteed (Kauffman 1998; O'Faircheallaigh 1995). This bargaining strength has been formalized in Australia through the 'right to negotiate', with developers under a legal obligation to negotiate with registered claimants. If no agreement is reached within six months, the NNTT can be requested to arbitrate and impose a decision that might, in theory, be more onerous than the conditions of an agreement. If there has been a finding of bad faith, another six-month period is launched. Moreover, an NNTT decision can be overridden by the Minister. In theory, the impact of these delays on development projects, and the possibility of an adverse decision, gives developers something to gain from genuinely seeking a consensual agreement, and thus grants an endowment to Indigenous parties.

In practice, however, the tribunal has never refused an application, and has only once, when the grantee party was making little effort to engage with the native title party, made a finding of bad faith (Corbett and O'Faircheallaigh 2006/7). Out of 17 determinations, 10 imposed conditions, but in 9 instances the conditions had either already been agreed to by the parties, were in keeping with existing state government policies imposing conditions on mining, or were justified precisely because they were not onerous. In contrast, for native title

17 Although for this zero-sum approach see Menkel-Meadow 1983.

parties, there is the incentive that, because the NNTT is not authorized to make a decision awarding payment based on profit-sharing (s. 38(2)), their only chance to secure a proportional and ongoing interest in the proposed development will be via negotiation. Where a native title determination is yet to be made, monies that are awarded as compensation when the NNTT finds against the developer in the process of determining whether 'future acts' will be approved may be ordered to be held on trust for the native title holders pending the positive determination, and so Indigenous parties risk delay in accessing compensation money, or losing it altogether (ss. 36(C) and 52).[18] The crux of criticisms of these provisions is usually that the substantive rights of native title are undermined by poor procedural protection (Bartlett 1996), or that a stronger bargaining position for Indigenous parties could have been afforded through something like the near veto of the Northern Territory Land Rights Act.

Analyses of formal rights as bargaining chips tend to include a detailed appreciation of the context in which rights operate. Robert Blowes and David Trigger, for example, note that bargaining positions are not only fixed by 'the minimum legal position', but also, among other things, by the company's policies on Aboriginal affairs and the environment, mineral prices and other industry variables, media sympathy or antipathy, the susceptibility of the company to public controversy, the extent to which native title is present in state and national politics, the diversity of interests among relevant Aboriginal people, the strength and unity of Aboriginal representative organizations, the personality, attitudes and experience of company officers and the amount of funding available for negotiations (Blowes and Trigger 1999: 97–8).[19] A survey of mining agreements shows that the most advantageous agreements as far as Indigenous peoples are concerned correlate either with rights of veto or with the political weight of the Indigenous organization (O'Faircheallaigh and Corbett 2005; O'Faircheallaigh 2004).

But how do these various factors play off against one another? The language of the bargaining chip, or the image of the shadow of the law, treats law as something determinate and finite: a discrete object that exists independently of the parties. With some reflection on how 'chips' get used, or how the shadow might fall over a negotiation process, however, it becomes obvious that the law does not simply land on parties' plates pre-formed and objective. To the extent that the shift in bargaining endowment in the above example – from (substantive) native title rights, to the (procedural) right to negotiate, to the (statistical) unlikely refusal of grant in arbitration – affects parties' behaviour and the outcome of the negotiations, it depends on their awareness of legal rules and their application, and on their own assessment of what the rules mean and the likely risks or benefits of appearing before a formal decision-maker. As Marc Galanter (1981) has written, '[t]he impact of courts on disputes is to an important extent accomplished by the

18 See Altman 1998.

19 See also Alcantara (2007: 194–200) on internal and external factors affecting Comprehensive Land Claim outcomes in Canada.

dissemination of information. Courts produce not only decisions, but messages' (13). Although courts and legislatures are influential messengers as to what the law is, so are academics, lawyers, journalists, politicians, bureaucrats, institutions and communities. To the extent that formal law governs people's behaviour, we are all authoritative interpreters (and indeed, even if we trust our lawyer as having privileged access to 'the law', the lawyer's advice must itself be interpreted). We self-administer the law a great deal of the time (Galanter 1985: 545). Law is more effective, Galanter (1981) continues, as 'a system of cultural and symbolic meanings than as a set of operative controls' (13).

Of course, the ability of negotiating parties not just to access information about the law and interpret it, but then to use that interpretation successfully to convince the other party, is not equally distributed. Lawyers, for instance, may have the training and skills that allow them to assess legal information more or less consistently with the way a court would decide.[20] They can use this special standing – and the cultural capital that comes with it, such as a certain confidence in speaking legalese – to persuade those across the table that they have produced the 'correct' interpretation. But not all lawyers are equally persuasive, and some may have rhetorical skills that cause the bargaining endowment of the shadow of the law to fall in one spot rather than another. Further, what is persuasive to a judge, listening with ears attuned to what he or she knows to be a cogent legal argument, is not necessarily what will be persuasive to government ministers, miners, forestry operators, pastoralists or Indigenous negotiators. The chips dealt by legislation or court decisions may have to be delivered in different languages depending on one's audience; they may have to be packaged in arguments based on changing principles depending on the context. Then again, since those packagings are perpetually changing, the solidity of the chips dissolves. The legal pluralist argument against the determinate ontology of law emerges here as a realization that – as provisional, personal and indeterminate as it may be – the law *is* interpretation.

Moreover, there is a porosity between overt interpretations of the legal rules and other principled arguments and rhetorical forms in the general attempts to convince the other party to agree to what is suggested. One former native title mediator in Australia commented to me that distinct kinds of arguments emerged from different groups engaged in native title negotiations: a kind of Lockean labour theory from pastoralists, together with the inertia of (recent) tradition ('the land is yours if you work it' and 'why should we change what we've been doing for three generations?'); the moral claim based on prior presence or dispossession from Indigenous parties; the self-evident good of development ('if not you're still just squatting in the dirt') from miners; and the obligation to act in the public interest from state governments ('we hold the land on trust for all the people' and 'it's not ours to give).[21]

20 This is described as 'sharing a legal consciousness' in Kennedy 1980.

21 Interview #1, 24 July 2003.

Others have noted the existence of principles (similar to the rhetorical *topoi* discussed in Chapter 3) such as 'good neighbourliness', 'actions speak louder than words' and 'authority is final' that seek to generate accord by invoking what (presumably) all parties will recognize as common sense. Further, while they may be shared at one level between groups and depend upon this for their rhetorical impact, the inversion of the substance of *topoi* can effectively stake a claim to difference and undermine the naturalness of the original. For instance, when a government negotiator on the Cape York/Century Zinc project in Australia stressed that his offer on compensation money was final and said 'I've consulted the Premier', an Aboriginal man interjected: 'Yeah, and I've consulted my grandmother! And she's higher than anybody ... !' (Blowes and Trigger 1999: 113). The inversion of the *topoi* of authority, and the dissonance it sounds, strikingly brings home the point that the Aboriginal man was operating according to a different set of values; the government man may well have thought twice the next time he invoked this rationale or at least have been made aware that he was invoking the hierarchy of state power and not some neutral fact of life.

Negotiation is thus not a norm-free process in which the fittest gain victory through brute strength, nor merely an economic transaction exchanging quantifiable chips, but is rather characterized by 'the invocation, elaboration and distinction of principles, rules and precedents' (Eisenberg 1976: 638–9). And neither are these 'invocations' (always) just deliberate strategies chosen from a deck of argument cards, if I may mix my gambling metaphors. They make sense to the parties and persuade them because they constitute (or can be imagined to constitute) the normative world in which they are embedded, or because they are accepted, as with Hart's 'external point of view', as a fact of the world, even if not an obligation to be upheld personally (Galanter 1981: 12). The negotiation is thus shot through with norms both shared and not shared by the parties: privacy, freedom of speech, fairness, restitution, responsibility, reasonableness, professional standards, personal honour or the importance of harmony. As Santos (1977) has pointed out, given the background of uncertainty in written laws, legal reasoning must always resort to the inventive art of finding common points of view, or argumentative *topoi*, to fill gaps and render the conclusion convincing: a constant process of fusion 'by which the legal system remains open to (and an integral part of) social life' (14–16).

Topoi, like narratives, must compete for legitimacy or primacy, and disadvantaged groups more than others will have to confront negative histories, stereotypes and cultural myths that undermine the ability of their rhetorical strategies to compete effectively (Gunning 1995: 68). At the end of the day, the track record of the Australian Native Title Tribunal on mining arbitration may effectively have removed Indigenous negotiators' capacity to say no or to insist on their own proposals. When Indigenous actors do have some leverage due to external factors such as media sympathy or time-sensitive development projects, negotiations may resemble 'dirty politics'. But as careful analysis – such as the one written by Blowes and Trigger on the Century Zinc negotiations – shows, bargaining and politicking happen through the medium of charged language, rhetorical strategies and 'unofficial' principles. Critics may see this as nothing more than law manipulated by the powerful, but even the exercise of power in this situation must happen through discursive and symbolic means: not only parties' understanding of legislation and the common law but a whole range of normative arguments get pressed into service. The significant meaning of the law, in that case, is not locked into some 'essence of statute' but – partially and temporarily – played out between the parties.

De Facto Recognition

> Whatever the strength of the denials of co-existing sovereignty in the Aboriginal nations of Australia, we are, in fact, operating on the basis that the Courts will acknowledge rights flowing from laws and customs which belong to those Aboriginal groups which might describe themselves as nations (Chaney 2001: 4).

In contrast to the previous two approaches that see negotiated agreements as separate from the law to varying degrees, in this section I turn to characterizations of agreement-making that explicitly locate legal meaning in practices other than in declarations made in official texts. The most extensive of these is the claim that, in locating the operative basis of Indigenous rights in nation-like, jurisgenic Indigenous groups making autonomous decisions about their land, negotiated agreements constitute a de facto recognition of Indigenous sovereignty, particularly where there have been explicit or implicit denials of its survival following colonization. In Australia, this denial has even led to a refusal to use the term 'treaty' to designate agreements. But because native title agreements are being made on a regional basis, covering diverse topics from land use to the provision of services and joint decision-making, and because the process involves Indigenous groups as polities, there is an argument that there is an implicit treaty-making process, with agreements being made on a 'government to government' basis. As the co-coordinators of the Agreements, Treaties and Negotiated Settlements (ATNS) project at the University of Melbourne argue, agreements are a 'surrogate instrument' of self-government (Langton and Palmer 2003).

Referring to the growing culture of agreement-making as the '*de facto* recognition' of Indigenous sovereignties evokes the use of this phrase in international law (Langton and Palmer 2003). There, it is used where an organized political leadership, effectively governing a territory but lacking official status as a state in international law, might nevertheless be treated as a state through acts of trade or diplomatic relations. In the case of Indigenous sovereignty, in part it is the instrumental attitudes of governments and businesses that makes this so: consent is required, not just because it is desirable to respect group autonomy as we saw above, but because 'agreements' reached through force will not be stable in the long run (Astor and Chinkin 1992: 85–6; Lane 2000b: 51). Indeed, one observer has suggested that it is only through the micro-rationale of self-interest – such as when protest threatens development – that states are compelled to negotiate treaties (de Costa 2003). Public opinion has also impacted on this change towards a culture of agreement-making with Indigenous peoples. For example, the popularity of 'triple bottom line accounting' (measuring corporate success by environmental and social performance rather than raw profit alone) in some sectors has led corporations to institutionalize processes of consultation and agreements with stakeholders, including Indigenous groups.

The political autonomy of Indigenous groups is a logical postulate of doctrines of Indigenous rights, at least in jurisdictions that include 'traditional laws and customs' as an element of the definition of rights; proof of Indigenous rights is a factual acknowledgement both of these traditional laws and of the Indigenous polity. In addition, negotiated agreements as the practical working out of rights actually require claimants or rights holders to *exercise* the capacities of a decision-making polity. These two aspects of Indigenous rights engender the following observations. First, it is through the process rather than the outcome of an agreement or determination that the recognition of rights starts. In Australia, for instance, some have considered this an exercise of what is often considered the primary native title right from an Indigenous perspective, the 'right to speak for country'. Second, at the local level, the need to consent to agreements is developing Indigenous decision-making institutions and so working functionally towards self-determination. Third, the growing 'culture of agreement',[22] whereby parties from many sectors are adapting to this new practice as the norm, is said to constitute an implicit recognition of Indigenous sovereignty. As Tim Rowse (2002/3) puts it, 'every time an organised Indigenous interest makes an agreement (about land use or about service delivery) with a non-Indigenous interest (whether government or private), something small but important is added to a growing edifice of Indigenous self-determination. Self-determination is arguably analogous to the growth of a coral reef'.

In Australia, the claim that regional agreements are a *de facto* treaty process is very controversial, however, and government representatives have been quick to differentiate between agreements (which are seen as progressive and beneficial) and calls for a treaty (which is subversive). Precisely because a treaty confronts head-on the question of Indigenous nationhood and sovereignty, and thus the foundations of the state, the government quashes the tendency to see agreements in this symbolic frame.[23] On the other hand, some commentators are wary of the uncritical support for agreement-making *per se*, arguing either that what counts is whether the micro-processes themselves present an opportunity

22 See Phillip Ruddock, quoted in Aboriginal and Torres Strait Islander Justice Commissioner 2002: Chapter 3; Fred Chaney 2002.

23 See comments by former Minister for Immigration and Multicultural and Indigenous Affairs, Phillip Ruddock, quoted in Aboriginal and Torres Strait Islander Justice Commissioner 2002: Chapter 3.

to exercise self-determination (Agius et al. 2003) or that agreement-making is just fancy rhetoric unless outcomes substantively benefit Indigenous participants (O'Faircheallaigh 2004: 304).

Interestingly, in Canada, an inverted claim of recognition has been made for modern treaties and negotiated agreements: that without a just and consensual settlement of the question of control over Indigenous territories, it is *Canada's* claims of sovereignty that will be legally deficient (Slattery 2005: 438). This claim is based on a shift in the language of the Supreme Court. In contrast to the Court's 1990 statement in *R v. Sparrow* that 'there was from the outset never any doubt that sovereignty ... and indeed the underlying title, to such lands, vested in the Crown', more recent developments have framed contemporary negotiations as the 'reconciliation of prior Aboriginal occupation with *de facto* Crown sovereignty' (McLachlin CJ, *Haida* 2004: [42]). That is, effective control over land and resources did not create the legal legitimacy of British or French claims of sovereignty, which will only happen through a treaty process. Thus, contradicting the instinct of Australian politicians, while contemporary treaties may necessarily problematize historical Crown sovereignty, they provide an occasion for its legitimation in the present.

A further statement from the *Haida* case indicates for the first time in Canadian jurisprudence that it is 'pre-existing Aboriginal sovereignty' (rather than the fact of physical occupation) that must be reconciled with 'assumed Crown sovereignty' through the process of honourable negotiation ([20]). Felix Hoehn (2012) then argues that, since Aboriginal peoples are unlikely to voluntarily relinquish their sovereignty or to have done so in the past, it follows that Canada is to be a country of shared Aboriginal and Crown sovereignty (35–6). However, the *de facto* nature of state sovereignty does not mean that it is not real, and Hoehn refers us to an earlier Canadian decision accepting the temporary applicability of invalid laws made by a body without *de jure* sovereignty if to quash them would leave a vacuum in the rule of law (43–5).

The suggestion that phenomena such as states, polities, sovereignty, treaties or constitutions can exist *de facto* even if not *de jure* is based on the same reasoning which finds that legal pluralism exists, not because of the official recognition of state law, but because in practice there are norms, principles, and sanctions which order people's lives. In Chapter 3 we saw how this 'social scientific' approach to legal pluralism ran into definitional difficulties: if to find law outside of the state one looks to equivalent function or form, the term 'law' then becomes both too wide in application, extending broadly into what is merely social phenomena, and too narrow, because it misses other things that we consider law to do or to be. This problem turns on the importance of linguistic convention to functional meaning.

The agreement debates get tied up in similar definitional knots: if a large element of a treaty relationship *is* the symbolic element of mutual respect as partners with equal formal status, then claiming *de facto* recognition in the face of recalcitrant government policy towards sovereignty, a treaty and self-determination is wishful thinking. To a large degree these entities cannot be seen to have a substantive existence if the key element of mutual respect is missing, which it arguably will be as long as the government resists the *symbolic* significance of admitting the full import of the process, one aspect of which is naming.

In Chapter 4 I suggested that one solution to the 'naming' dilemma for law was to note that linguistic conventions are living things, changing dialectically through use. Property, law, estate, nation; these can evolve new meanings that come with new associations in new contexts. So too the power of using 'treaty' or 'sovereignty' in the context of native title and other agreements may be to shift understandings of what a treaty needs to be, that is, other than a means to achieve a secessionist Indigenous state within the geographical bounds of the larger nation. Equally as powerfully, there is a potential for a new language, drawn from Indigenous traditions (such as *makarrata* (~treaty) in Australia, *pachamama* (~nature) in Ecuador, or the Two-Row wampum/*gaswenda* in North America), to counter the repression of a discourse of Indigenous self-government during the colonial period.

In giving agreements a consolidated public profile, the ATNS project mentioned above – which aims to document agreement-making through an extensive database, and promotes the necessity for close analysis of the benefits of agreement-making – is also playing an important part in this symbolic conversation.[24] Agreements are given a presence through the database, in company with some of the most monumental of both historical and contemporary treaties, such as the 1840 Treaty of Waitangi in New Zealand, or the creation, in 1993, of the new territory of Nunuvut formalizing self-governmentforo the Inuit majority in that region of Canada. Creating a public profile for the culture of agreement-making is a way of building alliances with people belonging to the electoral bases that will need to be won over if Indigenous Australians try to seek amendments to the Constitution in support of a treaty.

The idea that legal or constitutional arrangements are to be found in convention and usage has previously been taken up by James Tully in his re-imagination of North American constitutionalism laid out in *Strange Multiplicity* (1995). Following Wittgenstein, Tully seeks an understanding of constitutionalism, not in a grand universal theory, but in the uses to which the word and its cognates and associated terms are put – the language in which both the problems and the solutions arise (35, 103–16). In contrast to the dominant language of modern constitutionalism and its empire of uniformity, he re-reads the history of Crown and Aboriginal relations in North America in order to find, in the practice of treaty making and the language in which claims and counter claims were couched, suppressed conventions of 'common constitutionalism' which are capable of accommodating a multiplicity of culturally different voices (116–39). Three of these which, he claims, pre-date modern constitutionalism and continue today in the recognition claims of minorities, are mutual recognition, consent and the continuity of self-rule. In this 'hidden history' of constitutionalism, a constitution

24 See <http://www.atns.net.au>.

is not a piece of paper or an orderly structure imposed or brought into being by the 'will of the people' at a single point in time, but literally 'how we constitute ourselves': the labyrinth of forms of association that we develop over time.

Although some of this language of contemporary constitutionalism is derived from the discourse of imperialism and nation-states, the valuable input of Tully's analysis here is to see that even this language is the result of histories of struggle and resistance, as well as domination and control. As he puts it:

> [i]n the course of the contests for recognition, the language of constitutionalism has been shaped and formed by other cultures in ways that the European imperial writers would find unrecognisable. Indeed, to decry the language of contemporary constitutionalism as solely an European, imperial monolith, imposed from the centre to the periphery without any change or interaction is, ironically, uncritically to accept the very self image the most chauvinistic imperial theorists of modern constitutionalism sought to uphold (38).

Indigenous contributions to this language are most visible when they are not in English, when they pre-date colonization, or when they are in another form of expression. Tully cites the *wampum* beaded belts exchanged in the treaty between the Haudenosaunee confederacy and settler governments, and the sculpture *The Spirit of Haida Gwaii* by artist Bill Reid, which is on the cover of *Strange Multiplicity* (17–8, 127–8). In the Australian context, we might note the painting adopted as the symbol of the South Australian Congress of Native Title Management Committees (Agius et al. 2002: 8) or the *Ngurrara Canvas* discussed in Chapter 5.

Importantly, the ATNS project and other writings on agreement-making stress that the culture of agreement-making is not necessarily about large-scale symbols but about changing habits at the local level. As Langton and Palmer (2003) conclude:

> the emerging culture of agreement making in Australia has led to the establishment of principles and rules for managing the relationship between native title, public law and private rights. It has created a corpus of experience and negotiation practices. The agreement-making process provides its own momentum and establishes communities of interest among parties who are engaged in the negotiations. Although they may have entered the process under the duress of native title procedures, parties often make considerable commitments to the ensuing negotiations, which creates relationships between the parties that, once established, assist in creating processes by which agreement making becomes a part of everyday business.

This 'momentum' is due to a lived pattern of behaviour, where groups, identities and relationships that are created through the very process of negotiating and the discourse that goes with it, exert a kind of force: the normative force of interdependence.

Intersecting Law: The Venn Diagram Approach to Legal Pluralism

The previous three parts have considered how law operates in the negotiation space through different practices – through mediation techniques that procure kinds of selves, through rhetorical strategies, interpretation and argument, through concrete acts that build decision-making structures and relations between groups, and through the creative capacity of symbolic invocation. In this final part, I want to use these insights to help conceptualize the legal pluralism of negotiation, the encounter between what is identified as 'Indigenous law' and 'national law', or, more diffusely, the broader norms of many different cultural groups coming together: the legal profession and other industry-specific professionals, bush and city, Indigenous and non-Indigenous.

One way of characterizing this situation would be as the co-existence of legal systems or normative orders in the same social field (Griffiths 1986: 1; Merry 1988: 870). The spatial imagery of overlapping zones or objects became current in analyses of native title in Australia through Noel Pearson's notion of the 'recognition space' and its later graphic representation by other authors as two intersecting circles.[25] It matches an intuitive sense of legal pluralism – repeated in some theoretical models such as Michael Walzer's (1983) spheres of justice, Leopold Pospisil's (1958: 273–8) legal levels, or Sally Falk Moore's semi-autonomous fields (1978)[26] – probably because we are used to thinking of law in reified and spatial terms. The 'Venn diagram' image requires two 'things' that have a defined content as well as a defined boundary, two things that are ontologically separate but which may interact, intersect or overlap. My argument here is that this model does not address the internal and relational aspects of legal pluralism that I have demonstrated, and further, that the problems it seeks to elucidate are better served by this stronger version of legal pluralism.

One analysis of native title mediation – that of mediator Craig Jones – explicitly characterizes conflict resolution in native title as a system of overlapping domains; for example, Indigenous, pastoral and native title (Figure 6.1). Each domain is said to represent all areas of life influencing the parties. Jones cautions that this visualization is a heuristic and not a description of the social field. He is interested, first, in making a case for a place for Indigenous law in native title mediation (making this clearly an argument for legal pluralism), and second, in helping mediators understand the limits of the purview of their role and assist in the design of the conflict resolution programme. While the influences on parties may come from anywhere within their 'domain', Jones clarifies that the mediator is only responsible for those issues, and has control of solely those processes that fall within the cross-section.

25 See Mantziaris and Martin 2000: 9.

26 And discussed in Griffiths 1986.

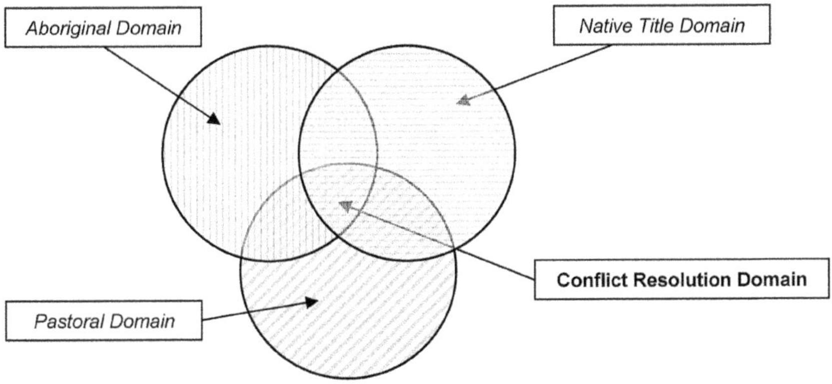

Figure 6.1 The Mediation Space[27]

He gives as an example a dispute between two Indigenous groups about boundaries, which overlaps with the 'native title domain', in which the NTA requires one group per area. The problem could be solved by recourse to anthropological reports, which would be situated in the larger overlap between the settler domain to which native title belongs and the Aboriginal domain. The real point in this dispute, however, is not to produce an objective map of country, but to achieve a stable decision on which to ground the rest of the mediation process. The best way to do this is to recognize that the dispute itself, he argues, is properly a matter for decision-making processes according to traditional law, and is thus situated in the overlap between the two Aboriginal domains, rather than in the cross-section with the native title domain.

Jones's heuristic mirrors the argument of legal pluralists who contest the monopoly of state law with a claim that other orders exist in the same social space. Like them, his reasons are political, empirical and pragmatic. Jones argues that failing to recognize Indigenous law is disrespectful to Indigenous people, and gives us a false picture of the mediation space. Furthermore, legal practitioners of the official system ignore it to their detriment: native title mediations that do not heed the obligations faced by Indigenous participants under their own law will produce unstable outcomes (Jones 2002). With the official law having the role of a management tool for social order, the Venn diagram is used in Jones' schema to underscore the point that although the influences on parties affect them throughout their domain, and so become part of the conflict resolution domain, the source of those influences may be outside of the responsibility of the mediation domain.

Despite Jones's disclaimer, there is necessarily a model of law, culture and the social field implicit in his analysis. Like the popular concept of the 'recognition

27 Adapted from Jones 2005.

space' at the base of Jones's mediation graph, his overlapping circles tap into a widespread notion of culture: that it is a bounded notional space with a location and a 'wholeness'. The Venn diagram also requires that we can postulate the existence of discrete and separate Indigenous and settler worlds within contemporary states. Finally, the recognition space becomes a supervening intersection between two things that already exist.

From an anthropological perspective, there is of course scepticism about a 'whole of culture' view that is not always and already a partial view from 'somewhere', an intersection with something else. We have seen in Chapter 4, for instance, that contemporary critical anthropology assumes its role as partial creator and not just observer of culture. An anthropological account of a given culture is at best the result of a dialogue with local interlocutors, at worst an exercise of imperial imagination. Whether through colonial practices of management or knowledge making, this intersection has, in most settler-colonial states, been complex and far reaching for several hundred years. However, this is not to say that the colonial intrusion represents a sudden distortion of something previously whole and intact either. Post-colonial thinkers such as Edward Said and Homi Bhabha have focused on the colonial encounter as the site of the production of difference so as to undo the assumption of 'pre-given ethnic or cultural traits set in the fixed tablet of tradition' (Bhabha 1994: 2) but the more general point is that culture is already 'internally' the result of overlap, continually negotiated by its practitioners, seen differently by each.

The encounters produced by the recognition of Indigenous rights are often characterized by a similarly hypostasized view of law on both (Indigenous and non-Indigenous) sides: emerging from something foundational, and containing distinct traits or practices. This is a legal pluralism that imagines a world containing multiple legal systems, where each system on its own is objectively knowable, occupying a determinate space. On the non-Indigenous side, however, work on the foundations of law show those foundations to constitute a kind of modern mythology, an attempt to cover over the contradictions that abound in human affairs, and the violence inherent in 'enforcing' the law (Fitzpatrick 1992b; Derrida 1990). The foundations of law are held in place, not by the undiluted truth of some past event, but by a constant re-iteration through symbols, ritual and discourse. The indeterminacy of law, as we saw in Chapter 3, is likewise a function of language. Whether things belong in or out of the 'legal domain' is not just unclear on the vague edges of words, but because 'meaning' itself can never be pinned down in any objective way. If, by and large, we function as if it can be, it is because we have experienced a range of uses that we are comfortable in assuming are 'the same'.

On the Indigenous side, the 'foundation' might be expressed to lie in Creation (such as the Dreaming in Australia) and the origin events that make the world what it is, in the land or nature, in stories, or in 'the people'. Certainly many Indigenous speakers seem to ascribe a monist rather than relational character to their law.

Statements such as 'the law was the same from the very start',[28] 'only one law', 'our law cannot change, we did not make it',[29] 'it's not our idea'[30] or the hope that once the land claim is over, they can just 'go back to the blackfella way' (Merlan 1997: 7) seem to express both the separateness of Indigenous and settler domains and the experience of law as beyond human control, unified and unchanging.

On the one hand, while this sounds similar to a European monist, positive and reified law, there are good reasons to be cautious in assuming these characteristics. First, we need to keep in constant focus the context in which these kinds of statements are offered. Is it in a land claim in which everything is digested in terms of the antiquity of traditions and a ritualized difference between settler law and Indigenous law? Is it when the speaker wishes to distinguish Dreaming law from the apparent inconstancy of White law or its human authority? What kinds of legal language are available to the speaker to express what they are trying to say in English? What subtle messages have been communicated over two hundred years about the valences of tradition and change? Second, we may be misreading claims to unity and constancy. As we saw in Chapter 3, just as a claim to one law in relation to territory seems to imply sovereignty, a claim to one law over time may imply a kind of objective constancy that we associate with written positive law. Both implications may be mistaken.

Third, in contrast to the kinds of expressions indicated above, there are also many accounts of the way reference to the Dreaming gives wide scope to personal interpretation and constant adaptation to new things: a stone dug up by grader work is interpreted as a dugong[31] because some local residents came from the coast (Merlan 1997: 8); colourful rock exposed by erosion is the entrails of a gutted kangaroo, adding a chapter to an already known story where, five miles away, two men killed a kangaroo in the Dreaming (Myers 1986: 66). That this is seen to be a discovery rather than an invention emphasizes the enduring nature of the Dreaming, but makes of it a 'vast repertoire by which the world can be re-imagined, and in being re-imagined be remade' (Verran 1998: 242). The authority for interpretation is also localized by land tenure relationships – 'the fact of localised knowledge is itself Law' – so although there might be one law, there is one law for each country whose content is the preserve of local law men and women.

On the other hand, any sense of separation between law and the world has to be qualified: in this way the Dreaming is not at all pretending *not* to be a mythology. The hardening and naturalization of boundaries in modern law sublimates the work – mythological, imaginary – that goes on to create and maintain those boundaries, and skips over the paradox inherent in meaningfulness that comes about because what is excluded from one thing is, in a semantic sense, inherent

28 Paul Sampi, witness cited in *Sampi v Western Australia* (2005: [316]) to support the claim that Bardi and Jawi people shared native title.

29 Mussolini Harvey, cited in Rose 1996a: 27.

30 Pintupi elder cited in Myers 1986: 53.

31 Marine mammal.

to it. In at least one account of the Dreaming, based on Yolngu practice, this 'boundary-maintaining' work is said to be explicitly acknowledged (Verran 1998: 247–8). If what happened in the eternal time plane of *Wangurr* is the foundational myth required to make material life meaningful – that turns other people into kin or the need for land into a relationship to 'sacred sites' – the boundary between 'myth' and 'reality' is not hidden but celebrated. In ceremonies these boundaries are ritually and publicly crossed in a multitude of ways: the original creation of meaningful places and connections are re-enacted, flesh is broken, substances exchanged between bodies and the environment.[32] In any case, the separateness implied by boundary is mitigated by the kinship relations that one has with animals, places, and all features of the natural world. The relationship between objects in the physical world and the Dreamings that, according to the stories, put them there, has been characterized as 'consubstantiality' or unity rather than representation of the world through the story (Munn 1984; Stanner 1998: 229). As the Yolngu say, 'a boundary is to cross' (Williams 1982).

The Venn diagram of native title mediation combines both the geometry of bounded space in legal positivism, and the geography of overlapping fields in legal pluralism. For all their differences, both theories assume law as a reified object. It is a pervasive trait of modernism that time, space and law 'are treated as a thing which exists aside from our human construction and interpretation of them, as abstractions in which we happen to find ourselves rather than as regulatory constructions devised by human minds to serve specific social purposes' (Manderson 2000: 159). Once something is experienced as outside ourselves it becomes naturalized and placed beyond criticism. It can easily become a 'powerful instrument of social discipline' (Manderson 2000: 159). This book has proposed an alternative geography of legal pluralism as one that recuperates the human element: boundaries and spaces become scale dependent (who is looking at which map and for what purpose?), non-linear relations defy determinative links between cause and effect. In fact, despite the neatness of Jones's Venn diagram and his tendency to describe law in this corporate fashion (proceeding 'under' Australian law and Aboriginal law, for instance) his actual mediation strategy affirms the centrality of Aboriginal people as the authors of their law: a boundary is not an objective fact, but a matter for decision-making.

We should be careful in treating these matters as 'purely internal' in any ontological sense, however. The dispute over boundaries is not simply a social given that is called into the public arena once native title arrives on the scene. It is provoked by the fact that a native title claim must name a single group and a bounded area, funded (sometimes) by Native Title Representative Bodies, historically exacerbated by forced displacement, and fed by scholarly writing on tribal territories. These complexly intertwined matters confound any attempt to locate a bounded intersection for Indigenous law and Australian law in native title. A similar point could be made for matters supposedly 'purely internal' to the

32 See the account of Arrernte ritual in Povinelli 2002: 99–107.

common law – which, as Fitzpatrick (1989) argues, has since the beginning of the modern era defined itself precisely in opposition to 'custom' and the 'lawlessness' of Indigenous peoples (353) – or to government bodies, the mining industry and pastoral groups. And by the same token, the corporate entity 'Indigenous peoples' did not pre-exist the arrival of settlers – these identities come to be through such diverse experiences as being the object of racial slurs, joining an Indigenous organization, ticking a box in the census or playing games with babies.[33]

Conclusion

The standard model of negotiation would assume that the two parties, with their separate laws, come together to create a third entity – an agreement. What I have suggested in this chapter instead is that not only does the law of each party inform and shape what they create together, but the experience of agreement-making, and the language, understanding, structures, procedures and relationships that come out of it, causes a re-evaluation of what has been understood as law. Both parties and their law are ultimately changed in some way by the negotiated settlement. They have a new language and a new set of experiences to call on in future instances of the elaboration of their law. A critical or discursive legal pluralism would thus place law in and through the negotiation space, not just as an external factor, a bargaining chip or an objective rule, but as something creatively engaged in a new ritual: one where differences are articulated, relationships, alliances and antagonisms consolidated, and laws enacted. This allows both a critical perspective on the role of the technologies, practices and processes associated with native title negotiations, and a role for Indigenous law beyond its bounded 'official recognition' or its status as an anthropological artefact of intra-Indigenous life.

For those writers who have tried to take on board the warning against both the fallacy of coherence and the alienation of reification, legal pluralism is something hosted by human selves: there is not a clash of two distinct systems in a social field, but a permanent interplay of ideas and principles in peoples' minds, gleaned from innumerable sources, that resolves itself into 'the law' for any one person in any one situation (Kleinhans and Macdonald 1997; Santos 1987). In our native title example, a person may experience multiple sources of obligation, accepted with differing degrees of legitimacy: to respect rights recognized by the courts, to submit proof in order to have rights recognized, to accede to the commercial reality of mining timetables, to maintain the goodwill of one's community, to make a decision in accordance with Indigenous law. In the Hartian sense, some may be experienced from the 'internal point of view' as genuine commitments, and

33 'You're an Aborigine' repeats the Bourke mother to the small baby on her knee. 'Lynette uses her daughter's position as the named to parody the accepted conventional status of the "white language" and show the hypocrisy, contradictions, and injustice embedded in it' (Cowlishaw 2004: 83).

others from the 'external point of view' to be taken into account in instrumental behaviour. Not all will be identified as 'law'.

In this way, an Indigenous party may accede to the requirements, as understood by him or her, stemming from jurisprudence or legislation, but may consider this to be the 'book' law of the conquerors, a false law that has not respected the law of the land, or not law at all but the consequence of white ignorance and power. Non-Indigenous persons may experience Aboriginal law 'second hand', by experiencing another person's sense of obligation, or 'first hand', such as when a judge in an 'on country' hearing for the Karrajarri claim accepts to blow on a handful of water in approaching a sacred site as an introduction to the spirits there,[34] when a government official is given the role and responsibilities of a host in a Gitxsan feast hall as a reconciliation event commemorating residential school survivors (Regan 2010: 193–212), or when a mediator claims to see 'Aboriginal agency, and perhaps even the agency of the country, working, acting on [him] as a settler' (Brigg and McIntyre 2005: 2). These actors' understanding of these events as being experiences of Aboriginal law is refracted through a multitude of texts and experiences, representations and stories, just as the Karrajarri elders cited in Chapter 5, for instance, understand their own law filtered through (a different set of) cultural texts and experiences.

If law is decentred through its irreducibly interpretive quality, if pure and bounded cultures or legal systems do not exist, then why is life experienced as a structured landscape rather than an indistinguishable cacophony in which so many individual voices form a blanket of white noise? The answer is that we cannot make meaning on our own. Individual acts of interpretation always take place in relation to others, and, as Wittgenstein showed us, it is the accumulation of these exchanges – in topographically varied patterns – that gives us a conventional understanding. The weight of convention that restricts our interpretations through habits is counterbalanced by the degree of 'play' entailed in our individual performance of meaning, which is always in response to something else and never either the re-iteration of a pure interior or anterior something, nor the deliberate and self-conscious construction of individuals.

It is for these reasons that Weiner urges a 'figure-ground' reversal in observing the 'recognition space' of native title. Instead of looking at institutions or moments of interaction between coherent 'cultures' (or 'laws') as if they result from, or are applied to, these essentially separate entities, he invites us to imagine ourselves as inhabiting one world, and to take as our subject those things which give any rarefied cultural group a place: not differences (how can we distinguish between differences emerging within one culture and between two cultures?) but the culturally differentiating activities in the world (Weiner 2006: 17). The governments, courts, NGOs, Aboriginal organizations, and companies that make the world of native title business and its components go round are then the new myth-makers, because they conceal the 'mechanisms that financially support it,

34 Interview with Justice North, 29 September 2003.

define it, translate it, make it visible, adjudicate it, manage it, assess it, evaluate it, regulate it, and so forth' (Weiner 2006: 19).

The focus on differentiating activities and their dialogic character avoids what is, for the simple constructivist version of culture, the risk of getting caught in a trap of its own making. One example of this trap was pointed out by David Scott (2003) with respect to Tully's reliance on the Wittgensteinian method in his new aspectival account of culture : 'surely on the very anti-foundationalist grounds established by the new theory itself, the unboundedness or otherwise of culture cannot be something given but must, rather, be something that *gets established* in forms of authoritative discourse' (101). And what happens if people *do* think of their culture as bounded, uniform and their law as imposed from above, like the Pintupi who claim that 'It's not our idea. It's a big law' (Myers 1986: 53)? A critical (but non-discursive) legal pluralism, with its focus on the individual's capacity to imagine the world, seems to suggest a constructivist approach. Therein lies the trap: because our ideology affects our understanding of the law and thus what law *is* for us, then, if we universally believe in the single normative order of the state, the 'inherent' plurality of law is nonsense. In that case, as Manderson (2000) asks, '[w]ould not any alternative norms thus have lost their power to guide conduct and affect behaviour?' (170).

The proviso is that, by the same token, these conventions are always contingent and open to dialogue. In fact, because this is how they have been produced (dialogically), one must always enquire of a proposition the question that it sought to answer and the argument in which it is participating.[35] For example, the characteristics of the modern state that can now in some contexts seem repressive, such as formal equality or the suspicion of legal pluralism, were devised in response to the perceived oppression of religious and aristocratic hierarchies. Contemporary descriptions of Indigenous law are the products of encounters with settlers such that parliaments, courts, the media and other public institutions are, as Weiner (1999) calls them, the 'elicitory mechanisms' of Indigenous culture; they are part of the same conversation rather than 'external intrusions' (6–7). The flip side of this is that in devising a theory, formulating a proposition or stating a fact – never the whole account or a view from nowhere – we have to consider what question we are answering and why we want to know.

With this in mind, I could now start this chapter again asking how it is that legislation, court and tribunal decisions and mediator techniques (to pick the few I have focused on) elicit particular articulations of law, culture and identity *as* traditional versus modern, Indigenous versus settler, farmer versus lawyer, and so on, that are experienced as having different sources. Each of the actors in a web of communities has his or her own response to legal questions, and these influence the responses of other actors in a never-ending cycle of intensifying perturbations. Law is generated by constant iterations and reiterations, each related to the other but ultimately unpredictable.

35 This is Quentin Skinner's take on the hermeneutic method (1988: 274).

Chapter 7
Conclusion

A declaration that human beings are dependent on each other should be news to no one; after all, this is what it is to be social and political creatures. And yet if John Donne's 'No man is an Island' ('Every man is a piece of the continent, A part of the main') has become a cliché after having lain dormant for 300 years, it may be because a need to express community in the wake of individualism, and connectivity in the face of modernist alienation and anomie, became pressing after 1940 when the lines appeared as the epigraph to Hemingway's novel *For Whom The Bell Tolls* (Beer 1997: 43). Still, there is something about our interdependence that is not captured by the simple agglomeration of individuals into a social group, or in the metaphor of islands and continents. As beings in time we are works in progress, ones that become graspable through our words and deeds in public. Our identity is shaped and narrated via interactions with others that are unpredictable, and over which we have imperfect control. Our very self is dependent on others.

No less than the individual, law developed island qualities in the modern era, expressed as jurisdiction and sovereignty in the usual territorial sense, but also as distinctness from the social and the political, and as a determinative control over the constitution of legal meaning. In fact, this last characteristic can also be considered a kind of sovereignty, and my argument in Chapter 2 borrowed from the work of Patchen Markell on recognition to make this point: purporting to arrive at a clear or complete knowledge of past phenomena in order to ground future action securely (surely an apt description of the application of law in orthodox legal theory) is an expression of a desire to be 'an independent, self-determining agent' (2003: 11). As with the self, interdependence became somewhat of a theme in Anglo-American legal theory from the 1950s onwards. The Law and Society movement argued that the two spheres of life are not islands but are mutually constituted, while Critical Legal Studies insisted on the thoroughly political qualities of the law. Literary approaches stress the importance of acts of reading, interpretation and context to underscore the instability of legal meaning over time. In statutory interpretation, even the idea of a controlling original intention is understood in the writing of Lon Fuller and others to be worked out dialogically, as we come to draw out the meaning of a text by situating it with respect to a range of real or hypothetical examples.

Indigenous claims trouble different aspects of law's sovereignty and test the degree to which interdependence is supported in official accounts. First, whether claims to land, resources and jurisdiction are read in terms of equality or of the distinctiveness of Indigenous peoples, the mechanical process of deciding claims turns on the recognition of some fact of the claimants' lives as something 'else':

sometimes occupation, sometimes tradition, sometimes law. It is a process of linguistic and cultural translation that requires Indigenous lives to be both legible and rendered into the terms of another law. The translation is always imperfect if not impossible. And yet the validity of claims depends on a finding that there is a genuine original for the translation, something with a prior, verifiable existence. Orthodox legal theory does not support the insights of philosophy, literary theory and anthropology that the very processes of recognition and translation are constitutive of, at the very least, the public version of the original. Lawyers and judges are still caught up in the pretention to temporal mastery over meaning.

Unless the productive activities associated with Indigenous rights regimes are appreciated, state law officials will continue to demand interminably unrealistic things of Indigenous claimants. To illustrate what I see happening in Indigenous rights processes, I will refer to the work of legal academic Pierre Schlag (1997) who critiques legal positivism by drawing on, of all things, the debunked nineteenth-century science of phrenology. Phrenologists sought to correlate the observable differences in human intellectual faculties and propensities in individuals with respect to an area of the brain that manifests as a cranial feature: large eyes or a prominent brow, for instance. From the empirical observation of behaviour, phrenologists implied distinct human faculties, and that these were associated with a specific part of the brain. From the observation of cranial features, they implied an association with that part of the brain. Empirical confidence then allowed the logical leap necessary to turn phrenology into an explanation and a predictive theory: human behaviour is *caused by* faculties, and faculties and head shape are *caused by* prominent parts of the brain. Faculties became real and elaborately defined; there were fundamental categories, combined categories and subsidiary categories.

The interesting question is how a science that appeared entirely credible and had countless adherents failed so spectacularly. Schlag suggests that this is due to its epistemological paradigm, but that other disciplines like law employ the same flawed paradigm without having succumbed to phrenology's failure. The paradigm involves the circularity of the explanatory categories: behaviours are described and classified, and then the categories are hypostatized and projected back onto a faculty defined as that which is wont to produce the behaviour in question. The faculty explains the behaviour. As Schlag notes, '[t]he core problem with this kind of explanation lies in the unthinking transformation of classifications designed to describe behaviour … into effective ontological agencies' (888).

In my view, official versions of Indigenous rights perform the same transposition from 'epistemic heuristics' to 'ontological actualities' as Schlag puts it. Faced with claims by Indigenous peoples for legal recognition, courts come up with an explanation that seems to reconcile history, anthropology and law. In the colonial period, Indigenous peoples' rights to land were ignored *because* the doctrines of *terra nullius* or discovery led colonists to denigrate Indigenous peoples and their ways. Now, Indigenous title can be recognized *because* Indigenous peoples had a normative system that gives them rights or because they occupied the land.

Now, the court has the authority to make this decision *because* the crown gained sovereignty at some point in the past. Now, the claimants must prove continuity *because* law and society are inextricably entwined.

The solid, enduring thing that is traditional laws and customs, or distinctive practices, is hard to recognize as a construction because often it gels well with how Indigenous people talk. This may be, as Julie Cruikshank (1998) has noted, because in the same era in which the social sciences were turning away from positivist methodologies and towards representation, polyvocality and indeterminacy, Indigenous peoples were discovering the strategic benefits of positivist claims to objective truth (162). However, because it is forgotten that these 'originals' are back-projections of the translation of Indigenous rights, the role of courts and other forums as elicitors of Indigenous difference is overlooked. The 'epistemic heuristic' of traditional law becomes a test of authenticity.

It may also be a misreading: the solidity demanded by positive law is not the eternity of the land or the knowledge of belonging to a community; it is the constancy of abstractions such as rules, systems or culture. Further, Indigenous traditions have plenty to offer to an account of interdependence and the 'non-sovereign character' of human life. Whether through the kind of connectivity glossed as holism and the prominence of kinship models in relating to other (human and non-human) persons, through gift economies that would see, for example, the use of territories for hunting as a matter of mutual gift exchange largely controlled by the species instead of seeing them as mastery of or dominion over the territory (Nadasdy 2007), or the structure of languages that do not easily permit talking about definitive objects independently of time, relationship or context (Henderson 2006: 116–77; Christie 1994: 27), future projects could develop further this aspect of legal pluralism by drawing on Indigenous knowledges.

Theory is inescapably circular – we tend to see what we look for – which is itself a problem of recognition. But if we are aware of this, we might change the way we use it. As Jacques Derrida (1987a) puts it in relation to the question of the theoretical definition of art and the recognition of a work of art: 'the hermeneutic circle has only the (logical, formal, derived) appearance of a vicious circle. It is not a question of escaping it, but on the contrary of engaging in it and going all around it' (32). That act of going round focuses our attention on the craft of thinking, on the activity of meaning-making that, in some Indigenous cultures at least, is celebrated, rather than hidden, in the mythological (Verran 1998: 247). Pragmatically, a subject of a phrenological experiment could never be asked to prove that they had a faculty for kindness, only that they had acted kindly. Likewise, the contemporary articulation by Indigenous peoples of their identities and laws as an expression of belonging to their land is what counts, and not a set of laws and customs that existed in 1788.

If the 'Just So' stories of modern law are unacceptable because they refuse to take Indigenous law ways seriously as law and cling to a vision of one law determined by the court, *Declarations of Interdependence* offers a way to understand that the court's law is already implicated in legally plural processes.

Try as it might to be the one law, the court is too dependent on uncontrollable and efflorescent meaning made elsewhere. It is already responsible to Indigenous law; it has constructed its own law against and in dialogue with, the arguments of Indigenous peoples. It participates in the rituals that mark Indigenous difference and that give rise to particular understandings of traditional laws and customs.

By the same token, Indigenous law as it is expressed and experienced is responsive to its interlocutors. In Markell's reading of sovereignty through the problems of recognition, seeking proper recognition of an authentic self expresses a mistaken attempt to be free of the instability and uncertainty that comes from interdependence. Thus, and this is a delicate point to make, Indigenous self-determination as the aspiration to construct a communal self free from outside interference is no more a viable objective than the autonomy of state law, even as that aspiration can be understood in the context of oppressive levels of interference and dependence that have been experienced as a result of colonization. Self-determination as the ability of a community to make political decisions about how its members will be educated, housed and fed, how its territories will be cared for, and how its social relations will be managed is essential, but these decisions and their consequences will always be taking shape in relation to other communities and governments, at different scales (Borrows 2002: 141). The justice question that emerges from our critique of sovereignty is not whether autonomy is being guaranteed, but whether patterns of recognition attempt to place a disproportionate burden of the fact of human finitude on one group, something that happens when the identity of the state and its claims are taken for granted, while Indigenous peoples have to establish their authenticity according to terms that are not of their making.

A second aspect of sovereignty challenged by Indigenous claims is the more usual one of a monopoly of law-making within a particular geographic space, for the obvious reason that, in some jurisdictions, claims depend on proof of Indigenous law, and are, either explicitly or implicitly, grounded in Indigenous sovereignty. The usual approach seems to reconcile overlapping claims to sovereignty by distinguishing Indigenous law as a species of fact, or, as in Canada's self-government agreements or constitutional arrangements for tribal sovereignty in the US, by formally organizing sovereignty or self-government into distinct territories and subject matters. A more complex account of co-existence is of course provided in the idea of productive encounters in the previous paragraphs. Further, the very spatial dimensions of territorial sovereignty – which relies on an essentially placeless or uniform law within a particular boundary – may be disrupted by Indigenous articulations of law as 'emplaced' in a highly differentiated landscape known in terms of its multiple connections – between places, different timescales and people – as my studies of the Yorta Yorta Aboriginal Community and the *Ngurrara Canvas* suggested.

Interdependence has important critical purchase on the spatial dimension of sovereignty. If legal positivism, like recognition, attempts to anchor sovereignty in determinate knowledge of law and facts, spatial dominion anchors it in the unencumbered control of things within a boundary. These days absolute territorial sovereignty is somewhat of a caricature, as is the equivalent idea in Blackstone's account of property as a 'sole and despotic dominion' (see Schorr 2009). Absolute state sovereignty is compromised by obligations within the international order just as real property rights are relative to other rights enshrined by law. However, despite this reality, efforts to maintain dominion persist. But just as temporal sovereignty – mastery over meaning – is an illusion purchased at the expense of subordinate groups, spatial sovereignty is an illusion because, in the long term, there are inherent limits to what can be done on the land. Human finitude is both a social and an ecological phenomenon. The burden of pursuing, for example, resource extraction, as if we were not interdependent with all living things, is displaced both onto communities (human and non-human) dispossessed and disrupted by development, and onto future generations (human and non-human). Although a fuller exploration of this idea will have to wait for another occasion, Indigenous legal traditions that have proven themselves sustainable in their particular places through notions of interdependence are a crucial intervention in the critique of sovereignty.[1]

This book began with an enquiry into what it means to say that state law and Indigenous law coexist, and the problems with approaching co-existence through the paradigm of recognition. My aim has been to develop a legal theory that can address some of the contradictions and ethical binds that orthodox understandings of the state recognition of Indigenous law provokes: in particular, the half-hearted legal pluralism that situates Indigenous law as a social fact, but maintains that the state has a monopoly over law, and the difficulties faced by Indigenous peoples who see their practices and understandings mistranslated, and then authoritatively fixed, by courts. Discursive, critical legal pluralism allows for both state law and Indigenous law to be understood *as law* and highlights how they can, and already do, exist in a mutually constituting relation to one another. Part of this has involved telling a counter story about law as provisional and open rather than fixed and determinative. However, if law is always and already plural, then why would legal actors need to do anything differently, according to my argument? From the perspective I have taken in this book, the answer lies in the displaced burden of interdependence. Understanding that one is implicated in creating, and not just responding to, social phenomena and human identities instils a different sense of responsibility for legal decision making. And understanding oneself as subject to others calls for some humility with respect to the grounds we assume for our actions. I have undertaken this analysis in the hope that, by seeing themselves in the mirror more clearly, those who call state law their own will have taken the first step in a new direction.

1 For a critique of property law along similar lines, see Graham 2011, in particular 197–202.

Bibliography

Abel, R. 1981. The contradiction of informal justice, in *The Politics of Informal Justice* (Vol 1), edited by Abel, R. London: Academic Press, 267–320.

Agius, P., Davies, J., Howitt, R. and Johns, L. 2002. Negotiating Comprehensive Settlement of Native Title Issues: Building a New Scale of Justice in South Australia. *Land, Rights, Laws: Issues of Native Title*, 2(20), 1–11.

Alcantara, C. 2007. Explaining Aboriginal treaty negotiation outcomes in Canada: the cases of the Inuit and the Innu in Labrador. *Canadian Journal of Political Science*, 40(1), 185–207.

Alcoff, L. 1991–92. The problem of speaking for others. *Cultural Critique*, 20(Winter), 5–32.

Alcoff, L. and Potter, E. 1993. (eds), *Feminist Epistemologies.* New York: Routledge.

Althusser, L. 1971. *Lenin and Philosophy, and Other Essays*, translated by Brewster, B. London: New Left Books.

Altman, A. 1986. Legal realism, critical legal studies and Dworkin. *Philosophy and Public Affairs*, 15(3), 205–35.

Altman, J. 1998. Compensation for native title: land rights lessons for an effective and fair regime. *Land, Rights, Laws: Issues of Native Title*, 8(20), 1–11.

Andersen, C. 1999. Governing Aboriginal justice in Canada: constructing responsible individuals and communities through 'tradition'. *Crime, Law & Social Change*, 31(4), 303–26.

Anderson, L. 2003. The law in the desert: alternative methods of delivering justice. *Journal of Law & Society*, 30(1), 120–36.

Anker, A. 2005. The truth in painting: cultural artefacts as proof of native title. *Law Text Culture*, 9(1), 91–130.

Appadurai, A. 1996. *Modernity at Large: Cultural Dimensions of Globalisation.* Minneapolis: University of Minnesota Press.

Appiah, K.A. 1994. Identity, authenticity, survival: multicultural societies and cultural reproduction, in *Multiculturalism: Examining the Politics of Recognition*, edited by Gutman, A. Princeton, NJ: Princeton University Press, 149–63.

Appleton, J. 1975. *The Experience of Landscape.* London: John Wiley & Sons.

Arendt, H. 1959. *The Human Condition.* Chicago: University of Chicago Press.

Aristotle. 1961. *Poetics*, translated by Butcher, S.H. New York: Hill & Wang.

Asad, T. 1973. The concept of cultural translation in British anthropology, in *Anthropology and the Colonial Encounter*, edited by Asad, T. New York: Humanities Press, 141–64.

Asch, M. 2000. The judicial conceptualizaton of culture after *Delgamuukw* and *Van der Peet*. *Review of Constitutional Studies*, 5(2), 119–37.
Astor, H. and Chinkin, C. 1992. *Dispute Resolution in Australia.* North Ryde, NSW: Butterworths.
Atkinson, W. 1996. Yorta Yorta struggle for justice continues, in *Majah: Indigenous Peoples and the Law*, edited by Bird, G. et al. Sydney: Federation Press, 281–9.
Atkinson, W. 2002. Mediating the mindset of opposition. *Indigenous Law Bulletin*, 5(15), 8–11.
Atkinson, W. 2008. Ngariarty: speaking strong, in *First Australians Unillustrated*, edited by Perkins, R. and Langton, M. Carlton, Vic: Miegunyah Press, 185–216.
Attwood, B. (ed.), 1996. *In the Age of Mabo: History, Aborigines and Australia.* St Leonards, NSW: Allen & Unwin.
Austin, J. 1954. *The Province of Jurisprudence Determined.* London: Weidenfeld & Nicholson.
Austin, J.L. 1962. *How to Do Things With Words.* Oxford: Oxford University Press.
Bakhtin, M. 1981. *The Dialogic Imagination: Four Essays*, translated by Emerson, C. and Holquist, M. Austin, TX: University of Texas Press.
Baird, M. 2013. The breath of the mountain is my heart: Indigenous cultural landscapes and cultural heritage. *International Journal of Heritage Studies*, 19(4), 327–40.
Banks, N. 2006. *Marshall and Bernard*: ignoring the relevance of customary property laws. *University of New Brunswick Law Journal*, 55, 120–34.
Banner, S. 2005. *How the Indians Lost Their Lands: Law and Power on the Frontier*. Cambridge, Mass: Belknap Press.
Barnett, K. 2000. *Western Australia v Ward* – one step forward, two steps back: native title and the bundle of rights analysis. *Melbourne University Law Review* 24(2), 462–77.
Barrett, J. and Barrett, J. 2004. *A History of Alternative Dispute Resolution: The Story of a Political, Cultural and Social Movement.* San Fransisco: Jossey-Bass.
Barrett, M. 1991. *The Politics of Truth: From Marx to Foucault*. Stanford: Stanford University Press .
Barsh, R.L. and Henderson, J.Y. 1997. The Supreme Court's *Van der Peet* trilogy: naïve imperialism and ropes of sand. *McGill Law Journal*, 42(4), 993–1009.
Bartlett, R. 1996. Dispossession by the native title tribunal. *University of Western Australia Law Review*, 26(1), 108–37.
Bartlett, R. 1997. A return to dispossession and discrimination. *University of Western Australia Law Review*, 27(1), 44–65.
Bartlett, R. 2000. *Native Title in Australia.* Sydney: Butterworths.
Bartlett, R. 2003. An obsession with traditional laws and customs creates difficulty establishing native title claims in the south: Yorta Yorta. *University of Western Australia Law Review*, 31(1), 35–46.

Basso, K. 1996. *Wisdom Sits in Places: Landscape and Language Among the Western Appache.* Albuquerque, NM: University of New Mexico Press.

Bauman, T. and Williams, R. 2004. The business of process: research issues in managing Indigenous decision making and disputes in land. *AIATSIS Research Discussion Paper No. 13.* Canberra: AIATSIS Research Publications.

Beckett, J. 1994. The Murray Island land case and the problem of cultural continuity, in *Mabo and Native Title: Origins and Institutional Implications*, edited by Sanders, W. Canberra: CAEPR, ANU, 7–24.

Beer, G. 1997. The making of a cliché: 'no man is an island'. *European Journal of English Studies*, 1(1), 33–47.

Behrendt, L. 1995. *Aboriginal Dispute Resolution.* Sydney: Federation Press.

Behrendt, L. 2003. *Achieving Social Justice: Indigenous Rights and Australia's Future*. Sydney: Federation Press.

Bell, D. 1983. *Daughters of the Dreaming.* North Sydney: Allen & Unwin.

Bell, D. 1998. *Ngarrindjeri Wurruwarrin: A World That Is, Was, and Will Be.* Melbourne: Spinifex Press.

Benda-Beckmann, F. von, 1984. Law out of context: a comment on the creation of traditional law discussion. *Journal of African Law* 28(1–2), 28–33.

Bender, B. 1999. Subverting the western gaze: mapping alternative worlds, in *The Archeology and Anthropology of Landscape*, edited by Ucko, P. and Layton, R. London: Routledge, 31–45.

Benjamin, W. 1969. *Illuminations*, edited by Arendt, H., translated by Zohn, H. New York: Schocken Books.

Berger, P. and Luckmann, T. 1966. *The Social Construction of Reality: A Treatise in the Sociology of Knowledge.* London: Penguin.

Bettinger, B. 1991. *Hunter-Gatherers: Archaeological and Evolutionary Theory.* New York: Plenum Press.

Bhabha, H. 1994. *The Location of Culture.* London: Routledge.

Bhandar, B. 2001. Plasticity and Post-Colonial Recognition: 'Owning, Knowing and Being' *Law & Critique* 22(3), 227–49.

Bhandar, B. 2007. Re-covering the limits of recognition: the politics of difference and decolonization in John Borrows' Recovering Canada: the resurgence of Indigenous law. *Australian Feminist Law Journal*, 27(Dec), 125–55.

Bhandar, B. 2011. Plasticity and post-colonial recognition: owning, knowing and being. *Law & Critique*, 22(3), 227–49.

Bix, B. 1999. *Jurisprudence: Theory and Context* (2nd ed). Durham, NC: Carolina Academic Press.

Black, C. 2011. *The Land is the Source of the Law: A Dialogic Encounter with an Indigenous Jurisprudence*. London, UK: Routledge-Cavendish.

Black, M. 2002. Developments in practice and procedure in native title cases. *Public Law Review*, 13(March), 16–25.

Blackburn, C. 2000. *Harvest of Souls: The Jesuit Missions and Colonialism in North America 1632–1650.* Montreal: McGill-Queens University Press.

Blackstone, W. 1800. *Commentaries on the Laws of England* (13th ed.), edited by Christian, E. London: T Cadell & W Davies.
Blainey, G. 1993. Drawing up a balance sheet of our history. *Quadrant*, 37(7–8), 10–15.
Blomley, N. 1998. Landscapes of property. *Law & Society Review* 32(3), 567–612.
Blowes, R. and Trigger, D. 1999. Negotiating the Century Mine Agreement: issues of law, culture and politics, in *Regional Agreements: Key Issues in Australia: Volume 2 Case Studies*, edited by Edmonds, M. Canberra: Australian Institute of Aboriginal and Torres Strait Islanders Studies, Native Title Unit, 85–135.
Borrows J. 1996. With or without you: First Nations law (in Canada). *McGill Law Journal*, 41(3), 629–65.
Borrows, J. 1997. Wampum at Niagara: the Royal Proclamation, Canadian legal history, and self-government, in *Aboriginal and Treaty Rights in Canada*, edited by Asch, M. Vancouver: UBC Press, 169–72.
Borrows, J. 1997/98. Frozen rights in Canada: constitutional interpretation and the trickster. *Northern American Indian Law Review* 22(1), 37–64.
Borrows, J. 1999. Sovereignty's alchemy: an analysis of *Delgamuukw v British Columbia*. *Osgoode Hall Law Journal* 37(3), 537–96.
Borrows, J. 2002. *Recovering Canada: The Resurgence of Indigenous Law.* Toronto: University of Toronto Press.
Borrows, J. 2005. Creating an Indigenous legal community: 5th annual John Tait memorial lecture. *McGill Law Journal*, 50(1), 153–82.
Borrows, J. 2010. *Canada's Indigenous Constitution.* Toronto: University of Toronto Press.
Bourdieu, P. 1977. *Outline of a Theory of Practice*, translated by Nice, R. Cambridge: Cambridge University Press.
Bowker, G. and Star, S.L. 1999. *Sorting Things Out: Classification and its Consequences.* Cambridge, Mass: MIT Press.
Boyle, J. 1987. Thomas Hobbes and the invented tradition of positivism: reflections on language, power and essentialism. *University of Pennsylvania Law Review*, 135(2), 383–426.
Brehaut, L. and Vitenbergs, A. (eds), 2001. *The Guruma Story = Guruma-yharntu Wangka* (told by the Guruma Elders Group, led by Stevens, P. ed.). Alice Springs, NT: Jukurrpa Books.
Brennan, S. 2004. Native title and the 'acquisition of property' under the Australian constitution. *Melbourne University Law Review*, 28(1), 28–79.
Brigg, M. 2003. Mediation, power, and cultural difference. *Conflict Resolution Quarterly*, 20(3), 287–306.
Brigg, M. 2007. Governance and susceptibility in conflict resolution: possibilities beyond control. *Social & Legal Studies*, 16(1), 27–47.
Brown, W. 1995. *States of Injury: Power and Freedom in Late Modernity.* Princeton, NJ: Princeton University Press.
Bushnell, I., Sai, F. and Mullin, J. 1989. Neonatal recognition of the mother's face. *British Journal of Developmental Psychology*, 7(1), 3–15.

Butler, J. 1999. *Subjects of Desire: Hegelian Reflections in Twentieth Century France*. New York: Columbia University Press.
Cairns, A. 2011. *Citizens Plus: Aboriginal Peoples and the Canadian State.* Vancouver: UBC Press.
Carey, M. 2004. From whiteness to whitefella: changing white race power in Australia. *Balayi: Culture, Law & Colonialism* 6, 9–22.
Carter, P. 1988. *The Road to Botany Bay: An Exploration of Landscape and History.* New York: Alfred A. Knopf.
Case, N. 1998/99. Tide of history or tsunami? *The Members of the Yorta Yorta Aboriginal Community v The State of Victoria & Ors*. *Indigenous Law Bulletin*, 4(17), 17–19.
Chamberlain, L. 1988. Gender and the metaphorics of translation. *Signs*, 13(3), 454–72.
Chance, I. 2001. *Kaltja Now.* Adelaide: Wakefield Press.
Charlton, G. 2007/08. Letting go of culture: a comment on *R v Sappier*; *R v Gray*. *Ottawa Law Review*, 39(2), 317–32.
Chartrand, P. 2006. *R v Marshall*; *R v Bernard*: the return of the native. *University of New Brunswick Law Journal*, 55, 135–45.
Chatwin, B. 1986. *Songlines.* London, UK: Franklin Press.
Cheng, C. 1997. Touring the museum: a comment on *R v Van der Peet*. *University of Toronto Faculty of Law Review*, 55(2), 419–34.
Chesterman, S. 1998. 'Skeletal legal principles' the concept of law in Australian land rights jurisprudence. *Journal of Legal Pluralism*, 40, 61–88.
Cheyfitz, E. 1991. *The Poetics of Imperialism: Translation and Colonization from The Tempest to Tarzan.* Philadelphia: University of Pennsylvania Press.
Christie, G. 1998. Aboriginal rights, Aboriginal culture and protection. *Osgoode Hall Law Journal*, 36(3), 447–84.
Christie, M. 1994. Grounded and ex-centric knowledges: exploring Aboriginal alternatives to western thinking, in *Thinking: International Interdisciplinary Perspectives*, edited by Edwards, J. Melbourne: Hawker-Brownlow Publishing, 24–34.
Christie, M. and Perrett, B. 1996. Negotiating resources: language, knowledge and the search for 'secret English' in northeast Arnhem land, in *Resources, Nations and Indigenous Peoples,* edited by Howitt, R. and Hirsch, J. Oxford: Oxford University Press, 57–65.
Christie, N. 1977. Conflicts as property. *The British Journal of Criminology*, 17(1), 1–15.
Clarkson, S. 2001. Yorta Yorta: the effect of changes in traditional laws and customs in native title determinations. *University of Queensland Law Journal*, 21(2), 235–39.
Clifford, J. 1988. *The Predicament of Culture: Twentieth-Century Ethnography, Literature, and Art.* Cambridge, Mass: Harvard University Press.
Cobb, S. 1997. The domestication of violence in mediation. *Law & Society Review*, 31(3), 397–437.

Cockayne, J. 2001. *Members of the Yorta Yorta Aboriginal Community v Victoria*: Indigenous and colonial traditions in native title. *Melbourne University Law Review* 25(3), 786–809.

Conklin, W. 2001. *The Invisible Origins of Legal Positivism.* Dordrecht: Kluwer Academic Publishers.

Connolly, A. 2010. *Cultural Difference on Trial: The Nature and Limits of Judicial Understanding.* Farnham, Surrey: Ashgate.

Constable, M. 1994. *The Law of the Other: The Mixed Jury and Changing Conceptions of Citizenship, Law, and Knowledge.* Chicago: University of Chicago Press.

Constable, M. 2005. *Just Silences: The Limits and Possibilities of Modern Law.* Princeton: Princeton University Press.

Constable, M. 2014. Law as language. *Critical Analysis of Law*, 1(1), 63–74.

Coombs, H.C. 1994. *Aboriginal Autonomy: Issues and Strategies.* Cambridge: Cambridge University Press.

Cooray, M. 1994. The High Court in Mabo – legalist or l'egotiste, *Make a Better Offer: The Politics of Mabo*, edited by Goot, M. and Rowse, T. Leichhardt, NSW: Pluto Press, 82–96.

Corbett, T. and O'Faircheallaigh, C. 2006/7. Unmasking the politics of native title: the National Native Title Tribunal's application of the NTA's arbitration provisions. *University of Western Australia Law Review*, 33(1), 153–77.

Cornell, D. 1992. *The Philosophy of the Limit.* London, UK: Routledge.

Correy, S. 2006. The reconstitution of Aboriginal sociality through the identification of traditional owners in New South Wales. *The Australian Journal of Anthropology*, 17(3), 336–47.

Cosgrove, D. 1984. *Social Formation and Symbolic Landscape.* London: Croom Helm.

Coulthard, G. 2007. Subjects of empire: Indigenous peoples and the 'politics of recognition' in Canada. *Contemporary Political Theory*, 6(4), 437–60.

Cover, R. 1983. The Supreme Court 1982 term foreword: nomos and narrative. *Harvard Law Review*, 97(1), 4–68.

Cover, R. 1986. Violence and the word. *Yale Law Journal*, 95(8), 1601–29.

Cowlishaw, G. 1995. Did the earth move for you? The anti-Mabo debate. *The Australian Journal of Anthropology*, 6, 43–64.

Cowlishaw, G. 2004. *Blackfellas, Whitefellas, and the Hidden Injuries of Race.* Carlton, Vic: Blackwell Publishing.

Cross, R. and Tapper, C. 1985. *Cross on Evidence* (6th edn). London: Butterworths.

Cruikshank, J. 1992. Invention of anthropology in British Columbia's Supreme Court: oral tradition as evidence in *Delgamuukw v BC. BC Studies*, 95(Autumn), 25–42.

Cruikshank, J. 1998. *The Social Life of Stories: Narrative and Knowledge in the Yukon Territory.* Vancouver: UBC Press.

Culhane, D. 1992. Adding insult to injury: Her Majesty's loyal anthropologists. *BC Studies*, 95(Autumn), 66–92.

Curr, E. 1883. *Recollections of Squatting in Victoria, Then Called Port Phillip District*. Echuca, Vic: Rich River Printers.
Curr, E. 1886. *The Australian Race: Its Origin, Languages, Customs, Place of Landing in Australia and the Routes by Which It Spread Itself Over That Continent*. Melbourne, Vic: J. Ferres.
Davies, M. 2002. *Asking the Law Question: The Dissolution of Legal Theory* (2nd edn). Pyrmont, NSW: Lawbook Co.
Davies, M. 2005. The ethos of pluralism. *Sydney Law Review*, 27(1), 87–112.
de Certeau, M. 1984. *The Practice of Everyday Life*, translated by Rendall, S. Berkeley: University of California Press.
de Costa, R. 2003. Treaty How? *The Drawing Board: An Australian Review of Public Affairs*, 4(1), 1–22.
de Costa, R. 2006a. Identity, authority, and the moral worlds of Indigenous petitions. *Comparative Studies in Society and History*, 48(3), 669–98.
de Costa, R. 2006b. National encounters between Indigenous and settler peoples: some Canadian examples, in *What Good Condition? Reflections on an Australian Aboriginal Treaty 1986–2006*, edited by Read, P. et al. Canberra: ANU Press, 15–30.
Delgado, R. 1995. Rodrigo's final chronicle: Cultural power, the law reviews, and the attack on narrative jurisprudence. *Southern California Law Review*, 68(3), 545–75.
Delgado, R., Dunn, C., Brown, P., Lee, H. and Hubbert, D. 1985. Fairness and formality: Minimizing the risk of prejudice in alternative dispute resolution. *Wisconsin Law Review*, 1985(6), 1359–404.
Delgado, R. and Stefanic, J. (eds), 2000. *Critical Race Theory: The Cutting Edge.* Philadelphia: Temple University Press.
Delgado, R. and Stefancic, J. 2001. *Critical Race Theory: An Introduction.* New York: New York University Press.
Derrida, J. 1974. *Marges de la Philosophie*. Paris: Minuit.
Derrida, J. 1976. *Of Grammatology*, translated by Spivak, G.C. Baltimore: John Hopkins University Press.
Derrida, J. 1978. *Writing and Difference*, translated by Bass, A. Chicago: University of Chicago Press.
Derrida, J. 1982. Différance, in *Margins of Philosophy*, translated Bass, A. Chicago: Chicago University Press, 1–27.
Derrida, J. 1982. White mythology: metaphor in the text of philosophy, in *Margins of Philosophy*, translated by Bass, A. Chicago: Chicago University Press, 207–71.
Derrida, J. 1986. Declarations of independence. *New Political Science*, 7(1), 7–15.
Derrida, J. 1987a. *The Truth in Painting*, translated by Bennington, G. and McLeod, I. Chicago: University of Chicago Press.
Derrida, J. 1987b. *Psyche: Inventions de l'Autre*. Paris: Galilé.
Derrida, J. 1990. Force of law: the mystical foundation of authority. *Cardozo Law Review*, 11(5/6), 919–1046.

Detmold, M. 1993. Law and difference: reflections of Mabo's case, in *Essays on the Mabo Decision.* North Ryde, NSW: Law Book Company.

Dick, C. 2009. 'Culture and the courts' revisited: group-rights scholarship and the evolution of s.35(1). *Canadian Journal of Political Science*, 42(4), 957–79.

Dilthey, W. 1914. The construction of the historical world in the human sciences, in *W. Dilthey: Selected Writings*, edited by Rickman, H.P. (1976) Cambridge: Cambridge University Press, 168–245.

Dodson, M. 1996a. Indigenous culture and native title. *Alternative Law Journal*, 21(1), 2–5.

Dodson, M. 1996b. Power and cultural difference in native title mediation. *Aboriginal Law Bulletin*, 3(84), 8–18.

Dorsett, S. and McVeigh, S. 2002. Just so: the law which governs Australia is Australian law. *Law & Critique*, 13(3), 289–309.

Douzinas, C. 2002. Identity, recognition, rights: what can Hegel teach us about human rights? *Journal of Law & Society*, 29(3), 379–405.

Durkheim, E. 1995. *Elementary Forms of the Religious Life*, translated by Fields, K. New York: Free Press.

Dworkin, R. 1975. Hard cases. *Harvard Law Review* 88(6), 1057–109.

Dworkin, R. 1986. *Law's Empire*. London, UK: Belknap Press.

Eades, D. 1988. They don't speak an Aboriginal language, or do they?, in *Being Black: Aboriginal Cultures in 'Settled' Australia*, edited by Keen, I. Canberra: Aboriginal Studies Press, 97–115.

Eagleton, T. 1991. *Ideology: An Introduction*. London: Verso.

Edmond, G. 2004. Thick decisions: expertise, advocacy and reasonableness in the Federal Court. *Oceania*, 74(3), 190–230.

Ehrlich, E. 1975. *Fundamental Principles of the Sociology of Law*, translated by Moll, W. L. New York: Arno Press.

Eisenberg, M.A. 1976. Private ordering through negotiation: dispute-settlement and rulemaking. *Harvard Law Review*, 89(4), 637–81.

Eisler, W. 1995. *The Furthest Shore: Images of Terra Australis from the Middle Ages to Captain Cook.* Cambridge: Cambridge University Press.

Elkin, A.P. 1954. *The Australian Aborigines: How to Understand Them* (3rd edn). Sydney: Angus & Robertson.

Elkin, A.P. 1969. Elements of Australian Aboriginal philosophy. *Oceania*, 40(2), 85–98.

Ellickson, R. 1991. *Order Without Law: How Neighbors Settle Disputes.* Cambridge, Mass: Harvard University Press.

Ermine, W. 1995. Aboriginal epistemology, in *First Nations Education in Canada: The Circle Unfolds*, edited by Battiste, M. and Barman, J. Vancouver: UBC Press, 101–12.

Fanon, F. 1967. *Black Skin, White Masks,* translated by Markmann, C.L. New York: Grove Press.

Fanon, F. 2004. *The Wretched of the Earth*, translated by Philcox, R. New York: Grove Press.

Feuchtwang, S. 1973. The discipline and its sponsors, in *Anthropology and the Colonial Encounter*, edited by Asad, T. New York: Humanities Press, 153–72.

Figueira, D. 1991. *Translating the Orient: The Reception of* Śākuntala *in Nineteenth Century Europe.* Albany: State University of New York.

Findlay, L. 2000. Always Indigenise! the radical humanities in the postcolonial Canadian university. *Ariel*, 31(1–2), 307–26.

Fisher, R. and Ury, W. 1991. *Getting to Yes – Negotiating an Agreement without Giving In.* New York: Penguin Books.

Fishkin, J. 1992. *The Dialogue of Justice: Toward a Self-Reflective Society.* New Haven, CT: Yale University Press.

Fitzpatrick, P. 1984a. Law and societies, *Osgoode Hall Law Journal*, 22(2), 115–38.

Fitzpatrick, P. 1984b. Traditionalism and traditional law. *Journal of African Law*, 28(1/2), 20–27.

Fitzpatrick, P. 1989. 'The desperate vacuum': imperialism and law in the experience of enlightenment. *Droit et Societé*, 13, 343–58.

Fitzpatrick, P. 1992a. *The Mythology of Modern Law.* London: Routledge.

Fitzpatrick, P. 1992b. The impossibility of popular justice. *Social & Legal Studies*, 1(2), 199–215.

Fitzpatrick, P. 2007. 'What are the gods to us now?': secular theology and the modernity of law. *Theoretical Inquiries in Law*, 8(1), 161–90.

Fitzpatrick, P. and Darian-Smith, E. 1999. Laws of the postcolonial: an insistent introduction, in *Laws of the Postcolonial*, edited by Fitzpatrick, P. and Darian-Smith, E. Ann Arbor: University of Michigan Press, 19–38.

Flood, S. 1993. *Mabo: A Symbol of Sharing: The High Court Judgment Examined and Commentary on the Native Title Act (Cth) and a Section for Students and Teachers* (3rd edn), Glebe, NSW: E. Fink.

Flyvbjerg, B. 2001. *Making Social Science Matter: Why Social Inquiry Fails and How It Can Succeed Again.* Cambridge: Cambridge University Press.

Foley, D. 2003. Indigenous epistemology and indigenous standpoint theory. *Social Alternatives*, 22(1), 44–52.

Ford, R. 1999. Law's territory (a history of jurisdiction). *Michigan Law Review*, 97(2), 843–930.

Foucault, M. 1979. Governmentality. *Ideology & Consciousness*, 6(Summer), 5–21.

Foucault, M. 1980. *Power/Knowledge: Selected Interviews and Other Writings, 1972–77*, translated by Gordon, C. New York: Pantheon Books.

Foucault, M. 1995. *Discipline and Punish: The Birth of the Prison* (2nd edn), translated by Sheridan, A. New York: Vintage.

Frankenburg, R. (ed). 1997. *Displacing Whiteness.* Durham: Duke University Press.

Fraser, N. 1997. *Justice Interruptus: Critical Reflections on the 'Postsocialist' Condition.* New York: Routledge.

Fraser, N. 2000. Rethinking recognition. *New Left Review,* 3(May/Jun), 107–20.

Fraser, N. 2002. Recognition without ethics, in *Recognition and Difference*, edited by Lash, S. and Featherstone, M. London: SAGE Publications, 21–42.
French, R. 1997. Local and regional agreements. *Land, Rights, Laws: Issues of Native Title (Regional Agreements Paper)*, 2, 1–9.
French, R. 2002. The role of the High Court in the recognition of native title. *University of Western Australia Law Review*, 30(2), 129–66.
French, R. and Lane, P. 2002. The common law of native title in Australia. *Oxford University Commonwealth Law Journal*, 2(1), 15–46.
Friedrich, H. 1992. On the art of translation, in *Theories of Translation: An Anthology of Essays from Dryden to Derrida*, edited by Schulte, R. and Biguenet, J. Chicago: University of Chicago Press, 11–16.
Fuller, L. 1956. Human purpose and natural law. *Journal of Philosophy*, 53(22), 697–705.
Fuller, L. 1957/58. Positivism and fidelity to law – a reply to Professor Hart. *Harvard Law Review*, 71(4), 630–72.
Furnival, J. 1939. *Netherlands India: A Study of Plural Economy.* Cambridge: Cambridge University Press.
Gadamer, H.G. 1979. *Truth and Method.* London: Sheed &Ward.
Galanter, M. 1981. Justice in many rooms: courts, private ordering and Indigenous law. *Journal of Legal Pluralism & Unofficial Law*, 19(1), 1–47.
Galanter, M. 1985. Presidential address: the legal malaise; or, justice observed. *Law & Society Review*, 19(4), 537–56.
Geertz, C. 1973. *The Interpretation of Cultures*. New York: Basic Books.
Geertz, C. 1983. *Local Knowledge: Further Essays in Interpretive Anthropology.* New York: Basic Books.
Ghandi, L. 1998. *Postcolonial Theory: A Critical Introduction.* New York: Columbia University Press.
Gilligan, C. 1982. *In Different Voice: Psychological Theory and Women's Development.* Cambridge, Mass.: Harvard University Press.
Girardot, N. 2002. *The Victorian Translation of China: James Legge's Oriental Pilgrimage.* Berkeley: University of California Press.
Glaskin, K. 2004. An anthropological perspective on writing for the courts. *Land, Rights, Law: Issues of Native Title*, 2(29), 1–15.
Goldberg, C., Clinton, R., Tsosie, R. 2010. *American Indian Law: Native Nations and the Federal System: Cases and Materials* (6th edn). New Providence, NJ: LexisNexis Matthew Bender.
Golder, B. 2004. 'Law, history, colonialism: an Orientalist reading of Australian native title law. *Deakin Law Review*, 9(1), 41–60.
Goodrich, P. 1987. *Legal Discourse: Studies in Linguistics, Rhetoric and Legal Analysis*. New York: St Martin's Press.
Graham, N. 2011. *Lawscape: Property, Environment, Law*. Milton Park, Oxon: Routledge.

Gray, K. and Gray, S. 1998. The idea of property in land, in *Land Law: Themes and Perspectives*, edited by Bright, S. and Dewar, J. Oxford: Oxford University Press, 15–51.

Gray, S. 1993. Wheeling, dealing and deconstruction: Aboriginal art and the land post-Mabo. *Aboriginal Law Bulletin*, 3(63), 10–12.

Greatbatch, D. and Dingwall, R. 1989. Selective facilitation: some observations on a strategy used by divorce mediators. *Law & Society Review*, 23(4), 613–41.

Green, L. 1996. The concept of law revisited. *Michigan Law Review*, 94(6), 1687–717.

Grillo, T. 1991. The mediation alternative: process dangers for women. *Yale Law Journal*, 100(6), 1545–610.

Griffiths, J. 1986. What is legal pluralism? *Journal of Legal Pluralism & Unofficial Law*, 24, 1–55.

Gumbert, M. 1981. Paradigm lost: an analysis of anthropological models and their effect on Aboriginal land rights. *Oceania*, 52(2), 103–23.

Gunning, I. 1995. Diversity Issues in Mediation: Controlling Negative Cultural Myths. *Journal of Dispute Resolution*, 1995(1), 55–94.

Gurvitch, G. 1932. *L'idée du droit social.* Paris: Recueil Sirey.

Gurvitch, G. 1935. *L'Expérience Juridique et la Philosophie Pluraliste du Droit.* Paris: A. Pedone.

Haldar, P. 1994. In and out of court: on topographies of law and the architecture of court buildings (a study of the Supreme Court of the State of Israel). *International Journal for the Semiotics of Law*, 7(20), 185–200.

Hamilton, M. 1987. The elements of the concept of ideology. *Political Studies*, XXXV, 18–38.

Harmon, L. 1999. Etchings on glass: reflections on the science of proof. *South Texas Law Review*, 40(2), 483–507.

Harris, M. 2003. Mythologising 'Recollections of squatting in Victoria': law's intersection with colonial memory. *Law, Social Justice & Global Development*, [online] 1. Available at: http://www2.warwick.ac.uk/fac/soc/law/elj/lgd/2003_1/harris/ [accessed 29 December 2013].

Hart, H.L.A. 1958. Positivism and the separation of law and morals. *Harvard Law Review*, 71(4), 593–29.

Hart, H.L.A. 1961. *The Concept of Law.* London: Oxford University Press.

Hartog, H. 1985. Pigs and positivism. *Wisconsin Law Review* (4),899–935.

Harvey, D. 1996. *Justice, Nature and the Geography of Difference.* Malden, Mass: Blackwell Publishers.

Hay, D. 1976. Property, authority and the criminal law, in *Albion's Fatal Tree: Crime and Society in Eighteenth-Century England*, edited by Hay, D., Linebaugh, P., Rule, J., Thompson, E.P. and Winslow, C. London: Allen Lane, 17–63.

Healy, C. 1997. *From the Ruins of Colonialism: History as Social Memory.* Cambridge: Cambridge University Press.

Hegel, G.W.F. 1967. *Philosophy of Right (1820)*, translated by Knox, T.M. Oxford: Oxford University Press.

Hegel, G.W.F. 1977. *Phenomenology of Spirit (1807)*, translated by Miller, A.V. Oxford: Oxford University Press.

Heisenberg, W. 1958. *Physics and Philosophy: The Revolution in Modern Science.* New York: Harper Row.

Henderson, J.Y., Benson, M. and Findlay, I. 2000. *Aboriginal Tenure in the Constitution of Canada*. Scarborough, Ont.: Carswell.

Henderson, J.Y. 2006. *First Nation Jurisprudence and Aboriginal Rights: Defining the Just Society*. Saskatoon, Sask: Native Law Centre.

Henderson, J.Y. and McCaslin, W.D. 2005. 'Exploring justice as healing, in *Justice as healing: Indigenous* ways, edited by McCaslin, W.D. St Paul, MN: Living Justice Press, 3–12.

Highland, H. 2007. The mote in the common law's eye: dislodging europecentric barriers to just recognition of native title in the wake of Yorta Yorta. *Washington and Lee Journal of Civil Rights and Social Justice*, 13(2), 349–87.

Hinchman. 1984. *Hegel's Critique of the Enlightenment*. Gainesville, FL: University of Florida Press.

Hobbes, T. 1996. *Leviathan (1651)*, edited by Gaskin, C.J.A. Oxford: Oxford University Press.

Hobbes, T. 2005. *A Dialogue Between a Philosopher and a Student of the Common Laws of England (1681)*, edited by Cromartie, A. Oxford: Clarendon Press.

Hoebel, E.A. and Lewellyn, K.N. 1941. *The Cheyenne Way: Conflict and Case Law in Primitive Jurisprudence.* Norman: University of Oklahoma Press.

Hoehn, F. 2012. *Reconciling Sovereignties: Aboriginal Nations and Canada.* Saskatoon: Native Law Centre, University of Saskatchewan.

Hohfeld, W.N. 1913. Some fundamental legal concepts as applied in judicial reasoning. *Yale Law Journal*, 23(1), 16–59.

Honneth, A. 1995. *The Struggle for Recognition: The Moral Grammar of Social Conflicts,* translated by Anderson, J. Cambridge, Mass.: Polity Press.

Honneth, A. 2002. Recognition or redistribution: changing perspectives on the moral order of society. *Recognition and Difference*, edited by Lash, S. and Featherstone, M. London: Sage Publications, 43–55.

Hooker, M.B. 1975. *Legal Pluralism: An Introduction to Colonial and Neo-Colonial Laws.* Oxford: Clarendon Press.

hooks, b. 1981. *Ain't I a Woman? Black Women and Feminism*. Boston: South End Press.

Howard, M. 2000. *Phipson on Evidence* (15th edn). London: Sweet & Maxwell.

Howitt, R. and Suchet-Pearson, S. 2003. Spaces of knowledge: ontological pluralism in contested cultural landscapes, in *Handbook of Cultural Geography*, edited by Anderson, K. et al. London: Sage Publications, 557–69.

Humphrey, C. 1998. Compensation for native title: the theory and the reality. *E-LAW Murdoch University Electronic Journal of Law* [online], 5(1). Available at: http://www.murdoch.edu.au/elaw/indices/issue/v5n1.html [accessed 29 December 2013].

Hunter, P. 1997. The *Wik* decision: unnecessary extinguishment, in *The Wik Case: Issues and Implications*, edited by Hiley, G. Sydney: Butterworths, 6–18.

Hutchinson, A. and Monahan, P. 1984. Law, politics and critical legal scholars: the unfolding drama of American legal thought. *Stanford Law Review*, 36(2), 199–245.

Imai, S. 2003. Sound science, careful policy analysis, and ongoing relationships: integrating litigation and negotiation in Aboriginal land and resource disputes. *Osgoode Hall Law Journal*, 41(4), 587–628.

Isenberg, A. 2007. Reasoning about the identity of Aboriginal peoples, in *Accommodating Cultural Diversity*, edited by Tierney, S. Aldershot, Hants: Ashgate, 34–53.

Jackson, B. 1988. *Law, Fact and Narrative Coherence*. Merseyside: Deborah Charles Publishing.

Jackson, B. 1995. *Making Sense in Law*. Liverpool: Deborah Charles Publications.

Jackson, B. 1996. *Making Sense in Jurisprudence*. Liverpool: Deborah Charles Publications.

Jackson, S. 1996. *When History Meets the New Native Title Era at the Negotiating Table: A Case Study in Reconciling Land Use in Broom, Western Australia*. Darwin: North Australia Research Unit.

Jacobson, M. F. 1999. *Whiteness of a Different Color: European Immigrants and the Alchemy of Race*. Cambridge, Mass: Harvard University Press.

James, A. 2003. *Yanagai! Yanagai!* Sydney: Currency Press.

Jennings, F. 1975. *The Invasion of America: Indians, Colonialism, and the Cant of Conquest*. Chapel Hill: University of North Carolina Press.

Johnson, B. 1985. Taking fidelity philosophically, in *Difference in Translation*, edited by Joseph Graham. Ithaca: Cornell University Press, 142–8.

Jonas, W. 2001. 'Unfinished business' – the recognition of Aboriginal and Torres Strait Islander rights. *Newcastle Law Review*, 5(1), 53–64.

Jones, C. 2002. Aboriginal boundaries: the mediation and settlement of Aboriginal boundary disputes in a native title context. *National Native Title Tribunal Occasional Paper Series* 2, 1–14. Available at: http://www.nntt.gov.au/Mediation-and-agreement-making-services/Research-services/Pages/Occasional-Paper-Series.aspx [accessed 29 December 2013].

Kamir, O. 2005. Cinematic judgment and jurisprudence: a woman's memory, recovery, and justice in a post-traumatic society (a study of Polanski's Death and the Maiden), in *Law on the Screen*, edited by Sarat, A., et al. Stanford: Stanford University Press, 27–81.

Kauffman, P. 1998. *Wik, Mining and Aborigines*. St Leonards, NSW: Allen & Unwin.

Keen, I. (ed.), 1988. *Being Black: Aboriginal Cultures in 'Settled' Australia*. Canberra: Aboriginal Studies Press.

Keen, I. 1995. Metaphor and the metalanguage: 'groups' in northeast Arnhem land. *American Ethnologist*, 22(3), 502–27.

Kelsen, H. 1967. *The Pure Theory of Law*, translated by Knight, M. Berkeley: University of California Press.

Kennedy, D. 1976. Form and substance in private law adjudication. *Harvard Law Review*, 89(8), 1685–1778.

Kennedy, D. 1980. Toward an historical understanding of legal consciousness: the case of classical legal thought in America 1850–1940. *Research in Law & Society*, 3, 3–24.

Kennedy, D. 1983. The political significance of the structure of the law school curriculum. *Seton Hall Law Review*, 14(1), 1–16.

Keon-Cohen, B. 2000. The Mabo litigation: a personal and procedural account. *Melbourne University Law Review*, 24(3), 893–951.

Kerruish, V. and Perrin, C. 1999. Awash in colonialism: a critical analysis of the Federal Court decision in the matter of *The Members of the Yorta Yorta Aboriginal Community v The State of Victoria and Ors* (1998). *Alternative Law Journal*, 24(1), 3–8.

Kerruish, V. and Purdy, J. 1998. He 'look' honest – big white thief. *Law Text Culture*, 4(1), 146–71.

Kirby, Justice M. 2005. HLA Hart, Julius Stone and the struggle for the soul of law. *Sydney Law Review*, 27(2), 323–38.

Kleinert, S. and Neale, M. (eds), 2000. *The Oxford Companion to Aboriginal Art and Culture.* Oxford: Oxford University Press.

Kleinhans, M. and Macdonald, R. 1997. What is a *critical* legal pluralism. *Canadian Journal of Law & Society*, 12(2), 25–46.

Koch, G. 2013. We have the song, so we have the land: song and ceremony as proof of title in Aboriginal and Torres Strait Islander land claims. *AIATSIS Research Discussion Paper No. 33.* Canberra: AIATSIS Research Publications.

Kojève, A. 1980. *Introduction to the Reading of Hegel*, translated by Nichols, J.H. Ithaca, NY: Cornell University Press.

Kramer, M. 1988. The rule of misrecognition in the Hart of jurisprudence. *Oxford Journal of Legal Studies*, 8(3), 401–33.

Kristeva, J. 1989. *Language, The Unknown: An Initiation Into Linguistics*, translated by Menke, A. New York: Columbia University Press.

Kymlicka, W. 1995. *Multicultural Citizenship: A Liberal Theory of Minority Rights*. Oxford: Clarendon Press.

Ladner, K. and McCrossan, M. 2009. The road not taken: Aboriginal rights, in *Contested Constitutionalism: Reflections on the Canadian Charter of Rights and Freedoms*, edited by Kelly, J. and Manfredi, C. Vancouver: UBC Press, 263–83.

Lake, M. 1999. *Getting Equal: The History of Australian Feminism*. St Leonards, NSW: Allen & Unwin.

Lakoff, G. 1987. *Women, Fire and Dangerous Things.* Chicago: University of Chicago Press.

Lane, P. 2000a. Native title – the end of property as we know it? *Australian Property Law Journal*, 8(March), 1–37.

Lane, P. 2000b. Have we got a deal for you? Mediating native title, in *Native Title in perspective: Selected papers from the Native Title Research Unit 1998–2000*, edited by Strelein, L. and Muir, K. Canberra: Aboriginal Studies Press, 35–64.

Langton, M. and Jonas, W. 1994. *The Little Red, Yellow and Black (and Green and Blue and White) Book: A Short Guide to Indigenous Australia.* Canberra: AIATSIS.

Langton, M. and Palmer, L. 2003. Modern agreement making and Indigenous people in Australia: issues and trends. *Australian Indigenous Law Reporter*, 8(1), 1–31.

LaRocque, E. 1997. Re-examining culturally-appropriate models in criminal justice applications, in *Aboriginal and Treaty Rights in Canada: Essays on Law, Equality and Respect for Difference*, edited by Asch, M. Vancouver: UBC Press, 75–96.

Latour, B. 1993. *We Have Never Been Modern*, translated by Porter, C. Cambridge, Mass.: Harvard University Press.

Lavery, D. 2004. The recognition of the native title claim group: a legal and policy perspective. *Land, Rights, Laws: Issues of Native Title*, 2(30), 1–11.

Le Dœuff, M. 1990. *The Philosophical Imaginary*, translated by Gordon, C. Stanford: Stanford University Press.

Lefebvre, H. 1991. *The Production of Space,* translated by Donaldson-Smith, N. Oxford: Basil Blackwell.

Leiter, B. 2007. *Naturalizing Jurisprudence: Essays on American Legal Realism and Naturalism in Legal Philosophy*. Oxford: Oxford University Press.

Levine, H. 2002. The Maori *Iwi* – contested meanings in contemporary Aotearoa/New Zealand, in *Politics of Indigeneity in the South Pacific: Recent Problems of Identity in Oceania*, edited by Kolig, E. and Mückler, H. Hamburg: LIT, 73–84.

Levi-Strauss, C. 1963. *The Structural Study of Myth.* New York: Basic Books.

Levi-Strauss, C. 1967. *The Scope of Anthropology*, translated by Paul, S.O. and Paul, R. London: Jonathan Cape.

Levi-Strauss, C. 1968. *Structural Anthropology*, translated by Jacobson, C. and Schoepf, B.G. London: Allen Lane.

Ligertwood, A. 1993. *Australian Evidence.* Sydney: Butterworths.

Locke, J. 1764. *Two Treatises of Government II,* edited by Thomas Hollis. London: A Millar et al.

Lokan, A. 1999. From recognition to reconciliation: the functions of Aboriginal rights law. *Melbourne University Law Review*, 23(1), 65–120.

Lyotard, J.F. 1984. *The Postmodern Condition: A Report on Knowledge*, translated by Bennington, G. and Massumi, B. Minneapolis: University of Minnesota Press.

Macdonald, G. 1988. A Wiradjuri fight story, in *Being Black: Aboriginal Cultures in 'Settled' Australia*, edited by Ian Keen. Canberra: Aboriginal Studies Press.

Macdonald, R. 1998. Metaphors of multiplicity: civil society, regimes and legal pluralism. *Arizona Journal of International and Comparative Law*, 15(1), 69–91.

Macdonald, R. 2003. The legal mediation of social diversity, in *The Conditions of Diversity in Multinational Democracies*, translated by Gagnon, A. et al. Montreal: Institute for Research on Public Policy, 85–111.

Macdonald, R. 2006. Here, there … and everywhere: theorizing legal pluralism; theorizing Jacques Vanderlinden, in Étudier *et* énseigner *le droit: hier aujourd'hui et demain:* Études *offertes* à *Jacques Vanderlinden*, edited by Castonguay, L. and Kasirer. N. Montreal, QC: Éditions Yvon Blais, 381–413.

Macdonald, R. 2011. Custom made – for a non-chirographic critical legal pluralism. *Canadian Journal of Law & Society*, 26(2), 301–327

Macdonald, R. and Sandomierski, D. 2006. Against nomopolies. *Northern Ireland Legal Quarterly*, 57(4), 610–33.

Mackinnon, C. 1987. *Feminism Unmodified: Discourses on Life and Law.* Cambridge: Harvard University Press.

MacIntosh, C. 2007. Developments in Aboriginal law: the 2006–2007 term. *Supreme Court Law Review* 38, 1–53.

Macklem, P. 2001. *Indigenous Difference and the Constitution of Canada.* Toronto: Toronto University Press.

Malinowski, B. 1926. *Crime and Custom in Savage Society*. New York: Harcourt Brace.

Malinowski, B. 1961. *Argonauts of the Western Pacific: An Account of Native Enterprise and Adventure in the Archipelagos of Melanesian New Guinea.* New York: EP Dutton.

Manderson, D. 2000. *Songs Without Music: Aesthetic Dimensions of Law and Justice.* Berkeley: University of California Press.

Manderson, D. 2003. From hunger to love: myths of the source, interpretation, and constitution of law in children's literature. *Law & Literature*, 15(1), 87–141.

Manderson, D. 2012. *Kangaroo Courts and the Rule of Law: The Legacy of Modernism.* London: Glasshouse.

Mantziaris, C. and Martin, D. 2000. *Native Title Corporations: A Legal and Anthropological Analysis.* Sydney: Federation Press.

Markell, P. 2003. *Bound by Recognition*. Princeton: Princeton University Press.

Martin, D. 2003. Rethinking the design of Indigenous organisations: the need for strategic engagement. *CAEPR Discussion Paper No 248.* Available at: http://caepr.anu.edu.au/Publications/DP/2003DP248.php [accessed 31 December 2013].

Martin-Booran Mirraboopa, K. 2003. Ways of knowing, being and doing: a theoretical framework and methods for doing Indigenous and Indigenist re-search. *Journal of Australian Studies*, 27(76), 203–57.

Matson, J.N. 1991. The language, the law, and the Treaty of Waitangi. *Journal of the Polynesian Society*, 100(4), 343–64.

Matthews, R. (ed.), 1988. *Informal Justice?* London: Sage Publications.

McCarthy, T. 1988. *The Critical Theory of Jürgen Habermas.* Cambridge, Mass.: MIT Press.

McCool, D. 2002. *Native Waters: Contemporary Indian Water Settlements and the Second Treaty Era.* University of Arizona Press.

McHugh, P. 2011. *Aboriginal Title: The Modern Jurisprudence of Tribal Land Rights.* Oxford: Oxford University Press.

McIntyre, G. and Bagshaw, G. 2002. Preserving culture in Federal Court proceedings: gender restrictions and anthropological evidence. *Land, Rights, Laws: Issues of Native Title*, 2(15), 1–12.

McNeil, K. 1989. *Common Law Aboriginal Title.* Oxford: Clarendon Press.

McNeil, K. 1999. The onus of proof in Aboriginal title. *Osgoode Hall Law Journal*, 37(4), 775–803.

McNeil, K. 2000. Aboriginal title as a constitutionally protected property right, in *Beyond the Nass Valley: National Implications of the Supreme Court's Delgamuukw Decisions*, edited by Lippert, O. Vancouver: The Fraser Institute, 55–75.

McNeil, K. 2001. *Emerging Justice: Essays on Indigenous Rights in Canada and Australia.* Saskatoon: Native Law Centre, University of Saskatchewan.

McNeil, K. 2001–2002. Extinguishment of Aboriginal title in Canada: Treaties, legislation and judicial discretion. *Ottawa Law Review*, 33(2), 301–46.

Melissaris, E. 2004. The more the merrier? A new take on legal pluralism. *Social & Legal Studies* 13(1), 57–79.

Melissaris, E. 2009. *Ubiquitous Law: Legal Theory and the Space for Legal Pluralism.* Farnham, Surrey: Ashgate.

Menkel-Meadow, C. 1983. Toward another view of legal negotiation: the structure of problem solving. *UCLA Law Review* 31(4), 754–842.

Merlan, F. 1997. Fighting over country: four commonplaces, in *Fighting Over Country: Anthropological Perspectives*, edited by Smith, D. and Finlayson, J. Canberra: Centre for Aboriginal Economic Policy Research, The Australian National University, 1–14.

Merlan, F. 1998. *Caging the Rainbow: Place, Politics and Aborigines in a North Australian Town.* Honolulu: University of Hawai'i Press.

Merry, S.E. 1988. Legal pluralism. *Law & Society Review,* 22(5), 869–96.

Miller, J.R. 1996. *Shingwauk's Vision: A History of Native Residential Schools.* Toronto: University of Toronto Press, 1996.

Mnookin, R. and Kornhauser, L. 1979. Bargaining in the shadow of the law: the case of divorce. *Yale Law Journal* 88(5), 950–97.

Mohr, R. 2002. Shifting ground: context and change in two Australian legal systems. *International Journal for the Semiotics of Law* 15(1), 1–24.

Monk, G. 2000. *Narrative Mediation: A New Approach to Conflict Resolution.* San Francisco: Jossey-Bass.

Moore, C. 2003. *The Mediation Process.* San Francisco: Jossey-Bass.

Moore, S.F. 1978. *Law as Process: An Anthropological Approach.* London: Routledge & Kegan Paul.

Moreton-Robinson, A. 2004. The possessive logic of patriarchal white sovereignty: the High Court and the Yorta Yorta decision. *Borderlands e-journal* 3(2). Available at: http://www.borderlands.net.au/vol3no2_2004/moreton_possessive.htm [Accessed 29 December 2013].

Morphy, F. 2007. Performing law: the Yolngu of Blue Mud Bay meet the native title process, in *The Social Effects of Native Title: Recognition, Translation, Coexistence*, edited by Smith, B. and Morphy, F. *The Social Effects of Native Title: Recognition, Translation, Coexistence*. Canberra: ANU E Press, 31–57.

Morphy, H. 1983. 'Now you understand': an analysis of the way Yolngu have used sacred knowledge to retain their autonomy, in *Aborigines, Land and Land Rights*, edited by Peterson, N. and Langton, M. Canberra: Aborigines, Land and Land Rights, Australian Institute of Aboriginal Studies Press, 110–33.

Morphy, H. 1991. *Ancestral Connections: Art and an Aboriginal System of Knowledge.* Chicago: University of Chicago Press.

Morphy, H. 1998. The art of Northern Australia, in *Traditional Aboriginal Society*, edited by Edwards, W.H. South Yarra, Vic: Macmillan Education Australia, 6–29.

Morphy, H. 1999. Australian Aboriginal concepts of time, in *The Story of Time*, edited by Lippincott, K. London: Merrel, 264–8.

Morris, C. 2001. Constitutional dreaming, in *Beyond the Republic: Meeting the Global Challenges to Constitutionalism*, edited by Sampford, C. and Round, T. Sydney: The Federation Press, 290–99.

Morris, S. 2012. Re-evaluating *Mabo*: the case for native title reform to remove discrimination and promote economic opportunity. *Land, Rights, Laws: Issues of Native Title*, 5(3), 1–13.

Motha, S. 1998. MABO: Encountering the epistemic limit of the recognition of difference. *Griffith Law Review* 7(1), 79–96.

Motha, S. 2005. The failure of postcolonial sovereignty in Australia. *The Australian Feminist Law Journal* 22, 107–25.

Munn, N. 1973. *Walpiri Iconography: Graphic Representation and Cultural Symbolism in a Central Australian Society.* Ithaca: Cornell University Press.

Munn, N. 1984. The transformation of subjects into objects in Walbiri and Pitjantjatjara myth, in *Religion in Aboriginal Australia: An Anthology*, edited by Charlesworth, M. et al. St Lucia, Qld: University of Queensland Press, 141–63.

Murphy, P. 1995. *Murphy on Evidence* (5th edn). London: Blackstone Press Ltd.

Murray, T. 2003. Down by law. *Meanjin* 62(1), 69–78.

Myers, F. 1986. *Pintupi Country, Pintupi Self: Sentiment, Place and Politics among Western Desert Aborigines.* Berkeley: University of California Press.

Myers, L.J. 1988. *Understanding an Afrocentric World View: An Introduction to an Optimal Psychology.* Dubuque, Iowa: Kendall/Hunt Publishing Co.

Myers, M. 2002. *Painting Culture: The Making of an Aboriginal High Art.* Durham: Duke University Press.

Myers, M.D. 2001. Federal recognition of Indian tribes in the United States. *Stanford Law & Policy Review* 12(2), 271–300.

Nadasdy, P. 2007. The gift in the animal: the ontology of hunting and human-animal society. *American Ethnologist* 34(1), 25–43.

Nader, L. 1991. Harmony models and the construction of law, in *Conflict Resolution: Cross-Cultural Perspectives*, edited by Avruch, K. et al. Westport, CT: Greenwood Press, 41–59.

Nader, L. and Ou, J. 1998. Idealization and power: legality and tradition in Native American law. *Oklahoma City University Law Review* 23(1/2), 13–42.

National Indigenous Working Group on Native Title. 1997. Co-existence: negotiation and certainty. *Indigenous Law Bulletin* 4(2), 10.

Nakayama, T. and Martin, J. (eds), 1999. *Whiteness: The Communication of Social Identity.* Thousand Oaks, Cal.: Sage Publications.

Nettheim, G. 1993. 'The consent of the natives': Mabo and Indigenous political rights, in *Essays on the Mabo Decision.* North Ryde, NSW: Law Book Company, 103–26.

Nettheim, G. 1997. Wik: on invasions, legal fictions, myths and rational responses. *University of NSW Law Journal* 20 (2), 495–501.

Newman, D. 2007. You still know nothin' 'bout me: toward cross-cultural theorizing of Aboriginal rights. *McGill Law Journal* 52(4), 725–56.

Newman, D. 2009. *The Duty to Consult: New Relationships with Aboriginal Peoples.* Saskatoon: Purich Publishing.

Newman, S. 2004. The Mawül Rom Project: an experience of cross-cultural mediation. *Indigenous Law Bulletin*, 6(6), 11

Nicholson, D. 2000. Gender, epistemology and ethics: feminist perspectives on evidence theory, in *Feminist Perspectives on Evidence*, edited by Childs, M. and Ellison, L. London: Cavendish Publishing, 13–37.

Nida, E.A. 1964. *Toward a Science of Translating: With Special Reference to Principles and Procedures Involved in Bible Translating.* Leiden, Netherlands: Brill Archive.

Nida, E.A. 1969. Science of translation. *Language*, 45(3), 483–98.

Nielsen, J. 2002. Dealing with the dilemmas: research, integrity, knowledge. *Southern Cross University Law Review* 6, 151–76.

Niezen, R. 2003. Culture and the judiciary: the meaning of the culture concept as a source of Aboriginal rights in Canada. *Canadian Journal of Law & Society*, 18(2), 1–26.

Niezen, R. 2009. *The Rediscovered Self: Indigenous Identity and Cultural Justice.* Montreal: McGill-Queens University Press.

Niranjana, T. 1992. *Siting Translation: History, Post-Structuralism, and the Colonial Context.* Berkeley: University of California Press.

Norris, C. 2002. *Deconstruction* (3rd edn). London: Routledge.

O'Faircheallaigh, C. 1995. Mineral development agreements negotiated by Aboriginal communities in the 1990s. *CAEPR Discussion Paper No 85.* Available at: http://caepr.anu.edu.au/Publications/DP/1995DP85.php [accessed 31 December 2013].

O'Faircheallaigh, C. 2004. Evaluating agreements between Indigenous peoples and resource developers, in *Honour Among Nations?*, edited by Langton, M. et al. Carlton, Vic: Melbourne University Press, 303–28.

O'Faircheallaigh, C. and Corbett, T. 2005. Indigenous participation in environmental management of mining projects: the role of negotiated agreements. *Environmental Politics* 14(5), 629–47.

O'Hair, R.B. 1993. Mabo and land rights: searching for a golden thread, in *Mabo: A Judicial Revolution*, edited by Stephenson, M.A. and Ratnapala S. St Lucia, Qld: University of Queensland Press, 63–74.

Oliver, K. 2001. *Witnessing: Beyond Recognition.* Minneapolis: University of Minnesota Press.

O'Malley, J. (ed.), 1970. *Marx's Critique of Hegel's Philosophy of Right (1843).* Cambridge: Cambridge University Press.

Otis, G. 1997. Opposing Aboriginality to modernity: the doctrine of Aboriginal rights in Canada. *British Journal of Canadian Studies* 12(2), 182–94.

Pannel, S. 1994. Mabo and museums: 'the Indigenous (re)appropriation of Indigenous things'. *Oceania* 65(1), 18–39.

Parsonson, A. 2001. Telling stories for land: oral narratives in the Maori land court, in *Telling Stories: Indigenous Histories and Memory in Australia and New Zealand*, edited by Attwood, B. and Magowan, F. Wellington: Bridget Williams Books, 21–40.

Patton, P. 1996. Mabo, difference and the body of the law, in *Thinking Through the Body of the Law*, edited by Cheah, P. et al. Sydney: Allen & Unwin, 43–62.

Patton, P. 2000. The translation of Indigenous land into property: the mere analogy of English jurisprudence. *Parallax* 6(1), 25–38.

Pavlich, G. 1996a. *Justice Fragmented: Mediating Community Disputes Under Postmodern Conditions.* London: Routledge.

Pavlich, G. 1996b. The power of community mediation: government and formation of self-identity. *Law & Society Review* 30(4), 707–33.

Pearson, N. 1993. 204 years of invisible title, in *Mabo: A Judicial Revolution*, edited by Stephenson, M.A. and Ratnapala, S. St Lucia, Qld: University of Queensland Press, 83–7.

Pearson, N. 1995. From remnant title to social justice. *The Australian Journal of Anthropology* 6(3), 95–100.

Penner, J. 1996. The 'bundle of rights' picture of property. *UCLA Law Review*, 43(3), 711–820.

Penrose, R. and Isham, CJ. 1986. *Quantum Concepts in Space and Time.* Oxford: The Clarendon Press.

Peperzak, A. 1993. *To the Other: An Introduction to the Philosophy of Emmanuel Levinas.* West Lafayette, IN: Purdue University Press.

Peterson, N., Keen, I. and Sansom, B. 1977. *Succession to Land: Primary and Secondary Rights to Aboriginal Estates.* Canberra: AGPS.

Pether, P. 1998. Principles or skeletons: Mabo and the discursive constitution of the Australian nation. *Law Text Culture* 4(1), 115–45.

Pitty, R. 2000. A poverty of evidence: abusing law and history in *Yorta Yorta v Victoria* (1998). *Australian Journal of Legal History* 5(1), 41–61.

Pomedli, M. 1995. Eighteenth-century treaties: amended Iroquois condolence rituals. *American Indian Quarterly* 19(3), 319–39.

Pospisil, L. 1971. *Anthropology of Law: A Comparative Theory*. New York: Harper & Row.

Pospisil, L. 1958. *Kapauku Papuans and Their Law*. New Haven: Yale University Publications in Anthropology, No. 54.

Postema, G. 1989. *Bentham and the Common Law Tradition*. Oxford: Clarendon Press.

Pottage, A. 1994. The measure of land. *The Modern Law Review* 57(3), 361–84.

Povinelli, E. 1993. 'Might be something': the language of indeterminacy in Australian Aboriginal land use. *Man* 28(4), 679–704.

Povinelli, E. 2002. *The Cunning of Recognition: Indigenous Alterities and the Making of Australian Multiculturalism*. Durham: Duke University Press.

Pyle, R. 2011. *The Thunder Tree: Lessons from an Urban Wildland* (2nd edn). Corvallis: Oregon State University Press.

Quartly, M., Janson, S. and Grimshaw, P. (eds), 1995. *Freedom Bound 1: Documents on Women in Colonial Australia*. St Leonards, NSW: Allen & Unwin.

Rawls, J. 1971. *A Theory of Justice*. Cambridge, Mass.: Harvard University Press.

Ray, A.J. 2003. Native history on trial: confessions of an expert witness. *Canadian Historical Review*, 84(2), 253–73.

Ray, A. 2010. From the US Indian claims commission to *Delgamuukw*: facts, theories, and evidence in North American land claims, in *Aboriginal Title and Indigenous Peoples: Canada, Australia and New Zealand*, edited by Knafla, L. and Westra, H. Vancouver: UBC Press, 37–52.

Raz, J. 2009. *The Authority of Law: Essays on Law and Morality* (2nd edn). Oxford: Oxford University Press.

Rees, R. 1982. Painting, place and identity: a prairie view, in *Environmental Aesthetics: Essays in Interpretation*, edited by Saddler, B. and Carson, A. University of Victoria, 117–41.

Regan, P. 2010. *Unsettling the Settler Within: Indian Residential Schools, Truth Telling, and Reconciliation in Canada*. Vancouver: UBC Press.

Reilly, A. 1998. Entering a dream: two days of a native title trial in the North-East Kimberley. *Law Text Culture* 4(1), 196–211.

Reilly, A. 2000. The ghost of Truganni: use of historical evidence as proof of native title. *Federal Law Review* 28(3), 453–75.

Reilly, A. 2001. History always repeats: *Members of the Yorta Yorta Aboriginal Community v State of Victoria*. *Indigenous Law Bulletin* 5(6), 25.

Reilly, A. 2002. From a jurisprudence of regret to a regrettable jurisprudence: shaping native title from Mabo to Ward. *E LAW – Murdoch University Electronic Journal of Law* [online] 9(4). Available at: http://www.murdoch.edu.au/elaw/issues/v9n4/reilly94_text.html [accessed 29 December 2013].

Reilly, A. 2003. Cartography and native title. *Journal of Australian Studies* 27(79), 3–14.

Reisman, M. 1985. Lining up: the microlegal system of queues. *University of Cincinnati Law Review* 54(2), 417–50.

Reynolds, H. 1996. After *Mabo*, what about Aboriginal sovereignty? *Australian Humanities Review* 1. Available at http://www.australianhumanitiesreview.org/archive/Issue-April-1996/Reynolds.html [accessed 29 December 2013].

Richland, J. 2008. *Arguing About Tradition: The Language of Law in Hopi Tribal Court*. Chicago: University of Chicago Press.

Ricoeur, P. 1971. The model of text: meaningful action considered as text. *Social Research* 38(3), 529–62.

Ricoeur, P. 2005. *The Course of Recognition.* Translated and edited by Pellauer, D. Harvard University Press.

Rigney, L. 1999. Internationalisation of an Indigenous anticolonial cultural critique of research methodologies: a guide to Indigenist research methodologies and its principles. *Wicazo Sa Review* 14(2), 109–22.

Ritter, D. 1996. The 'Rejection of *Terra Nullius*' in *Mabo*: A Critical Analysis. *Sydney Law Review*, 18(1), 5–33.

Ritter, D. 2004. The judgement of the world: the Yorta Yorta case and the tide of history. *Australian Historical Studies* 35 (123), 106–21.

Roberts, S. 1998. Against legal pluralism: Some contemporary reflections on the enlargement of the legal domain. *Journal of Legal Pluralism*, 30 (42), 95–106.

Rose, D.B. 1984. The saga of Captain Cook: morality in Aboriginal and European law. *Australian Aboriginal Studies* 2, 24–39.

Rose, D.B. 1992. *Dingo Makes Us Human: Life and Land in an Aboriginal Australian Culture.* Cambridge: Cambridge University Press.

Rose, D.B. 1996a. *Nourishing Terrains: Australian Aboriginal Views of Landscape and Wilderness.* Canberra: Australian Heritage Commission.

Rose, D.B. 1996b. Histories and rituals: land claims in the territory, in *In the Age of Mabo: History, Aborigines and Australia*, edited by Attwood, B. St Leonards, NSW: Allen & Unwin, 35–53.

Rose, D.B. 2004. *Reports from a Wild Country: Ethics for Decolonisation.* Sydney: University of New South Wales Press.

Rowse, T. 2002/03. Treaty talk 2002: notes on three conferences. *Arena* 62(Dec), 30–7.

Rumsey, A. 1989. Language groups in Australian Aboriginal land claims. *Anthropological Forum* 6(1), 69–79.

Rumsey, A. 2001. Tracks, traces, and links to land in Australia, New Guinea and beyond, in *Emplaced Myth: Space, Narrative and Knowledge in Australia and Papua New Guinea*, edited by Rumsey, A. and Weiner, J. Honolulu: University of Hawai'i Press, 19–42.

Russel, P. 2005. *Recognising Aboriginal Title: The Mabo Case and Indigenous Resistance to English-Settler Colonialism.* Toronto: University of Toronto Press.

Ryan, S. 1996. *The Cartographic Eye: How Explorers Saw Australia.* Cambridge: Cambridge University Press.

Sackett, L. 1976. Indirect exchange in a symmetrical system: marriage alliance in the western desert of Australia. *Ethnology* 15(2), 135–49.
Said, E. 1979. *Orientalism.* New York: Vintage Books.
Said, E. 1993. *Culture and Imperialism.* New York: Vintage Books.
Sampford, C. 1984. Legal systems and their place in legal theory, in *Essays in Legal Theory: A Collaborative Work*, edited by Galligan, D. Melbourne: Melbourne University Press, 165–86.
Santos, B. d. S. 1977. The law of the oppressed: the construction and reproduction of legality in Pasargada. *Law & Society Review* 12(1), 5–126.
Santos, B. d. S. 1987. Law: a map of misreading. Toward a postmodern conception of law. *Journal of Law & Society,* 14(3), 279–302.
Santos, B. d. S. 1995. *Toward A New Common Sense: Law, Science and Politics in the Paradigmatic Transition.* New York: Routledge.
Santos, B. d. S. 2002. *Toward A New Legal Common Sense: Law, Globalization, and Emancipation.* London: Butterworths LexisNexis.
Sapir, E. 1966. *Culture, Language and Personality*, edited by Mandelbaum, D. Berkeley: University of California Press.
Sarmas, L. 1994. Story telling and the law: a case study of *Louth v Diprose. Melbourne University Law Review* 19(4), 701–28.
Saul, J.R. 1993. *Voltaire's Bastards: The Dictatorship of Reason in the West.* New York: Vintage Books.
Saul, J.R. 2008. *A Fair Country*. Toronto: Viking Canada.
Sauvé, M. 1996. Mediation: towards an Aboriginal conceptualization. *Aboriginal Law Bulletin*, 3(80), 10–12.
Schaap, A. 2005. *Political Reconciliation.* London: Routledge.
Schauer, F. 1988. Formalism. *Yale Law Journal*, 97(4), 509–48.
Schauer, F. 2008. A critical guide to vehicles in the park. *New York University Law Review*, 83(4), 1109–34.
Scheppele, K.L. 1991. Facing facts in legal interpretation, in *Law and the Order of Culture*, edited by Post, R. Berkeley: University of California Press, 42–67.
Schlag, P. 1997. Commentary: law and phrenology. *Harvard Law Review*, 110(4), 877–921.
Scholtz, C. 2006. *Negotiating Claims: The Emergence of Indigenous Land Claim Negotiation Policies in Australia, Canada, New Zealand, and the United States.* New York: Routledge.
Schorr, D. 2009. How Blackstone Became a Blackstonian. *Theoretical Enquiries in Law*, 10(1), 103–26.
Schreiner, A. 2007. Landmarks for Aboriginal law in Australia, in *Interpretation, Law and the Construction of Meaning: Collected Papers on Legal Interpretation in Theory, Adjudication and Political Practice*, edited by Wagner, A., Werner, W. and Cao, D. Dordrecht: Springer, 195–204.
Scott, D. 2003. Culture in political theory. *Political Theory*, 31(1), 92–115.
Sen, A. 2009. *An Idea of Justice*. Cambridge, Mass.: Harvard University Press.

Sexton, S. 1996. Law, empowerment and economic rationalism. *Aboriginal Law Bulletin*, 3(81), 12–15.

Shapiro, S. 2007. The 'Hart-Dworkin' debate: a short guide for the perplexed, in *Ronald Dworkin*, edited by Ripstein, A. Cambridge: Cambridge University Press, 22–55.

Shaw, K. 2008. *Indigeneity and Political Theory: Sovereignty and the Limits of the Political*. London: Routledge.

Sheridan, J. and Longboat, R.D. 2006. The Haudenosaunee imagination and the ecology of the sacred. *Space and Culture* 9(4), 365–81.

Short, J. 1991. *Imagined Country: Environment, Culture and Society.* London: Routledge.

Simpson, A.W.B. 1986. The common law and legal theory, in *Legal Theory and Common Law*, edited by Twining, W. London: Basil Blackwell, 8–25.

Simpson, G. 1993. Mabo, international law, terra nullius and the stories of settlement: an unresolved jurisprudence. *Melbourne University Law Review* 19(1), 195–210.

Skinner, Q. 1988. Reply to my critics, in *Meaning and Context: Quentin Skinner and His Critics*, edited by Tully, J. Princeton, NJ: Princeton University Press, 231–88.

Slattery, B. 1992. The legal basis of Aboriginal title, in *Aboriginal Title in British Columbia: Delgamuukw v. The Queen*, edited by Cassidy, F. Montreal: Institute for Research on Public Policy, 113–32.

Slattery, B. 2005. Aboriginal rights and the honour of the Crown. *Supreme Court Law Review (2d)*, 29, 433–45.

Slattery, B. 2006. The metamorphosis of Aboriginal title. *Canadian Bar Review* 85(2), 255–86.

Smith, A. 1997. Indigenous research ethics: policy, protocol, practice. *Australian Journal of Indigenous Education* 25(1), 23–9.

Smith, D., Blagg, H. and Derricourt, N. 1988. Mediation in the shadow of the law: the South Yorkshire experience, in *Informal Justice?*, edited by Matthews, R. London: Sage Publications, 123–49.

Smith, D. and Finlayson, J. 1997. *Fighting Over Country: Anthropological Perspectives.* Canberra: Centre for Aboriginal Economic Policy Research, ANU.

Somerville, M. 2013. *Water in a Dry Land Place: Learning Through Art and Story.* New York: Routledge.

Spivak, G. 1988. Can the subaltern speak?, in *Marxism and the Interpretation of Culture*, edited by Nelson, C. and Grossberg, L. Champaign, IL: University of Illinois Press, 271–313

Stanner, W.E.H. 1998. The Dreaming, in *Traditional Aboriginal Society* (2nd edn), edited by Edwards, W. South Yarra, Victoria: Macmillan Education Australia, 227–38.

Steiner, G. 1992. *After Babel: Aspects of Language and Translation* (2nd edn). Oxford: Oxford University Press.

Strelein, L. 2001. Conceptualising native title. *Sydney Law Review*, 23(1), 95–124.

Strelein, L. 2005. Native title holding groups and native title societies: *Sampi v State of Western Australia* [2005]. *Land, Rights, Laws: Issues in Native Title* 3(4), 1–10.
Sutton, P. 2001. The politics of suffering: Indigenous policy in Australia since the 1970s. *Anthropological Forum* 11(2), 125–73.
Sutton, P. 2003. *Native Title in Australia: An Anthropological Perspective.* Cambridge: Cambridge University Press.
Sutton, P. 2006. Customs not in common: cultural relativism and customary law recognition in Australia. *Macquarie Law Journal*, 6, 161–75.
Szablowski, D. 2010. Operationalizing free, prior and informed consent in the extractive industry sector? Examining the challenges of a negotiated model of justice. *Canadian Journal of Development Studies* 3(1/2), 111–30.
Tait, D. 1999, Boundaries and barriers: The social production of space in magistrates' courts and guardianship tribunals. *Journal of Social Change and Critical Inquiry*, 1. Archived at: http://pandora.nla.gov.au/nph-wb/20000123130000/http://www.uow.edu.au/arts/joscci/tait.html. Accessed 2 May 2014.
Tamanaha, B. 1993. The folly of the 'social scientific' concept of legal pluralism. *Journal of Law & Society* 20(2), 192–217.
Tamanaha, B. 2000. A non-essentialist version of legal pluralism. *Journal of Law & Society* 27(2), 296–321.
Tamanaha, B. 2001. *A General Jurisprudence of Law and Society*. New York: Oxford University Press.
Tamanaha, B. 2008. Understanding legal pluralism: Past to present, local to global. *Sydney Law Review*, 30(3), 375–411.
Taylor, C. 1989. *Sources of the Self.* Cambridge, Mass.: Harvard University Press.
Taylor, C. 1992. The politics of recognition, in *Multiculturalism: Examining the Politics of Recognition*, edited by Gutmann, A. Princeton: Princeton University Press, 25–73.
Tebebu, T. 2010. *Hegel and the Third World: The Making of Eurocentrism in World History*. Syracuse, NY: Syracuse University Press.
Tehan, M. 2004. Negotiating co-existence, in *Honour Among Nations*, edited by Langton, M. et al. Carlton, Vic: Melbourne University Press, 173–5.
Teubner, G. 1992. The two faces of Janus: rethinking legal pluralism. *Cardozo Law Review* 13(5), 1443–62.
Tierney, B. 2004. The idea of natural rights: origins and persistence. *Northwestern Journal of Human Rights* 2(1), 2–12.
Thornton, M. 1996. *Dissonance and Distrust: Women in the Legal Profession.* Oxford: Oxford University Press.
Thuen, T. 2004. Anthropological knowledge in the courtroom: conflicting paradigms. *Social Anthropology* 12(3), 265–87.
Tilbury, F. 2000. What's in a name? Wadjula self-labelling and the process of reconciliation. *Balayi: Law, Culture and Colonisation* 1(2), 73–88.
Timony, J. 2000. Demeanor credibility. *Catholic University Law Review* 49(4), 903–44.

Tindale, N. 1974. *Aboriginal Tribes of Australia: Their Terrain, Environmental Controls, Distribution, Limits, and Proper Names.* Berkeley: University of California Press.

Tully, J. 1993. *An Approach to Political Philosophy: Locke in Contexts.* Cambridge: Cambridge University Press.

Tully, J. 1995. *Strange Multiplicity: Constitutionalism in an Age of Diversity.* Cambridge: Cambridge University Press.

Tushnet, M. 1984. Critical legal studies and constitutional law: an essay in deconstruction. *Stanford Law Review* 36(1), 623–47.

Twining, W. 1985. *Theories of Evidence: Bentham and Wigmore.* London: Weidenfelt & Nicolson.

Uhlmann, A. 2001. Law translating life and life translating law through stories: 'Bringing Them Home' and 'Benang' by Kim Scott'. *The Australian Feminist Law Journal* 15, 41–54.

Unger, R. 1976. *Law in Modern Society: Toward a Criticism of Social Theory.* New York: Free Press.

Vanderveld, K. 1980. The new property of the nineteenth century: the development of the modern concept of property. *Buffalo Law Review* 29(2), 325–67.

van Krieken, R. 2001. Legal informalism, power and liberal governance. *Social & Legal Studies* 10(1), 5–22.

Venuti, L. 1995. *The Translator's Invisibility: A History of Translation.* London: Routledge.

Verran, H. 1998. Re-imagining land ownership in Australia. *Postcolonial Studies*, 1(2), 237–54.

Vessey, D. 2011. Paul Ricoeur's and Hans-Georg Gadamer's diverging reflections on recognition, in *Gadamer and Ricoeur: Critical Horizons for Contemporary Hermeneutics*, edited by Mootz, F. and Taylor, G. London: Continuum, 142–55.

Vollenhoven, C. van, 1918. *Het Adatrecht van Nederlansch-Indië.* Leiden: EJ Brill.

von der Heydte, F.A.F. 1935. Discovery, symbolic annexation and virtual effectiveness in international law. *American Journal of International Law*, 29, 448–71.

Waldron, J. 2010. Legal pluralism and the contrast between Hart's jurisprudence and Fuller's. *The Hart-Fuller Debate 50 Years On*, edited by Cane, P. Oxford: Hart Publishing, 135–55.

Walters, M. 2006. The Morality of Aboriginal Law. *Queen's Law Journal* 31(2), 470–520.

Walzer, M. 1983. *Spheres of Justice: A Defence of Pluralism and Equality.* New York: Basic Books.

Ward, A. 1990. History and historians before the Waitangi tribunal: some reflections on the Ngai Tahu claim. *New Zealand Journal of History* 24(2), 150–67.

Watson, C. 2003. *Piercing the Ground: Balgo Women's Image Making and Relationship to Country.* Freemantle, WA: Freemantle Arts Centre Press.

Watson, I. 1997. Indigenous peoples' law-ways: survival against the colonial state. *The Australian Feminist Law Journal*, 8, 39–58.

Watson, I. 1998. The power of the Muldarbi, the road to its demise. *The Australian Feminist Law Journal*, 11, 28–45.

Watson, I. 2002. Buried alive. *Law & Critique*, 13(3), 253–69.

Webber, J. 1995. Relations of force and relations of justice: the emergence of normative community between colonists and Aboriginal peoples. *Osgoode Hall Law Journal*, 32(4), 623–40.

Webber, J. 2000. Beyond regret: Mabo's implications for Australian constitutionalism, in *Political Theory and the Rights of Indigenous People*, edited by Patton, P. et al. Melbourne: Cambridge University Press, 60–88.

Webber, J. 2006. Legal pluralism and human agency. *Osgoode Hall Law Journal* 44(1), 167–98.

Weber, M. 1954. *Max Weber on Law and Economy in Society*, translated by Shils, E. and Rheinstein, M. Cambridge, Mass: Harvard University Press.

Weiner, J. 1999. Culture in a sealed envelope: the concealment of Australian Aboriginal heritage and tradition in the Hindmarsh Island bridge affair. *Journal of the Royal Anthropological Institute*, 5(2), 193–210.

Weiner, J. 2001. Strangelove's dilemma or, what kind of secrecy do the Ngarrindjeri practice?', in *Emplaced Myth: Space, Narrative and Knowledge in Aboriginal Australia and Papua New Guinea*, edited by Rumsey, A. and Weiner, J. Honolulu: University of Hawaii Press, 139–60.

Weiner, J. 2002. Diaspora, materialism, tradition: anthropological issues in the recent High Court Appeal of the Yorta Yorta. *Land, Rights, Laws: Issues of Native Title*, 2(18), 1–12.

Weiner, J. 2003. The law of the land: a review article. *The Australian Journal of Anthropology*, 14(1), 97–110.

Weiner, J. 2006. Eliciting customary law. *The Asia Pacific Journal of Anthropology*, 7(1), 15–25.

Weir, J. 2009. *Murray River Country: An Ecological Dialogue with Traditional Owners*. Canberra: Aboriginal Studies Press.

Weyrauch, W. 2001. *Gypsy Law: Romani Legal Traditions and Culture*. Berkeley: University of California Press.

White, H. 1973. *Metahistory: The Historical Imagination in 19th-century Europe*. Baltimore: John Hopkins University Press.

White, J.B. 1990. *Justice as Translation: An Essay in Cultural and Legal Criticism*. Chicago: University of Chicago Press.

Wicken, W. 2002. *Mi'kmaq Treaties on Trial: History, Land and Donald Marshall Junior.* Toronto: University of Toronto Press.

Wilcock, D. and Brierley, G. 2012. It's about time: extending time-space discussion in geography through use of 'ethnogeomorphology' as an education and communication tool. *Journal of Sustainable Education* 3. Available at http://www.jsedimensions.org/wordpress/wp-content/uploads/2012/03/Wilcock BrierleyJSE2012.pdf [accessed 29 December 2013].

Williams, N. 1982. A boundary is to cross: observations on Yolngu boundaries and permission, in *Resource Managers: North American and Australian Hunter Gatherers*, edited by Williams, N. and Hunn, E. Canberra: Australian Institute for Aboriginal and Torres Strait Islander Studies, 131–54.

Williams, N. 1986. *The Yolngu and Their Land.* Stanford: Stanford University Press.

Williams, P. 1997. *Seeing a Colour-Blind Future: The Paradox of Race.* New York: The Noonday Press.

Williams, R. 1990. *The American Indian in Western Legal Thought: The Discourses of Conquest.* New York: Oxford University Press.

Winslade, J. and Monk, G. 2000. *Narrative Mediation: A New Approach to Conflict Resolution.* San Francisco: Jossey-Bass.

Winter, J. 2002. Native title business: traveling art exhibition 1 July 2002–31 October 2005. *Native Title Newsletter*, 3(May-June), 5–6. Available at: http://www.aiatsis.gov.au/ntru/newsletter.html Accessed 2 May 2014.

Wittgenstein, L. 1968. *Philosophical Investigations*, translated by Anscombe, G.E.M. Oxford: Basil Blackwell.

Wolfe, P. 1991. On being woken up: the dreamtime in anthropology and in Australian settler culture. *Comparative Studies in Society & History* 33(2), 197–224.

Wolfe, P. 1999. *Settler Colonialism and the Transformation of Anthropology: The Politics and Poetics of an Ethnographic Event.* London: Cassel.

Woodman, G. 1988. How state courts create customary law in Ghana and Nigeria, in *Indigenous Law and the State*, edited by Morse, B. and Woodman, G. Dordrecht: Foris, 181–222.

Woodman, G. 1999. The idea of legal pluralism, in *Legal Pluralism in the Arab World*, edited by Dupret, B. et al. The Hague: Kluwer Law International, 3–19.

Woolford, A. 2004. Negotiating affirmative repair: symbolic violence in the British Columbia treaty process. *Canadian Journal of Sociology* 29(1), 111–44.

Wootton, H. 1996. Mediating between Aboriginal communities and industry, in *Implementing the Native Title Act: The Next Step: Facilitating Negotiated Agreements*, edited by Meyers, G. Perth: National Native Title Tribunal, 161–82.

Yar, M. 2001. Recognition and the politics of humane desire. *Theory, Culture & Society* 18(2–3), 57–76.

Young, S. 2008. *The Trouble With Tradition: Native Title and Cultural Change.* Sydney: Federation Press.

Cases

The Alyawarr, Kaytetye, Warumungu, Wakay Native Title Claim Group v Northern Territory [2004] FCA 472 (Unreported, Mansfield J, 23 April 2004).

Amodu Tijani v Secretary, Southern Nigeria [1921] UKPC 80, 2 A.C. 399.

Bennell v Western Australia [2006] FCA 1243 (Unreported, Wilcox J, 19 September 2006).
Calder v British Columbia (Attorney General) [1973] 1 SCR 313.
Calvin's Case [1608] 7 Coke Report 1a, 77 ER 377.
Commonwealth v Yarmirr [2001] 208 CLR 1.
Daniel v Western Australia [2003] FCA 666 (Unreported, Nicholson J, 3 July 2003).
Delgamuukw v British Columbia [1997] 3 SCR 1010.
De Rose v South Australia [2002] FCA 1342 (Unreported, O'Loughlin J, 1 November 2002).
Fejo v Northern Territory [1998] 195 CLR 96.
Guerin v The Queen [1984] 2 S.C.R. 335.
Griffiths v Northern Territory [2006] FCA 903 (Unreported, Weinberg J, 17 July 2006).
Haida Nation v British Columbia (Minister of Forests) [2004] 3 SCR. 511, 2004 SCC 73.
Harrington-Smith on Behalf of the Wongatha Peoples v Western Australia [2007] FCA 31 (Unreported, Lindgren J, 5 February 2007).
Jango v Northern Territory [2006] FCA 318 (Unreported, Sackville J, 31 March 2006).
Kable v Director of Public Prosecutions [1996] 189 CLR 51.
In Re Southern Rhodesia [1919] AC 211.
Lardil, Kaiadilt, Yangkaal & Gangalidda Peoples v State of Queensland [2000] FCA 1959 (Unreported, Cooper J, 19 December 2000).
The Lardil Peoples v State of Queensland [2004] FCA 298 (Unreported, Cooper J, 23 March 2004).
Mabo v Queensland (No. 1) [1988] 166 CLR 186.
Mabo and Others v Queensland (No. 2) [1992] 175 CLR 1, [1992] HCA 23.
Members of the Yorta Yorta Aboriginal Community v State of Victoria [1998] 1606 FCA (Unreported, Olney J, 18 December 1998).
Members of the Yorta Yorta Aboriginal Community v Victoria (2001) 180 ALR 655.
Members of the Yorta Yorta Aboriginal Community v Victoria (2002) 194 ALR 538.
Milirrpum v Nabalco Pty Ltd [1971] 17 FLR 141.
Mitchell v Minister of National Revenue [2001] 1 SCR 911.
Neowarra v State of Western Australia [2003] FCA 1402 (Unreported, Sundberg J, 8 December 2003).
North Ganalanja Aboriginal Corp v Queensland [1996] 185 CLR 595.
Pueblo De Zia v United States [1962] 11 Ind. Cl. Comm. 131.
R v Gladstone [1996] 2 SCR 723.
R v Kapp [2008] 2 SCR. 483, 2008 SCC 41.
R v Marshall; R v Bernard [2005] 2 SC 220, 2005 SCC 43.
R. v. Sappier; R. v. Gray [2006] 2 SCR. 686, 2006 SCC 54.
R v Sparrow [1990] 1 SCR 1075, 70 D.L.R. (4th) 385.

R v Van der Peet [1996] 2 SCR 507.
Risk v Northern Territory [2006] FCA 404 (Unreported, Mansfield J, 29 August 2006).
Sampi v Western Australia [2005] FCA 777 (Unreported, French J, 10 June 2005).
Simon v. The Queen [1985] 2 SCR 387.
State of Western Australia v Ward [2000] FCA 191.
St Catherines Milling [1888] UKPC 70, 14 App Cas 46.
Svartskog Case [2001] NRt. 2001, 1229.
Wandarang People v Northern Territory [2000] 104 FCR 380.
Western Australia v Ward [2002] 191 ALR 1.
Western Australia v Ward [2000] FCA 191 (Unreported, North J, 3 March 2000)
The Wik Peoples v Queensland; The Thayorre Peoples v Queensland [1996] 187 CLR 1.
Winters v United States [1908] 207 US 564.
Yanner v Eaton [1999] 166 ALR 259.
Yarmirr v Northern Territory [No 2] [1998] 82 FCR 533.

Legislation

Aboriginal Land Rights (Northern Territory) Act 1976. (Cth., No. 191), Canberra: Parliament of Australia.
Commonwealth of Australia Constitution Act 1990. (Imp), Canberra: Parliament of Australia.
Comprehensive Land Claims Policy 1973. Ottawa: Indian Claims Commission.
Constitution Act 1982, being Schedule B to the Canada Act 1982 (U.K.), 1982, c. 11, Ottawa: Department of Justice.
Federal Court Rules 2011. Canberra: Federal Court of Australia.
Marine and Coastal Area (Takutai Moana) Act 2011. (11/3), Wellington: Parliamentary Counsel Office.
Native Title Act 1993. (Cth., No. 110), Canberra: Parliament of Australia.
Nisga'a Final Agreement 1999. Available at: http://www.aadnc-aandc.gc.ca/eng/1100100031292/1100100031293 [accessed 5 May 2014].
Racial Discrimination Act 1975. (Cth., No. 52), Canberra: Parliament of Australia.
Real Property Act 1900 (NSW). (No. 25), Sydney, NSW: Parliamentary Counsel's Office.
Treaty of Waitangi 1840. Wellington: Archives New Zealand.

News Media

ABC Radio National. 1997. Art work as evidence in native title claim. *Law Report* (15 July 1997). Available at: http://www.abc.net.au/rn/talks/8.30/lawrpt/lstories/lr970715.htm [accessed 20 April 2006].

Background Briefing. 1997. ABC Radio National Transcripts (11 May 1997). Available at: http://www.abc.net.au/radionational/programs/backgroundbriefing/yorta-yorta/3563904 [accessed 31 December 2013].

Brooks, G. 2003. The painted desert. *New Yorker*, 28 July, 60–67.

Morgan, S. 2013. Fight for our land: Pangerang elder wants to set the record straight. *Wangaratta Chronicle* Monday, 25 March 2013. Available at: http://wangarattachronicle.com.au/2013/03/25/fight-for-our-land/ [accessed 29 December 2013].

Peatling, S. 2006. Fear over native title land grab in cities. *Sydney Morning Herald*, 22 September. Available at http://www.smh.com.au/news/national/fear-of-native-title-land-grab-in-cities/2006/09/21/1158431843986.html [accessed 15 July 2009].

Raybould, T. 2007. Just who needs treaties? *Globe and Mail.* (April 4), Letters to the editor.

Ritter, D. 2004. Native title through the fog of history wars. ABC Radio National *Perspectives* (14 July 2004).

Other Papers and Reports

Aboriginal Affairs and Northern Development Canada. 2003. *Resolving Aboriginal Claims: A practical Guide to the Canadian Experience*. Available at: www.aadnc-aandc.gc.ca/eng/1100100014174/1100100014179 [accessed 31 December 2013].

Aboriginal and Torres Strait Islander Justice Commissioner. 1994. *HREOC Social Justice Report*. Available at: http://www.austlii.edu.au/au/other/IndigLRes/1994/2/index.html [accessed 31 December 2013].

Aboriginal and Torres Strait Islander Social Justice Commissioner. 1997. *HREOC Social Justice Report*. Available at: http://www.humanrights.gov.au/sites/default/files/content/pdf/social_justice/sj_report97.pdf [accessed 31 December 2013].

Aboriginal and Torres Strait Islander Justice Commissioner. 2002. *HREOC Social Justice Report*. Available at: http://www.humanrights.gov.au/sites/default/files/content/social_justice/sj_report/sjreport02/Social_Justice_Report02.pdf [accessed 31 December 2013].

Aboriginal and Torres Strait Islander Justice Commissioner. 2003. *HREOC Native Title Report*: Available at: http://www.humanrights.gov.au/publications/native-title-report-2003-index [accessed 31 December 2013].

Agius, P., Howitt, R., Jarvis, S. and Williams, R. 2003. *Doing Native Title as Self-Determination: Issues from Native Title Negotiations in South Australia*, Traditional Lands in the Pacific Region: Indigenous Common Property Resources in Convulsion or Cohesion, Brisbane, 7–9 September 2003.

Australian Institute for Aboriginal and Torres Strait Islander Studies, 2011. *Guidelines for Ethical Research in Australian Indigenous Studies*. Available at: http://www.aiatsis.gov.au/research/ethics/GERAIS.html [accessed 2 May 2014].

Australian Institute for Aboriginal and Torres Strait Islander Studies. 2013. *Connection*. Available at: http://www.aiatsis.gov.au/ntru/connection.html [accessed 31 December 2013].

Brigg, M. and McIntyre, P. 2005. *Cross-Cultural Mediation and Training: Problems and Prospects*, Native Title, Decision-Making and Conflict Management, AIATSIS Seminar Series, Canberra, 16 May 2005. Available at: http://www.aiatsis.gov.au/_files/research/pdfs2005/Brigg-paper.pdf [accessed 2 May 2014].

Chaney, F. 2001. *The National Native Title Tribunal and Reconciliation Australia*. Limits and Possibilities of a Treaty Process, AIATSIS Seminar Series, Canberra, 27 August 2001. Available at: http://www.aiatsis.gov.au/ntru/nativetitleconference/conf2001and2002/pdfs/fredchaney.pdf [accessed 31 December 2013].

Chaney, F. 2002. *Eddie Mabo Memorial Speech*, Unfinished Business Conference, Melbourne, 3 June 2002. Available at: http://www.nntt.gov.au/News-and-Communications/Speeches-and-papers/Pages/Eddie_Mabo_memorial_lecture.aspx [accessed 31 December 2013].

Jones, C. 2005. *Apples and Oranges: The Intersection of Aboriginal Law and Native Title Mediation*, Native Title, Decision-Making and Conflict Management, AIATSIS Seminar Series, Canberra, 11 April 2005. Available at: http://www.aiatsis.gov.au/_files/research/pdfs2005/Jones-paper.pdf [accessed 31 December 2013].

Keating, P. 1992. Redfern Park Speech to launch the International Year of Indigenous Peoples, Sydney, 10 December 1992.

McNaughton, C. and Rock, D. 2003. Opportunities in aboriginal research: results of SSHRC's dialogue on research and aboriginal peoples. SSHRC Aboriginal Backgrounder paper. Available at: http://www.sshrc-crsh.gc.ca/funding-financement/apply-demande/background-renseignements/aboriginal_backgrounder_e.pdf [accessed 31 December 2013].

National Statement on Ethical Conduct in Human Research. 2007. Canberra: National Health and Medical Research Council. Available at: http://www.nhmrc.gov.au/guidelines/publications/e72 [accessed 31 December 2013].

Neate, G. 1999. *ILUAs – What Certainty for Pastoralists?*, 69th Annual Conference of the Pastoralists' and Graziers' Association of WA, Scarborough, WA, 14 February 1999. Available at: http://www.nntt.gov.au/news-and-communications/speeches-and-papers/documents/1999/speeches%20iluas%20what%20certainty%20for%20pastoralists%20neate%201999.pdf [accessed 31 December 2013].

Neate, G. 2003. *Land, Law and Language: Some Issues in the Resolution of Aboriginal Land Claims in Australia*, International Association of Forensic Linguists, Sydney, 11 July 2003. Available at: http://www.nntt.gov.au/News-and-Communications/Speeches-and-Papers/Pages/Land_law_and_language.aspx [accessed 31 December 2013].

Neate, G., Jones, C. and Clark, G. 2003. *Against All Odds: The Mediation of Native Title Agreements in Australia*, 2nd Asia Pacific Mediation Forum, Singapore, 19–22 November 2003. Available at: http://www.nntt.gov.au/News-and-Communications/Speeches-and-Papers/Pages/Against_all_odds.aspx [accessed 31 December 2013].

Rigsby, B. 2001. *Representations of Culture and the Expert Knowledge and Opinions of Anthropologists*, Opening Address, Native Title Conference, Adelaide, 6–7 July 2001. Available at: http://www.aas.asn.au/publications/Conference%202001/Rigsby.pdf [accessed: 31 December 2013].

Shaw, B. 2001. *Bringing the Numinous into the Witness Stand. Expert Evidence in Native Title Court Cases: Issues of Truth, Objectivity and Expertise*, Adelaide, 6–7 July 2001. Available at: http://www.aas.asn.au/publications/Conference%202001/Shaw.pdf [accessed 31 December 2013].

Trees, K. 2002. *Respecting Difference: For Indigenous People Law and Cultural Memory is in the Land not Legislation*, Mediating Law: Theory, Production, Culture 11th International Conference of the Law and Literature Association of Australia, Melbourne, 29 November–1 December 2002.

Woodward, E. 1999. Submission to the Federal Parliamentary Committee Enquiry into the Reeves Report. Available at: http://www.aph.gov.au/parliamentary_business/committees/house_of_representatives_committees?url=/atsia/reeves/sub47.pdf [accessed 31 December 2013].

Index

For Product Safety Concerns and Information please contact our EU representative GPSR@taylorandfrancis.com
Taylor & Francis Verlag GmbH, Kaufingerstraße 24, 80331 München, Germany

www.ingramcontent.com/pod-product-compliance
Ingram Content Group UK Ltd.
Pitfield, Milton Keynes, MK11 3LW, UK
UKHW022132190926
475702UK00013B/1767

* 9 7 8 1 1 3 8 6 3 7 6 4 1 *